A Pictorial History of
SOCCER

A Pictorial History of
SOCCER
Dennis Signy

Hamlyn London/New York/Sydney/Toronto

Contents

Introduction by George Best   page 11

1   Birth and Development   12

2   The Game Today   56

3   Great Players and Great Teams   106

4   The European Scene   150

5   South America   190

6   North America   224

7   World Soccer Organization   250

8   Running a Top Club   274

   Glossary & Laws of the Game   292

   Index   311

   Acknowledgments   316

Published by THE HAMLYN PUBLISHING GROUP LIMITED
LONDON · NEW YORK · SYDNEY · TORONTO
Hamlyn House, Feltham, Middlesex, England

© Copyright The Hamlyn Publishing Group Ltd 1968
First published by Spring Books 1968
Second edition by Paul Hamlyn 1969
Third edition 1970
Fourth edition, first impression 1971 (fully revised)

ISBN 0 600 36978 1

Filmset in Great Britain by Oliver Burridge Filmsetting Ltd
Printed in Great Britain by Jarrold & Sons Ltd, Norwich

Introduction

Footballers, and the people who watch this great sport, live upon anecdote and incident from match to match. We are inveterate talkers behind the scenes, pooling our favourite stories of other players and of sporting moments great and small.

Memories are tossed about and, as they will, the facts behind the stories sometimes become distorted with time. The book you are about to read, A PICTORIAL HISTORY OF SOCCER, gets just about every record straight. It is a most fascinating account of the origins and workings of the world's most popular ball-game—a book which everyone, in and out of football, will enjoy having on his bookshelf.

In the dressing-room at Old Trafford, my Manchester United colleagues and I are forever on the look-out for new stories or legends from the past. Now, from reading this book before publication, I have a new hero-figure. He is the Hon. Arthur Kinnaird, later Lord Kinnaird, the majestic amateur who played in nine FA Cup Finals between 1873-83. I shall have great fun retelling one marvellous anecdote revealed in the book. I won't spoil it for you here, except to say that I could readily change the names to those of players performing in 1968 and get just as big a laugh!

When I was first shown the manuscript of this book, I was especially pleased to see how the records and statistics had been integrated with the general narrative, to make lively reading throughout. The book certainly represents the happiest marriage of education and entertainment I can ever recall. You will enjoy it.

George Best

1 Birth and Development

The essence of the game of soccer is its simplicity. Despite the commercial and big-business implications of the professional game in the 1960s, and the trend-setting applications of modern coaching methods, soccer is basically as simple today as it was in its early history.

It remains a game of the masses. It cuts through international barriers of language and, in an age of jet travel, has pushed aside political and religious differences to enable a divided world to meet in the common cause of sport.

A look at the origins of soccer in countries that today show world-class skill at the game reveals the English influence at the source of development.

Where did it all begin? A form of football was certainly played with a leather ball in China at least as early as 200 BC—according to learned research. The general emphasis in this game was placed upon the ability of players to dribble the ball.

Both soccer and rugby are branches of the same sporting tree and there is ample evidence of a common connection with the ball game played by the Greeks and the Romans. The Greek *episkyres* and the Roman *harpustum*, however, were ball-*carrying* games.

Football, in all its varied forms, is a development of these games and the mêlées of ancient and medieval Britain in which a round or oval object—generally the inflated bladder of an animal—was kicked, punched, carried or driven towards a goal.

The Roman *harpustum* game, which derived its name from the Greek word for 'handball', was started by throwing the ball into the air in midfield, and the players then tried to force it beyond a line drawn by the opposition.

From early times there was a game of football annually on Shrove Tuesday at Chester, and his-torians of the game also refer to Shrovetide matches in Derbyshire, and at Corfe Castle in Dorset and Scone in Perthshire. At Chester, it is said, the shoe-makers annually delivered a leather ball and the drapers played football with it between the hall of Rodehoe and the common hall of the city.

Tradition also has it that the first ball used was the head of a dead Danish brigand; but this particular game evidently became so violent that it was stopped and replaced by a running match.

Shrove Tuesday, the day immediately before Lent, was the date on which nearly all these medieval contests took place. At one centre the married women of the parish traditionally staged a match against the spinsters—and usually emerged sound winners.

As their popularity increased, these games were no longer confined to days of festival. Legend de-scribes how King Edward III decided in 1365 to prohibit football for military reasons—the troops preferred playing football to fighting; and their archery suffered too!

From the apprentices' games in Smithfield, Lon-don, grew the street games in Cheapside, Covent Garden and the Strand, and the Shrove Tuesday games at Derby, Nottingham, Kingston-on-Thames and elsewhere that came to be known as 'mob foot-ball'. The pitches were the length of the town, the players numbered up to 500, the conflict continued all day, vast numbers of windows and legs were broken—and there were some deaths.

Opposite page, above: a fourteenth-century carving in Gloucester Cathedral showing two medieval footballers vying for possession of the ball. Below: blowing up the ball for a game of *pallo*, one of the ancestors of modern football played in Italy during the sixteenth century.

Most early versions of football were wildly disorganized affairs, played on public holidays and the like, in which opposing teams tried to kick, carry or otherwise transport the ball to the other side of town, or across the parish boundary. Above, left to right: football played in Crowe Street, London, in 1721; next, an Easter Monday fixture from the same period, this time fought out across open countryside, and, from Naples, a more decorous display of ball-artistry by a group of seventeenth-century Mazzolas. Left: a reconstruction of how 'mob football', as it was sometimes known, must have looked in the fourteenth century, during the reign of Edward II: not unlike a modern-day crowd perhaps, going home one Saturday after a local 'derby'.

A survey of Cornwall published in 1602 records that goals were set three or four miles apart, and two or three parishes united to play two or three others 'hurling over country'. In this version, too, many of the characteristics of soccer were employed.

The basic simplicity of soccer is embodied in the words of Joseph Strutt, a famed historian of English sport, who wrote in 1801: '. . . an equal number of competitors take the field and stand between two goals placed at a distance of 80 to 100 yards the one from the other. The goal is usually made with two sticks driven into the ground about two or three feet apart. The ball, which is commonly made of a brown bladder and cased with leather, is delivered in the midst of the ground, and the object of each party is to drive it through the goal of their antagonists, which being achieved the game is won. The abilities of the performers are best displayed in attacking and defending the goals; and hence the pastime is more frequently called a goal at football than a game at football. When the exercise becomes exceedingly violent the players kick each others' shins without the least ceremony, and some of them are overthrown at the hazard of their limbs.'

The similarities with soccer in the 1960s do not have to be underlined. In its present-day form, soccer owes its origins to the public schools of England.

Although rules differed from place to place, it seems fair to record that Eton, Westminster and Charterhouse really laid the foundations for England's national sport. The game spread from schools to universities and eventually a number of Old Boys joined together and formed the first soccer club, at Sheffield in 1857.

The Sheffield club was much influenced by local men who went to Harrow School. It disapproved of handling the ball, which was not permitted in their school code, and so provided the opposition with white gloves and silver florins to hold in their fists.

The Hallam club was formed in 1857, as was Blackheath in the south. By 1860 the famous Wanderers were in existence, the Old Harrovians had formed and Forest Football Club, another product of Harrow missionaries, had started playing in Epping Forest near Snaresbrook.

Old Boys and university men also played a leading part in the foundation of the Football Association a few years later. There was certainly no trace of a cloth-cap-and-muffler approach to soccer in those early days.

Around 1850 the game was played with fifteen to twenty men on each side. In the late 1860s, when it was normal practice to field eleven or twelve, the Queen's Park club, of Glasgow, still turned out fifteen or more.

Nine forwards and two defenders, known as 'behinds', was the line-up formation when the first eleven-a-side matches began, but eleven players per team was not established as an all-round rule until 1870.

For a time sides consisted of a goalkeeper, who

wore the same dress as the others, a goal 'cover', a back and eight forwards, who roamed the field and relied almost entirely on mass dribbling and charging. Later, seven forwards and two half-backs were employed.

The next formation was a goalkeeper, two backs, two half-backs and six forwards, but from 1883 onwards the accepted formation became the present three half-backs and five forwards. The first steps towards modern-day massed defences!

In those early days, charging a goalkeeper out of the way of an expected shot or centre was a recognized feature, and Preston North End, the 'Proud Preston' we will refer to later, were great exponents of this method of clearing a path to the goal.

Of the historic clubs which survive today as Football League members, Notts County came into being in 1862, followed by Nottingham Forest (1865) and Sheffield Wednesday and Chesterfield (1866). The Sheffield FA was formed in 1867.

1863
One of the most significant dates in the history of soccer was Monday, 26 October 1863, when representatives of eleven clubs met at the Freemason's Tavern, Great Queen Street, Lincoln's Inn Fields, London, to form themselves into the Football Association. Since that time the formation of other national associations has spread, particularly in the last fifty years, until now there are over 100 member-nations of the world body—the Fédération Internationale de Football Association (FIFA).

The game is played in all countries under the same laws, framed and controlled by a universal authority, the International Football Association Board. This consists of the four British associations and an equal representation from FIFA.

The part played by the Football Association, and later by the Football League, in the progressive future of soccer cannot be stressed too highly. At every major stage the influence of the two bodies is clearly recognizable.

It is interesting to record that the inaugural meeting of the FA attracted representatives of eleven London and suburban clubs, one public school (Charterhouse) and a number of interested parties. Mr Pember, of

Opposite page, above: an engraving made in 1868 entitled 'Winter Amusements: Football'. As the players battle desperately for the ball, several figures reel away from the scrimmage clutching battered shins and aching heads—all part of the fun in those days when hacking, tripping and elbowing were permitted. Compared, however, with the earlier picture, below, of Shrove Tuesday 'mob football' at Kingston-on-Thames, we can see that the game had already come a long way in terms of organization and control: the playing area is confined within recognizable limits, the goals are clearly positioned and, what is more, each is manned by a specialist player.

No Names, Kilburn, was voted into the chair and the following clubs were enrolled: NN (No Names), Kilburn; Barnes, War Office; Crusaders, Forest, Leytonstone; Perceval House, Blackheath; Kensington School; Surbiton; Blackheath Proprietary School; Blackheath, and Crystal Palace. The subscription was fixed at one guinea a year.

It is also fascinating to note that shortly after the FA drew up their laws of the game the Blackheath club withdrew because they resented the rule which banned hacking. This withdrawal, shortly after Blackheath had been represented at the inaugural meeting, marks the establishment of the separate games of soccer and rugby.

At this stage the game was not confined to England. Football was introduced to the Argentine in the 1860s by Britishers engaged on building railways and, in 1865, the Buenos Aires FC was formed. Italians later emigrated to the Argentine, around the time of the First World War, and they too developed the game.

1867
The year 1867 saw the formation of the famous Queen's Park club in Glasgow, a club that has maintained an amateur tradition to the present day and still performs in the otherwise professional Scottish League, playing its home games at the massive Hampden Park stadium.

Queen's Park immediately became a power in the land of soccer. They did not have a goal scored against them by a Scottish side until Vale of Leven broke a seven-year-old record on 16 January 1875.

Even as late as 1904 an FA rule insisted that shorts should be long enough to cover the knees, but some of the colour variations of this period are interesting: Sheffield Norwich in 1868 wore violet and black jerseys and stockings, black knickerbockers, with a violet, black and yellow cap and tassel; Black Rovers, Hackney (1869) wore black jerseys with a white skull-and-crossbones on the breast, black caps and stockings and white knickerbockers.

Around 1870 Association rules were also played in Germany, and a team from Oxford University visited the country in 1875, the first overseas tour by a soccer team. As a result of this meeting several German universities were encouraged to take up the game.

English residents in Lisbon began introducing soccer there in 1870, and the Lisbon club was formed in 1875. The game acquired a national footing in Portugal in 1893.

Around this time there was, too, the first mention in FA rules of a goalkeeper being able to use his hands to stop the ball; a further development in 1872 was the adoption of the corner-kick by the national association, although the Sheffield rules had included it since 1868. In those early days a wing-half took a corner-kick and it was not until late in the 1890s that wing-forwards finally took over this task.

1871

Another significant year was 1871, which marked the inauguration of the FA Cup competition, now the premier of its kind in the world, with all the attendant glamour and excitement caused by giant-killing performances and the fitting climax of a Final tie at Wembley Stadium watched by crowds of 100,000. The Scottish Cup competition was started two years later.

Fifteen clubs entered the first FA knock-out competition, and in the Final Wanderers beat Royal Engineers 1—0 at Kennington Oval. The goal was scored by M. P. Betts, who played under the assumed name of A. H. Chequer. He was an Old Harrovian who had played for Harrow Chequers, but the chroniclers of that period do not record why he

The public schools did most to develop soccer as we know it. With their regard for order, and character-building team games, they established rules where few had existed before. Other pioneers took the game abroad, setting up teams wherever they went to work or settle, from Brazil to India. Opposite page: three photographs from the 1860s showing, above left, a public-school House team grouped with superb indifference around their trophy; above right, the Royal Engineers, India XI and, below, the Harrow School XI of 1867. On this page, below, is a cartoon sequence which first appeared in 1872 with the title 'Our Great Football Match—"Pelicans" *versus* "Phantoms"'.

WE DRIVE DOWN   OUR DRESSING ROOM—THE "PHANTOM" CAPTAIN (*loq.*), "IS THAT ALL?"

"ARE YOU READY?"—MR. DABSIE DETERMINED TO SPRINT A TOUGH SCRIMMAGE—"GET YOUR HEADS LOW, 'PELICANS'" AN ACCIDENT—"WINDED"

preferred not to use his real name. In 1873 Wanderers, as holders of the trophy, were allowed a bye right through to the next Final.

The fifteen teams that took part in the first Cup competition included eight from London, Wanderers, Harrow Chequers, Barnes, Civil Service, Crystal Palace, Upton Park, Hampstead Heathens and Clapham Rovers; five more from the south, Hitchin, Royal Engineers, Reigate Priory, Maidenhead and Great Marlow; and two from the north, Donington Grammar School and Queen's Park.

Queen's Park, because of two byes and a walkover, only played one match in the first competition, the semi-final. They held Wanderers to a 0—0 draw and surprised spectators, who were accustomed to the dribbling game, with their short-passing style. They could not stay in London for the replay, so they retired. Incidentally, Queen's Park subscribed one guinea towards the purchase of the Cup although the club's income for that year was only £6.

Amateur clubs, including Queen's Park, dominated the competition for the first decade. Wanderers, on winning the trophy for the third successive year in 1878, returned it to the FA on condition that in future no club could win it outright.

Wanderers, whose teams comprised the best of those who had played for public schools and universities, won five of the first seven finals. Their dominance declined after their win in 1878 because the growth of Old Boys' sides took away their best players, one of whom was the Hon. Arthur Kinnaird, who played in nine Cup Finals between 1873–83, three times for Wanderers and six for Old Etonians.

Kinnaird won five Cup-winners' medals and one cap for Scotland—and he was later President of the FA for thirty-three years. He played for Old Etonians in the last Final to be won by an amateur side, and celebrated victory by standing on his head in front of the pavilion at The Oval.

The story is told that Sir Francis Marindin, President of the FA before Kinnaird, called on Kinnaird's mother, who said, 'I'm afraid that one of these days Arthur will come home with a broken leg.' Marindin replied, 'Never fear, dear madam, it will not be his own!'

It was not until 1883 that the trophy went to the north of England for the first time when Blackburn Olympic were the winners. But from that date onwards the north and the Midlands had their full share of honours.

The Scottish clubs, once they had their own competition, soon dropped out, but a small number of Welsh clubs was admitted annually and finally, in 1927, the Cup went out of England for the only time—to Cardiff, who beat Arsenal 1—0 in the Final.

This page, above: a completed fixture-list showing the results of the Accrington Football Club in 1878–9. Opposite page, above: a soccer match at Yokohama, Japan, played in 1873 by a team of British visitors and viewed, incredulously, by the local population. Below: an artist's impression of an international match of 1872 between England and Scotland.

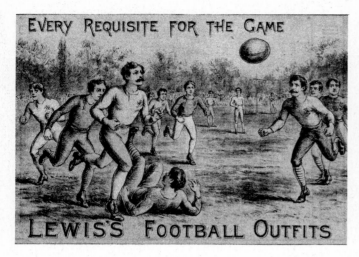

Up to the present time the highest numbers of victories in the Final have been won by Aston Villa (seven), Blackburn Rovers (six), Newcastle United (six), Wanderers (five) and Tottenham Hotspur (five). Since 1891 Newcastle and Tottenham are the only teams to have retained the trophy in the following year. Before that time, Wanderers and Blackburn Rovers each had won it three times in succession and twice in succession. Except in 1893 (Manchester), 1894 (Everton) and 1915 (Manchester), the Final has always been played in London, first at The Oval or Lillie Road, then at Crystal Palace, Stamford Bridge and, finally, at Wembley.

Immediately after the coming of professionalism the attendance at Cup-ties increased and over 100,000 people watched three of the Crystal Palace Finals, the record being 128,028 in 1913. After the Final was taken to Wembley in 1923 the FA decided to limit the attendance to 100,000 ticket-holders, but when Bolton Wanderers met West Ham United in the first Wembley Final the all-ticket decision had not been taken and the gates were rushed by people trying to pay at the turnstiles.

1872
To return, however, to the 1870s, the first Scotland–England match was staged in 1872. That same year the size of a football was defined, and a football club was formed at Le Havre following the introduction of the game by English sailors who visited France during the summer. But rugby kept a stronger hold on the affections of the French sporting public until after the First World War.

Opposite page: the first floodlit football match, held at the Bramall Lane Grounds, Sheffield, on 14 October 1878. The lamps were erected on 30-ft wooden towers, one in each corner of the ground. This page, above left: a poster by Lewis's of Liverpool advertising their range of 'requisites'. Above right: the Scottish team which faced England at Kennington Oval in 1879.

The first Scotland–England match, played on the ground of the West of Scotland cricket club at Partick, Glasgow, made a considerable impact. The *North British Mail* reported that the game 'at once established a record, as it was played in the presence of the largest assemblage previously seen at any football match in Scotland, close on four thousand, including a number of ladies, being present'.

The Queen's Park club represented Scotland and the England team was drawn from nine leading clubs. As the newspaper reported, 'The southerners had the choice of men from nearly 100 clubs, while in Scotland only ten clubs play Association rules, all without experience, except Queen's Park'. The game ended as a 0—0 draw, but 'England, especially forward, astonished the spectators by some very pretty dribbling, an art curious and novel'.

The English uniform consisted of white jerseys, with the arms of England as a badge on the left breast, dark-blue caps and white knickerbockers. The Scots played in dark-blue jerseys, with the Scottish lion rampant for a badge, white knickers, and blue-and-white stockings, with red cowls as headgear.

Bell's Life recorded, 'Altogether it was one of the jolliest, one of the most spirited and most pleasant matches that have ever been played according to Association rules'.

The idea of this first international was put forward by the FA secretary, Mr C. W. Alcock. The FA was then the only national association in the world, but the match led to the formation, in the following year, of the Scottish Association, and that in its turn to those of Wales (1876) and Ireland (1880).

1875
Cross-bars over the goalmouth were introduced into FA rules in 1875. Before this tapes were used, although the word 'bar' was mentioned in other rules back in 1863 and the Sheffield Association made bars obligatory some time before 1875.

In Doleful Memory
OF
EVERTON,
WHO FELL
Fighting for the Cup.
—
When shall we be in London town
Sing my laddies, oh !
Not this year for we are down,
Sing my laddies, oh !

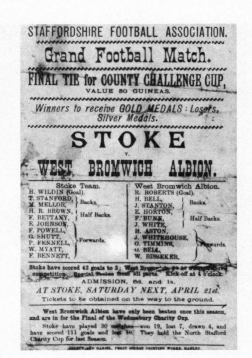

STAFFORDSHIRE FOOTBALL ASSOCIATION.
Grand Football Match.
FINAL TIE for COUNTY CHALLENGE CUP,
VALUE 50 GUINEAS.
Winners to receive GOLD MEDALS : Losers,
Silver Medals.
STOKE
v.
WEST BROMWICH ALBION.

Stoke Team.		West Bromwich Albion.	
B. WILDIN (Goal).		R. ROBERTS (Goal).	
T. STANFORD,	Backs.	H. BELL,	Backs.
M. MELLOR,		J. STANTON,	
H. R. BROWN,	Half Backs.	E. HORTON,	
F. BETTANY,		F. BUNN,	Half Backs.
E. JOHNSON,		J. WHITE,	
F. POWELL,		H. ASTON,	
G. SHUTT,	Forwards.	J. WHITEHOUSE,	Forwards.
P. FENNELL,		G. TIMMINS,	
W. MYATT,		G. BELL,	
F. BENNETT,		W. BISSEKER,	

Stoke have scored 42 goals to 3 ; West Brom. in the same competition. Special Trains from all parts. Kick-off at 4 o'clock.
ADMISSION, 6d. and 1s.
AT STOKE, SATURDAY NEXT, APRIL 21st.
Tickets to be obtained on the way to the ground.

West Bromwich Albion have only been beaten once this season, and are in for the Final of the Wednesbury Charity Cup.
Stoke have played 30 matches—won 19, lost 7, drawn 4, and have scored 111 goals and lost 40. They hold the North Stafford Charity Cup for last Season.

WEST BROMWICH
Albion Football Club.
—
SEASON TICKET.
1883-1884.
—
To Admit to all Matches on the
FOUR ACRES,
SITUATE IN SEAGAR STREET.
—
PRICE :—THREE SHILLINGS.
—
Mr

In Affectionate Remembrance
...of...
BLACKBURN ROVERS.
Who fell in the Competition for the
ENGLISH CUP.

WHEN the Football Match was over,
And they came to count the cost,
Then we heard poor Rovers wailing
For the Cup that they had lost.
Everywhere was desolation,
Silenced then was every tongue ;
Poor old Rovers they had fallen
Meek and lowly, once so strong.

Rise of the Professionals

This page, above: some footballing relics from the early years of the professional game. Left to right: a sardonic salute to the Everton team defeated in the 1893 Cup Final; a poster from the 1880s advertising the Final of the Staffordshire County Challenge Cup between Stoke and West Bromwich Albion, and a season ticket for 1883–4 issued to WBA fan Mr J. Stringer. Immediately above is another *In Memoriam*, which appeared following Blackburn Rovers' defeat in the 1882 Cup Final after an all-conquering season. This was but a temporary setback for the powerful Blackburn club, who came back to win the Cup in 1884; the lower picture, opposite, shows the victorious Rovers' team. This page, left: a collision in the 1895 Cup Final between West Bromwich Albion, striped shirts, and Aston Villa. Opposite page, above: a team photo taken in 1883 at the Royal Naval College, Greenwich.

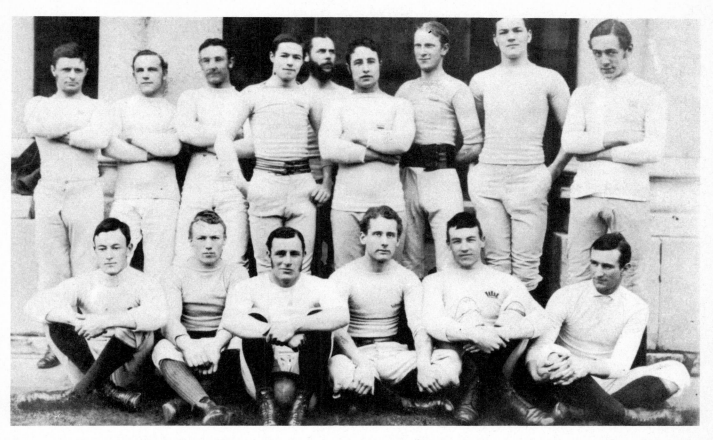

Opposite page: a group photograph of the Royal Arsenal Football Club (1888–9) and three pictures featuring historic clubs from the Midlands. Top: Bayliss (West Bromwich Albion) heads for goal in the 1887 Cup Final, played at the Oval; note the cross-bar tape, and the old-fashioned shinguards worn outside the players' stockings. Centre: police and mounted soldiers force back the crowd which spilled on to the pitch during a Cup-tie at Perry Barr in 1888 between Aston Villa and Preston North End. Bottom: the Press telegram sent from the Oval in 1892 announcing West Bromwich Albion's Cup victory over Aston Villa. This page, above: Blackburn Rovers attack the Notts County goal during their 1891 Cup battle at the Oval. Right: a reward notice posted by the Birmingham police in 1895 after the FA Cup was stolen from a local shopwindow where it had been on display following Aston Villa's victory that year.

British residents started football in Denmark in 1876; this country is a stronghold of the amateur game and has never embraced professionalism.

1878

The first game by floodlight was staged at Bramall Lane, Sheffield, on 14 October 1878, between teams chosen by the Sheffield Association from local clubs. Electric light was still a novelty in the provinces and the fixture, in the words of an observer at the time, 'attracted much attention'. The official attendance was 12,000 (the Cup Final only attracted 5,000!) but many more were thought to have been present.

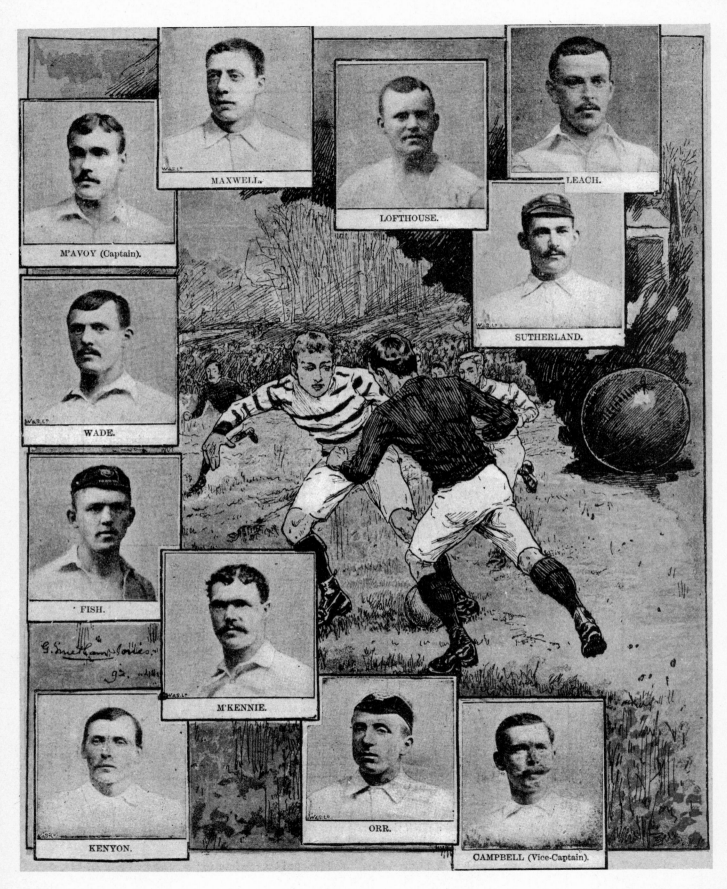

M'AVOY (Captain).

MAXWELL.

LOFTHOUSE.

LEACH.

WADE.

SUTHERLAND.

FISH.

M'KENNIE.

KENYON.

ORR.

CAMPBELL (Vice-Captain).

28

Opposite page: No. 1 in a series of illustrated club profiles, featuring the players of Darwen, a northern club which rose to fame in the FA Cup in 1879. This page, above: the first match of the British Ladies' Football Club, played in 1895.

The electric power was generated on the ground by two portable engines, one behind each goal. The lamps, one in each corner of the ground, were erected on thirty-feet-high wooden towers. The power of each lamp was 8,000 standard candles. The result of the match: a 2—0 win for the team captained by England international W. E. Clegg against a side skippered by his brother, J. C. Clegg, also an international and later President of the FA.

Two weeks later, at the Lower Aston grounds, a Birmingham representative side beat Nottingham Forest 2—1 under illumination provided by twelve electric lights spaced around the pitch. Unfortunately, wind and rain interfered and there were many stoppages.

1880

So we move into the 1880s, when shinguards were invented by Samuel W. Widdowson, a Nottingham Forest forward who played for England against Scotland. The British introduced soccer to Austria and helped form the Cricketers' club in 1889. Oxford University also played there that year.

The spread of the game was world-wide. Organized football in Australia dates from the early 1880s, and the Anglo-Australian Association was formed in 1884, although for some fifty years soccer was a poor

ALMOND HEDLEY SHEFFIELD'S THIRD GOAL BENNETT

NEEDHAM, THE SHEFFIELD CAPTAIN, MAKES SOME BRILLIANT DASHES

FRANK GILLETT

relation to the Rugby League and Australian Rules games.

Scottish immigrants introduced football to Canada in 1880, the year the Western Association was formed, but little real progress was made until the early 1950s. A Canadian team toured Britain in 1888, playing twenty-three matches. Scotland beat them 4—0 and the Prince of Wales saw them defeated 1—0 by the Swifts at The Oval.

1882
Blackburn Rovers played thirty-five matches without

defeat before losing 1—0 to Old Etonians in the Cup Final in March 1882. Old Carthusians, the Old Boys of Charterhouse, who beat Old Etonians 3—0 in the previous Final, were to make history as the only club to win both the FA and the FA Amateur Cup trophies. They beat Casuals 2—1 for the amateur trophy in 1894, and Stockton 4—1, after a 1—1 draw, three years later.

The Corinthians, formed in 1882 and who later amalgamated with Casuals in 1939, were quickly to become a force and an influence on the game.

Opposite page, above: two moments from the Sheffield United v. Derby Cup Final of 1899, showing the ball entering the net for Sheffield's third goal, and a characteristic dribble by Needham, the Sheffield captain. Below: Sheffield United bundle the ball into the Southampton goal during the 1902 Cup Final at Crystal Palace. The match ended in a 2—1 win for Sheffield. This page, above left: Glasgow Rangers FC (1896–7). Above right: Sheffield United again, this time on the defensive against Tottenham Hotspur in the 1901 Final, which resulted in a 2—2 draw (Tottenham won the replay 3—1). Below: the Aston Villa team which achieved a triumphant 'double' in 1896–7, winning the First Division championship and the FA Cup.

It was an unwritten law that only public-school or university men be admitted as members and Corinthians *never* entered for competitions until 1923. Their main object, it seems, was to try and improve England's poor international record against Scotland, and they also performed, with great success, at club level. In December 1884, they beat Blackburn 8—1 in an away match, when Rovers were FA Cup-holders and acknowledged as the best team in the country. In November 1888, they beat Preston, then Cup-holders and League-champions, 5—0, and in 1904

7th' June 1901.

Sir,

I have the honour to inform you that I have submitted to The King your letter of the 16th' Inst: and in reply I am commanded to say that His Majesty is pleased to accede to the request contained in it ,to grant his Patronage to The Football Association.

I am Sir,

Your obedient Servant,

General.
Keeper of H. M's Privy Purse.

TWO CORINTHIAN VETERANS
W. U. TIMMIS AND C. WREFORD BROWN

VASSALL HUGS THE TOUCH LINE AS USUAL

ONE OF MILESTONES SAVES

THE BRILLIANT CORINTHIAN FORWARDS CARRY ALL BEFORE THEM

they thrashed Bury, Cup-holders at the time, by 10—3. Between 1883 and 1890, fifty-two out of eighty-eight caps for internationals went to Corinthian players.

In 1897 Corinthians became the first English side to play outside Europe when they visited South Africa, and their influence on the game at home and abroad was considerable. They fielded great internationals such as G. O. Smith, who played twenty times for England, N. C. Bailey (nineteen) and E. C. Bambridge (eighteen).

An English professor at Montevideo University formed the first Uruguayan club in 1882, and British railway builders established another club there nine years later. The tentacles of soccer were reaching out.

Soccer was played in Prague before the formation of the Republic of Czechoslovakia, when Bohemia was part of Austria-Hungary. SK Slavia and AC Sparta were playing soccer in the 1880s and '90s; Slavia, now known as Bohemia, were formed in 1882.

1885
One domestic occurrence is worth noting for 1885: J. Petrie, an outside-right with Arbroath, created a soccer record by scoring thirteen goals against Bon Accord, from Aberdeen, in a Scottish Cup-tie.

1886
Professionalism was on the way and, on 16 January 1886, the Gentlemen beat the Players 1—0 in a representative match. In a return game at Kensington Oval the same season, the Players included six Scottish players against a Gentlemen's side represented by Corinthian members. The Players won 2—1 in a match described as one of the finest exhibitions of soccer ever seen. The Prince of Wales, later King Edward VII, attended. In all, the amateurs and professionals had fourteen meetings, the amateurs winning three of the encounters and the professionals nine, with two matches drawn.

Two pioneers in the southward movement of professional players were the Scots James Love and Fergus Sutar, of Partick, Glasgow, both members of the Darwen side that startled the south in 1879. Darwen was a team founded in 1875 by men employed

This page, above: the historic letter from Buckingham Palace advising the FA that King Edward VII had consented to become their Royal Patron. Below: some of the stars of the great Corinthians, perhaps the most celebrated of amateur clubs. In the bottom far right picture on the opposite page a group of Corinthians line up for the camera during their Budapest tour of 1904. Opposite page: the two individuals are, above, Alf Common, the first £1,000-player whose transfer from Sunderland to Middlesbrough in 1905 caused a great sensation, and the giant figure of W. Foulke, the Chelsea goalkeeper who topped twenty stone towards the end of his playing days. The team groups featured are, top, an England XI which drew 1—1 with Scotland in 1897 and, centre, Crook Town FC, winners of the FA Amateur Cup in 1900—1.

in the cotton mills. In '79 they were drawn against the Old Etonians in the fourth round of the Cup and a public subscription was raised locally to pay for their journey to The Oval, in London. They drew 5—5 against a side recognized as one of the greatest of the day; they returned to London for a replay and drew 2—2; then, with the FA and Old Etonians contributing to the subscription, they lost the third game.

Etonians went on to win the Cup, but people realized there was something stirring in soccer in the north and Darwen's achievements encouraged other northern clubs to pay for players.

C. W. Alcock, the FA's honorary secretary and the man behind the formation of the Cup competition, wrote: 'There is no use to disguise the speedy approach of a time when the subject of professional players will require the earnest attention of those on whom devolves the management of the Football Association.'

In 1883 it was proved that the Accrington club had been making payments to a player. The club was expelled from the FA and the player suspended for a year. The following year Preston North End played a draw in London against Upton Park, in the fourth round of the Cup, and were later charged with fielding professionals. Major Sudell, the Preston manager, appeared before an FA committee at The Oval and admitted the offence. He said he intended building the best team in the country. All of which came to a head on 20 July 1885, when a meeting at Anderton's Hotel, Fleet Street, legalized professionalism.

The British introduced the game to Russia and Rumania through engineers at coalfields around this time, and in Spain through mining engineers. Hamburg SV was formed, and two years later the English FA sent a representative side to Germany.

This page, above left: Hampton scores for Aston Villa in the 1905 Cup Final against Newcastle United. Above right: the famous Bob Crompton, left, captain of Blackburn Rovers, seen with the referee and his Tottenham counterpart, Danny Steele, before a Cup-tie at White Hart Lane, Tottenham, in 1912. Opposite page, above: the scene at Crystal Palace during the 1914 Cup Final in which Burnley beat Liverpool 1—0. Below left: a rare picture of FIFA President Sir Stanley Rous (kneeling, second from left) taken more than fifty years ago when he was playing for a village team. Below right: the England Amateur XI which won the Olympic Football Tournament staged at White City, London, in 1908.

1887

On 15 October 1887, another record was set in a Cup-tie. Preston beat Hyde 26—0 in a first series, first-round tie, which is still the record Cup score. Every player except the goalkeeper scored, although suggestions have been made that the game may have run an extra half an hour because of an error by the referee.

Preston, still managed by Major Sudell, were at their peak. They won the Cup the following year without conceding a goal. Their tally for five ties was 11—0. They were also Football League champions without losing a game and their goals' tally in that competition was seventy-four for and fifteen against.

1888

Before the founding of the League in 1888 there had been a rather haphazard approach to organized soccer.

Games were subject to last-minute cancellation or delay, almost at the whim or interest of the players. Spectators sometimes turned up to find a match called-off because a club could not raise a team or their opponents had failed to arrive.

Even when county associations were formed and county cup competitions organized, the same uncertainty about arrangements persisted. So, Mr William McGregor, a Scot living in Birmingham and associated with Aston Villa, conceived the idea of a League system and, on 2 March 1888, he wrote to five of the leading clubs suggesting organized home-and-away fixtures.

The first twelve clubs selected to constitute the League were: Accrington, Aston Villa, Blackburn Rovers, Bolton Wanderers, Burnley, Derby County, Everton, Notts County, Preston North End, Stoke,

West Bromwich Albion and Wolverhampton Wanderers. All have survived in the League except Accrington. In 1892 a Second Division was added and the First Division increased to 16 clubs. Soon the principle was adopted of promoting the first two clubs in the lower Division and relegating the bottom two from the First.

Development of tactics and formations progressed with the arrival of the professional game in England, generally accepted to have started with the influx of Scottish players south of the border.

The throw-in from touch at first was done with one hand, but so expert did some players become at reaching the goalmouth with throws that it was decided in the 1880s first to make the thrower use two hands and then to make him throw with his hands above his head from a standing position. And when

cross-bars replaced tapes, years of argument were finally ended.

Up to 1891 there were no linesmen; each side provided an umpire, and the referee was only called upon to arbitrate in case of dispute. The referees, who had used whistles since 1878, were eventually given control in 1891 and the Referees' Association was formed in 1893.

By this time international football was already under way. The brothers Jack and Roger Doughty, of Druids, scored seven of the eleven goals by which Wales beat Ireland in 1888.

The Netherlands FA was formed the next year, the oldest such association outside Great Britain. There had been a soccer club in Haarlem since 1879, but even so there was only limited progress in Holland for over fifty years because of the reluctance of the governing body to accept professionalism.

This page above: British soldiers playing football in Salonika on Christmas Day 1915. Opposite page, left: Scottish international Alan Morton, wearing the famous hooped jersey of amateur club Queen's Park, shakes hands with Corinthians' captain G. N. Foster in 1919. Right: programme of a wartime match, Corinthians v. Aldershot Command.

1890

The 1890s provided further change and development. The English introduced the game to Finland, where all the players are amateur. Because of the climate and the lack of pitches, it has been slow to develop there. The season in Finland runs from May–October.

Goal-nets were invented and patented in 1890 by J. A. Brodie, of Liverpool, and they were first used in the North v. South match at Nottingham in January 1891. They were also used at the Cup Final that year.

Soccer was first played in Greece in 1890, but

little progress was made there until the First World War.

There was a change in the rule about the charging of goalkeepers. Henceforth he was protected from charging except when he was playing the ball or was obstructing another player. At this time, too, penalty-kicks were introduced, following a proposal by the Irish FA.

Not only were the rules changing—so also was the appearance of players. It was customary at one stage for a player to sport knickerbockers fastened tightly below the knee, with long overlapping stockings. And the wearing of moustaches and caps was usual, with beards and top hats not unknown.

Once soccer became organized in England there were sweeping changes in style. Between 1880-96 the best sides added passing to their repertoires, and some of the brightest individual stars to emerge were J. Goodall (Preston and Derby), two famous cricketers, William Gunn (Notts County) and George Brann (Swifts), W. I. Bassett (West Bromwich Albion) and W. J. Townley (Blackburn Rovers).

In 1890 Sunderland were fined £50 and had two points deducted from their record for playing Scottish-international goalkeeper J. Doig against West Bromwich Albion in a Football League match, before he had completed the qualifying period of 14 days' registration. Birmingham, too, played an ineligible player, and were disqualified from the Cup.

1891

The New Zealand FA was formed in 1891, although soccer there has always come a bad second-best to rugby—and the great All Blacks.

Also in 1891, the first Inter-League match was played, between the Football League and the Football Alliance.

Wembley 1923

The pictures on these pages show just some of the remarkable scenes at Wembley Stadium in April 1923, on the occasion of the first Cup Final to be staged there. An enormous crowd turned up, entering the ground over the walls as well as through the gates, and pouring onto the playing area in a swarm so dense that the kick-off was delayed for some forty-five minutes. When a space was finally cleared, Bolton Wanderers, white shirts, beat West Ham 2—0; our action picture shows Pym, the Bolton goalkeeper, punching the ball clear from a West Ham attack.

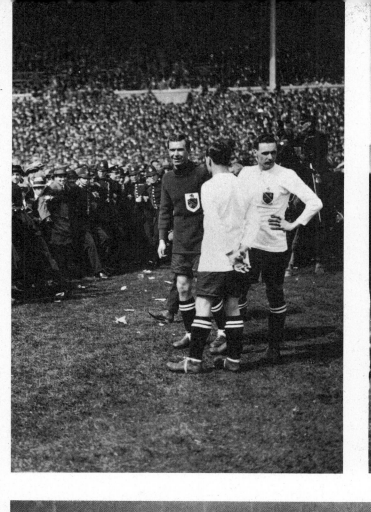

The FA introduced a rule the following year that club officials and players could not bet on matches. Clubs were made responsible for ensuring there was no wagering by spectators at football.

In that year, also, Liverpool achieved the longest run without defeat in Football League history. They won the Second Division championship with twenty-two wins and six draws in twenty-eight matches. At the other end of the scale, Northwich Victoria did not collect an away point all season.

1895

The Belgian FA was formed in 1895; so was Flamenge, the oldest club in Brazil, eleven years after the game was introduced into the country by British sailors.

Chile, too, saw the arrival of soccer. There the game is played nearly 2,000 feet above sea-level, and although the Chileans are rather overshadowed by the soccer deeds of other South American countries, a governing body was established which now controls 1,000 clubs.

The original FA Cup was stolen from a Birmingham shop where it had been on show following Aston Villa's victory in the 1895 Final. It was not recovered, and Lord Kinnaird donated a new trophy.

1896

The game was first played in Bulgaria in 1896, but their first club was not formed until 1909, and it was not until 1924 that they entered international football.

1898

High-scoring games were not uncommon in those

The Corinthians of the 1920s. This page: a group photo taken with the Queen's Park team before the annual match in Glasgow which that year, 1924, the Corinthians won 4—0. Opposite page, above left: the Corinthians in play against Blackburn Rovers and, above right, a telegram received after the match from Canada congratulating them on their victory. Below: Corinthians v. Brighton at Stamford Bridge.

formative years and Darwen suffered three 10—0 away defeats in the Second Division in 1898, against Manchester City, Walsall and Loughborough Town. On 26 November that year the First Division match between Sheffield Wednesday and Aston Villa was abandoned because of bad light after $79\frac{1}{2}$ minutes' play, with Wednesday leading 3—1. The remaining $10\frac{1}{2}$ minutes were played four months later, in March 1899. Wednesday scored another goal and the result was officially recorded as 4—1. Today, of course, clubs replay in full or the score at the time of abandonment is taken.

From 1896 onwards dribbling began to lose its appeal, except in Scotland. Emphasis was concentrated more on team-work than individual brilliance, although the game still provided household names. G. O. Smith, Steve Bloomer (Derby County), who scored twenty-eight goals in twenty-three matches in the international championships, Bob Crompton (Blackburn), capped forty-two times at full-back, Vivian Woodward (Tottenham)—these were a few names for the fan to conjure with as soccer moved beyond the turn of the century to the First World War.

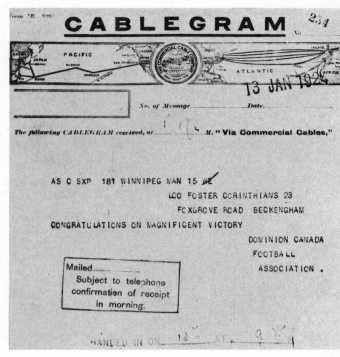

CABLEGRAM

13 JAN 1924

No. of Message_____ Date._____

The following CABLEGRAM received, at_____M. "Via Commercial Cables,"

AS C SXP 181 WINNIPEG MAN 15 WE

LCO FOSTER CORINTHIANS 23

FOXGROVE ROAD BECKENGHAM

CONGRATULATIONS ON MAGNIFICENT VICTORY

DOMINION CANADA

FOOTBALL

ASSOCIATION.

Mailed_____
Subject to telephone
confirmation of receipt
in morning.

HANDED IN ON_____

One of the most remarkable international records of all time was achieved by the 'Welsh Wizard' Billy Meredith, who played 669 Football League appearances for the two Manchester clubs and was picked for fifty full international matches for Wales between 1895–1920. Meredith played for Manchester City v. Newcastle in a Cup semi-final at the age of forty-nine years eight months, the oldest player to appear in a Cup-tie; and he was nearly forty-six when he played for Wales v. England on 15 March 1920.

The Argentinian FA was formed in 1895, and, in 1902, Sir Thomas Lipton presented a Cup to be competed for annually by Argentina and Uruguay.

1899

The buying and selling of players was now making sufficient impact for the FA to suggest to the League in 1899 that there should be a £10 limit on transfers. In fact, a £350 limit was imposed on 1 January 1908, but four months later this regulation was expunged by the FA. The Council decided there were too many loopholes permitting abuse of the system.

The growing popularity of the game as a spectator-sport provided fresh problems. The Sheffield United-Liverpool FA Cup semi-final at Fallowfield, Manchester, was abandoned at half-time because the crowd encroached on to the pitch.

Football had its first recorded fatality. Welsh international full-back D. Jones cut himself in training with Manchester City, lockjaw set in and he died.

R. E. Evans, an Englishman (who played for Aston Villa and Sheffield United), played for Wales v. England and England v. Wales at this time. He also represented both countries against Scotland and Ireland.

Fresh ground was broken in 1899 by the founding of the first club in Iceland. A national League was formed there in 1912, but Iceland still persists in being all-amateur; although the nation is very enthusiastic, it has little chance of much progress with a population about the size of a town like Southampton.

The German FA was formed in 1900 and today Germany has more registered players than England.

1901

The Hungarian FA was formed in 1901, as was the national League. Hungary's soccer success, it may be noted, does not stem from the wonderful Magyar side that became the first foreign international team to win on British soil in 1953—England were also

This page, from the top: happy Sheffield United players pictured after beating Cardiff City 1—0 in the 1925 Cup Final; a scene from a fifth-round tie the following year, with Gallacher of Newcastle rushing Wood, the Orient goalkeeper, and, bottom, Bolton in the white shirts keeping out the powerful Arsenal forward-line during a match at Highbury. Opposite page: two scenes from the 1926 Cup Final in which Bolton beat Manchester City 1—0.

victims of the Hungarians back in 1934, and the nation has a long footballing heritage.

1902

Although professionalism was firmly established, amateurs still figured in the national game at the highest level. Three amateurs, C. B. Fry at right-back, A. Turner (outside-right) and J. Turner (outside-left) were in the Southampton side which lost to Sheffield United in the 1902 Cup Final.

Bury emulated Preston's feat by winning the trophy in 1903 without conceding a goal—they themselves scored twelve.

Also in 1902, the Bohemian FA was formed, and, with British coaches visiting Prague in the years before the First World War, the game quickly developed.

1904

In February 1904 Aston Villa led Tottenham 1—0 in a second-round Cup tie when the crowd invaded the pitch. It was impossible to clear them and the match was abandoned at half-time. The FA ordered a replay at Villa Park, and Tottenham won the tie 1—0. But they were later fined £350 for the crowd incident.

There had been a crowd tragedy the previous season during the Scotland-England international at Ibrox Park, Glasgow. Part of the west stand collapsed when the match had been in progress for ten minutes. Twenty-five people were killed, twenty-four dangerously injured, 168 seriously injured and 172 slightly hurt. After half an hour's delay play was resumed and the game was drawn 1—1. This was later declared unofficial and the result deleted from international records.

Soon afterwards FIFA was formed. Its aims were: better control of the game on an international basis with provision for it to be played in all countries under the same set of rules. Belgium, France, Switzerland and the Netherlands originated the idea of a Federation and, together with Sweden and Spain, they held an inaugural meeting in Paris. In 1913 FIFA was given representation on the International Football Association Board.

The United Kingdom has twice ceased membership of FIFA. After the First World War the UK, Belgium, France and Luxembourg refused to be associated with Austria, Germany and Hungary, but they returned to membership in 1924. Four years later the UK left again after a disagreement over the definition of amateurism and broken-time payments. This time the rift lasted until 1946.

Back to 1904—and England were still the Masters. Woolwich Arsenal beat a Parisian XI 26—1 at Plumstead, a record win by a League side against a Continental team.

Opposite page: West Bromwich players walk off the pitch at Wembley after beating Birmingham 2—1 in the all-Midlands Final of 1931. This page, above: a skirmish round the Cardiff City goal on the day the Cup went to Wales, when Cardiff beat Arsenal 1—0 in 1927. Below left: Everton's marksman Dixie Dean, whose feat of scoring sixty goals in one season has still to be beaten. Below right: before the international with Spain in 1931, Ernie Blenkinsop, left, England's captain, shakes hands with Zamora, the famous Spanish goalkeeper.

1905
Transfer history was made in 1905 when the first four-figure fee changed hands. Middlesbrough paid £1,000 to Sunderland for Alf Common.

1906
The oldest Polish club was formed, in Cracow. In Brazil, the sailors of HMS Amethyst met Fuminese, and weeks later a League was formed in Rio. The Brazilian FA was established several years later, in 1914.

1907

The Finnish FA began in 1907, and the country had some success in the 1912 Olympics. But their first meeting with England brought an 8—0 defeat, all five English forwards scoring.

Because of the increase in professionalism, many old amateur clubs felt they were not receiving proper consideration from the FA. A meeting was called at the Holborn Restaurant and the Amateur FA formed. The clubs represented were: Cambridge University, Clapham Rovers, Corinthians, Old Carthusians, Old Etonians, Old Westminsters and the Swifts. Other clubs followed suit and there was a split with the FA until 1914. In May 1934, the title of the Association was changed to the Amateur Football Alliance.

1909

At Hampden Park, Glasgow, the replayed Scottish Cup Final between Rangers and Celtic ended in riot. Trouble started when the crowd realized there was to be no extra-time, the ground was wrecked, goalposts were uprooted and a great part of the stands, offices and club buildings set on fire. Hundreds were hurt in a long pitched battle with the police, firemen were attacked, their hoses cut and thrown on to the fire.

1910

England suffered her first-ever defeat abroad, beaten 2—1 in Copenhagen in an amateur international. That year Notts County sold their ground rights for a first round FA Cup-tie for £1,000. Bradford City won the match 4—2, but the gross takings fell short of the money they had paid. Such a procedure is now impossible, as clubs can only change venues by mutual arrangement.

1912

The FA of Canada was founded in 1912, but there has been no fully representative match between England and Canada since an England side beat the Canadians 6—1 at The Oval, although FA representative sides have toured the country.

England had already won the Olympic title at

This page, above: England attack the Scottish goal during the Wembley international of 1932. Below: the Arsenal team, League champions in 1932–3. Opposite page, above: Dixie Dean follows the ball into the Manchester City net after scoring for Everton in the 1933 Cup Final. Below: he receives the Cup from the Duchess of York (HM the Queen Mother). In this match players wore numbers for the first time in a Cup Final; Everton were numbered 1–11, Manchester City 12–22.

Shepherd's Bush, London, in 1908, and the same year they won the international championship without conceding a goal. In 1912 they captured the Olympic title for the last time to date, in Stockholm.

1913

The FA celebrated its fiftieth anniversary in 1913 with a lavish fifteen-course banquet; and a year later King George V went to Crystal Palace to make the Burnley-Liverpool Cup Final soccer's first Royal occasion. Freeman's goal won the match for Burnley in this, the last Final to be played at Crystal Palace.

Meanwhile, the Football League had ruled that goalkeepers had to play in distinctive colours. Another important change of rules was that goalkeepers had the privilege of using their hands restricted to within the penalty area. Just before the First World War the FA also amended the free-kick law to ensure that opponents stood ten yards from the ball.

The great Bloomer ended his career in 1913 with a record of 352 League goals. During the Cup replay at Hillsborough between Sheffield Wednesday and Wolverhampton, which Wednesday won 1—0, a wall collapsed and seventy-five people were injured.

1914

The outbreak of hostilities in 1914 brought about the formation of a Footballers' Battalion. In civilian life, soccer was able to carry on despite the war, although there were only a few hundred at Lincoln, the lowest attendance for a Cup-tie, when Norwich City and Bradford City played a third-round second replay 'behind closed doors'. This was done in order not to interfere with the production of armaments at nearby factories.

The First Division match between Middlesbrough and Oldham was abandoned after fifty-five minutes when the Oldham left-back Cook refused to leave the field after being ordered off. Middlesbrough led 4—1 at the time and the League ordered the result to stand. Oldham lost the championship by two points and Cook was suspended for twelve months.

1915

The 1915 Cup Final was played at Old Trafford, Manchester, and the first five clubs in the First Division came from Lancashire.

Entertainment Tax was applied to Soccer as a 'temporary measure' to help over expenditure on the war; it was removed in 1957.

Glasgow Celtic were undefeated in sixty-three games until 21 April 1917, when Kilmarnock ended the run with a 2—0 victory at Parkhead.

1920

The Football League was extended to forty-four clubs after the war and Division III (South) was formed in 1920. The International Board ruled that

in British championship matches goalkeepers should wear yellow jerseys.

Soccer started to become more popular in France. Forty clubs competed in the first Coupe de France, but professionalism did not come until 1932.

The Republic of Czechoslovakia was formed, and that same year (1920) a Czech international side reached the Final of the Olympic Games competition. But they disgraced themselves by walking off when losing 2—0 to Belgium after one of their players had been ordered from the field. In 1922 the new Czechoslovakian FA was formed.

The Royal Belgian FA was formed in 1920. Belgium has appeared in four World Cup Final tournaments but has lost every match bar one that was drawn.

The minimum admittance charge was raised from sixpence to one shilling after the war, and the next change was not made until 1942–3 when another threepence was added. The four-shilling minimum was brought into effect in 1965–6.

In season 1919–20 Motherwell outside-left R. Ferrier began a remarkable playing career of 626 matches in Scottish League football, spanning the years until 1937. Burnley won the English League championship, undefeated in thirty matches from their 2—0 defeat at Bradford in September 1920, to their 3—0 loss at Manchester City in March 1921.

1921

Stockport's ground was under suspension in 1921 and only thirteen people paid to see their Second Division match against Leicester at Old Trafford on 7 May. W. H. Minter, of St Albans, scored seven goals against Dulwich Hamlet in a replayed fourth qualifying round FA Cup-tie—but his side lost 8—7.

1923

The official attendance for the first Cup Final at Wembley was 126,047, but over 150,000 were inside to see a match that has gone into soccer's history-books as the 'White Horse Final'. This was so called because of a policeman on a white horse who helped control the people who invaded the stadium 'like some tidal wave carried along by its own momentum', according to one contemporary account. Traffic congested all approaches to Wembley and the match began some forty minutes late when the police had finally restored order. King George V watched the game, in which Bolton Wanderers beat West Ham United 2—0 with goals from David Jack and J. R. Smith.

Another Cup note in 1923: Corinthians took part in the competition for the first time. Liverpool won the championship for the second successive year, while S. Wynne, playing for Oldham v. Manchester United in a Second Division match, set a curious

This page, above: Moss, the Arsenal goalkeeper, saves in a match against Glasgow Rangers. Below: a two-referee system was tried out in the North v. South amateur international trial at Chester in 1935. Opposite page: two pictures of the mighty Arsenal side of the 1930s, in attack and defence. On the left, Alex James runs in to harass Holdcroft, the Preston goalkeeper, and, right, Eddie Hapgood clears a Chelsea attack, covered by Herbie Roberts, his 'stopper' centre-half.

record. He scored with a free kick and a penalty—but also put two goals into his own net!

A rare amateur in the professional game was W. V. Gibbins, who played for West Ham, Brentford, Bristol Rovers and Southampton in 176 League matches between 1923-34. He was West Ham's top scorer in 1930-1.

1924

A. Chandler created a record by scoring in sixteen consecutive League matches for Leicester in Division Two in 1924.

The laws were altered that year, the Scottish FA proposing that goals could be scored from corners. At first players taking corner-kicks dribbled the ball in and tried to score, and there was a certain amount of confusion. So the FA altered the wording of the law to make it clear that the taker of a corner could only have one kick. (There is only one recorded League match *without* a corner: when Newcastle and Portsmouth played a goalless draw in the First Division in December 1951.)

FA Cup competitions continued to provide many extraordinary occasions: also in 1924, Barrow and Gillingham had to meet five times, playing a total of nine and a half hours, before Barrow won 2—1.

1925

On the first day of the new offside rule Aston Villa beat Burnley 10—0. This rule had caused more trouble in soccer than any other. From 1886 it was defined: 'When a player plays the ball or throws it in from touch any player of the same side who, at such moment of playing or throwing-in, is nearer to his opponents' goal-line, is out of play and may not himself touch the ball or in any way interfere with an opponent until the ball has been played, unless there are, at such moment of playing or throwing-in, at least three of his opponents nearer their goal-line. A player is not out of play in case of a corner-kick or when the ball is kicked out from goal or when it has last been played by an opponent.'

The change from *three* opponents to *two* came about

because strategists such as Bill McCracken, a New-castle defender, became skilled in putting whole attacks off-side by clever anticipation and the simple ploy of moving upfield at the opportune moment.

The new rule also provided for a player not being offside under any circumstances in his own half. Since the offside rule was changed, the record number of League games in a season in which a club has stopped the opposition from scoring is twenty-nine, by Port Vale in 1953-4.

An odd family twist in 1925: Thomas Boyle and Harold Johnson won Cup medals with Sheffield United. Their fathers, Peter Boyle and Harold Johnson Senior, had also won medals with United in 1899 and 1902.

1926

Albert Geldard made his Second Division début for Bradford versus Millwall at the age of fifteen years 156 days; he remains the youngest player to make a début in English League football. Also in 1926, the first radio broadcast was made of a football match in England—Arsenal v. Sheffield United.

Huddersfield were a great side of the mid-1920s, winning the League championship title in three successive seasons. Manchester City, who reached Wembley in 1926 only to lose 1—0 to Bolton, had a still worse disappointment—they were relegated from the First Division that season.

1927

Dixie Dean, who scored thirty-seven hat-tricks in his eighteen seasons in top-class soccer, set a League record of sixty goals in a season for Everton in 1927-8. He beat by one goal the record set twelve months earlier by George Camsell, the Middlesbrough leader.

1928

The amateur club, Argonauts, tried to enter the Football League in 1928. They applied to join the Third Division (South) on their formation, but finished third in a poll of six clubs and only two were elected. Argonauts tried again the following year but again they came third in the poll. The next year they

did not collect one vote. Yet this ambitious side had provisionally booked to play at Wembley!

Other 1928 highlights: Ronnie Dix became the youngest goalscorer in the Football League—fifteen years 180 days—when he netted for Bristol Rovers against Norwich in a Third Division (South) match, having made his début the previous week.

Rotherham lost 11—1 to Bradford City and 10—1 to South Shields in the Third Division (North). Cardiff had the best defensive record in the First

Division (fifty-nine goals against), but were relegated.

What of soccer overseas? Argentina reached the Final of the Olympic Games tournament in 1928 and drew 1—1 with Uruguay, losing the replay 2—0.

1929
R. Suter played in goal for Halifax v. Darlington at the age of fifty years and nine months, the oldest Englishman ever to appear in the Football League.

1930
Austria, rated among the leading football nations for the greater part of the last forty years, produced its famous 'Wunderteam' in the early 1930s. This side beat Scotland 5—0, Germany 6—0 and just lost to England 4—3. The Austrians, recognized for their artistic football, were influenced in this period by Jimmy Hogan, the English coach with the Scottish-style methods. Austria was the last country to

Opposite page: Sunderland pierce the Preston defence to score in the 1937 Cup Final and, below, the victorious Sunderland team complete their lap-of-honour round the Wembley pitch. This page, below: soccer was televised direct for the first time in 1937 when a BBC mobile unit visited Highbury Stadium to film members of the Arsenal team in action. Our picture shows George Allison, Arsenal's manager, being interviewed.

England v. Rest of Europe, 1938. Opposite page, above: the Duke of Kent is introduced to the England team by Eddie Hapgood; on the far right is Willie Hall and, next to him, Stan Cullis. The other pictures show the dynamic Tommy Lawton menacing the Rest of Europe goal.

abandon the attacking centre-half, and the first to develop the art of funnel defence.

The Albanian FA was formed in 1930, but the country remained comparatively isolated from the international scene for many years.

England suffered her first defeat abroad in 1929—to Spain, by 4—3. The following year Uruguay won the first World Cup.

Brentford, then a Third Division (South) side, set a record in 1930 that can never be broken—they won all twenty-one of their home League matches.

Celtic goalkeeper J. Kennaway played for three countries. In 1928 he represented Canada against the USA; in 1930, America against Canada, and, while with Celtic, was selected for Scotland.

Manchester United lost their first twelve matches of the 1930 season. Their first victory was against Birmingham at Old Trafford on 1 November 1930—the worst-ever start to a season by a League club. In Division III (North), Nelson also had an unhappy time, losing every one of their away games.

1931
Arsenal, emerging as the mighty team of the 1930s, won the League title with a record total of sixty-six points in 1931, losing only four of their forty-two matches; and West Bromwich Albion celebrated a Cup victory and Second Division promotion in the same year. Attack-conscious Aston Villa set a First Division record by netting an impressive 128 goals.

Joe Hulme was a famous figure of the period. He

appeared in five Wembley Finals. He was outside-right for Arsenal in 1930 and 1936 as a winner; he was there in 1927 and 1932 as a loser. Hulme later moved to Huddersfield, and returned to Wembley in 1938, but unfortunately he collected another losers' medal. One of Hulme's losing Cup Finals in 1932 was memorable: Newcastle beat Arsenal 2—1, the deciding goal resulting from a centre that thousands thought was made after the ball had crossed the by-line.

The rules were changed to allow a goalkeeper to take four steps in possession of the ball instead of two.

1932
Stanley Matthews made his début for Stoke City in 1932—and went on to make 701 League appearances for Stoke and Blackpool before he retired in season 1964–5 at the age of fifty.

1933
Players were numbered in a Cup Final for the first time in 1933, the year Everton completed a notable hat-trick of winning the Second Division, the First and then the Cup in successive seasons. The numbering, incidentally, went from 1–11 for the Everton side, and from 12–22 for Manchester City. Johnny Arnold, who played football for Southampton and Fulham as an outside-left and cricket for Hampshire as a batsman, became a double international with his selection for England v. Scotland. He had already represented England at cricket, against New Zealand at Lord's in 1931.

1934
Herbert Chapman, manager of Huddersfield and then Arsenal, died in 1934. This was the year that Italy won the World Cup in Rome, and the England team that beat the world champions 3—2 at Highbury included seven Arsenal players.

Arsenal equalled Huddersfield's record of three

successive League championship wins, and London rivals Charlton made the ascent from Division III to Division I in two seasons.

S. Milton made an unhappy League début in goal for Halifax against Stockport on 6 January 1934, conceding thirteen goals. Joe Payne earned himself a place in the record books by scoring ten goals in a League match for Luton—he was known as 'Ten-Goal Payne' for the rest of his career—and Tranmere beat Oldham 13—4, the highest League aggregate score.

1935

In September 1935 N. Kernoghan, of Belfast Celtic, played for the Irish League against the Football League at the age of sixteen years and nine months.

1937

Millwall, renowned as Cup-fighters, became the first side from the Third Division to reach the semi-finals

The Cup Final of 1938 proved a thrilling battle, in which Preston beat Huddersfield 1—0 with a penalty by George Mutch scored in the last minute of extra-time. Above, left to right, King George VI meets the Preston team; Mutch forces a corner for Preston and, far right, his penalty-kick hits the back of the Huddersfield net.

of the competition in 1937, the year that the Scotland-England match at Hampden Park, Glasgow, attracted a British-record attendance of 149,547.

Denis Compton made the first of his seventy-eight Test appearances for England as a cricketer. He also played in wartime soccer internationals and in one Victory international against Scotland. Other well-known footballer-cricketers were: Andy Ducat (Surrey and Arsenal, Aston Villa and Fulham), Patsy Hendren (Middlesex and Manchester City, Coventry and Brentford), and the Hon. A. Lyttelton (Middlesex and Old Etonians).

Jimmy Delaney won a Scottish Cup medal with Glasgow Celtic in 1937, and went on to set a unique record by winning an English medal with Manchester United (1948), one for Northern Ireland with Derry City (1954) and another for Eire with Cork (1956).

Brechin City lost three games 10—0 in the Scottish League Division II, to Airdrieonians, Albion Rovers and Cowdenbeath.

1939
The numbering of players extended to League matches in 1939, and the same season saw the first and only six-figure attendance in a League match in Britain. Glasgow's 'Old Firm', Rangers and Celtic, attracted a crowd of 118,567.

The 1940s
An emergency committee was formed to manage football at the outbreak of the Second World War, during which the Football League ran two regional competitions. Soccer was disrupted, but never halted. Cameron Buchanan made his League début for Wolves against West Bromwich Albion at the age of fourteen in 1942, while goalkeeper Ron Simpson played in the Scottish League for Queen's Park at the same age.

Stan Mortensen made his international début in September 1943—against England at Wembley. Mortensen was reserve for England, but took over in the Wales side when Ivor Powell was unable to resume after the interval.

Interest in soccer was maintained despite the war. The Board of Trade allocated clothing coupons for football equipment. The boom years were ahead . . . but it was all a far cry from the public-school thinking that had set the machinery in motion in the nineteenth century by which soccer reached out to the far corners of the earth.

2

The Game Today

Soccer in the seventies is a far cry from the days of the enthusiastic amateurs of a century ago. It is a highly professional game that, through the vast network of the FIFA organization, is played in 130 countries by men of all creeds and colours.

Nations now honour their great players. One man, the Brazilian, Pele, who became a soccer immortal through the deeds of his country in World Cup competitions, certainly earns more money from the game than the Prime Minister of England, and is reputedly a multi-millionaire, Pele, now in his late twenties, was able to demand a salary of £2,700 per month, plus £700 for every international match, when his last three-year contract expired in 1970. The previous contract gave him a mere £1,680 a month!

Vast crowds watch the Peles of the world soccer scene and the record attendance for a match stands at 200,000, the crowd that watched the World Cup Final between Brazil and Uruguay at the Maracana Stadium, Rio de Janeiro, Brazil on 16 July 1950.

The World Cup, contested every four years by the cream of the world's footballing talent, is the peak of soccer achievement. Four hundred million viewers in Europe, Russia, North America and the Far East watched the 1966 Final on television and the final rounds, which were played in England, broke all previous crowd records.

A total of 1,458,043 spectators attended the thirty-two matches in the various centres in London, Sheffield, Manchester and the North-East of England, and in addition the 127 preliminary-round matches played all over the world were watched by 4,091,478. This made a grand total of 5,549,521 for the complete tournament, which was won by England for the first time.

Above: defeat of the champions, Mexico 1970. Gerd Müller rams the ball past England goalkeeper Bonetti to make it 3—2 to West Germany in extra-time of their World Cup quarter-final, thus putting England out of the championship and avenging for West Germany the Wembley defeat of 1966. Opposite page: Pele regains his crown as the world's most exciting goal-scorer. Here he scores his first goal of the 1970 World Cup in Brazil's opening match of the competition in which they defeated Czechoslovakia 4—1.

Geoff Hurst, of West Ham United, became the first player to score a hat-trick in a World Cup Final when England gained a 4—2 victory in extra-time against the West Germans on 30 July 1966. World-record receipts of £200,000 were paid by the 93,000 crowd.

The winners of the nine World Cup tournaments, with the host country shown in brackets, are:

	1930 (Uruguay)	
Uruguay 4		Argentine 2
	1934 (Italy)	
Italy 2		Czechoslovakia 1
	1938 (France)	
Italy 4		Hungary 2
	1950 (Brazil)	
Uruguay 2		Brazil 1
	1954 (Switzerland)	
W. Germany 3	Hungary 2	
	1958 (Sweden)	
Brazil 5		Sweden 2
	1962 (Chile)	
Brazil 3		Czechoslovakia 1
	1966 (England)	
England 4		W. Germany 2
	1970 (Mexico)	
Brazil 4		Italy 1

The World Cup has certainly developed since the Second World War into one of the most important of sporting competitions. The interest created in almost every part of the globe, through the medium of television in latter years, has had far-reaching effects well beyond the normal sporting spheres.

There has never been as much interest in the competition as there was in 1970. Even the United States had theatres packed for closed-circuit screening of matches.

In theory, international competition at this world-wide level should do nothing but good for soccer, but the win-at-all-costs attitude of some nations has often detracted from the purely sporting nature of the series. Politics have entered into World Cup calculations and, instead of ironing out national differences, football has sometimes been used as an end to a means, creating more harmful effects than good.

The World Cup itself, a gold cup known as the Jules Rimet trophy after the late Monsieur Jules Rimet, who was honorary president of FIFA from 1921 to 1954, was won outright by Brazil in 1970. The Brazilians retained the trophy after their third success. A FIFA Cup will replace it as the Everest of achievement among footballing nations.

The World Congress of 1928, inaugurated by FIFA, decided to hold a World Championship every four years. Uruguay organized the first series in 1930, but this was a shadow of the competition as it was to develop. Only thirteen nations took part and the host country became the first winners.

Italy were the next hosts, in 1934, and again the 'home side' were the winners, this time out of twenty-nine countries. Italy retained the title when the World Cup moved to France in 1938, with an entry of twenty-five, but because of the war the next competition did not take place until 1950. This was the first occasion on which the home associations—England, Scotland, Ireland and Wales—participated, as they were not members of FIFA between 1928 and the end of the war.

In 1950 the home international championship was made part of the qualifying competition for the World Cup finals, which took place in Brazil. England won the home championship and went to Brazil, but Scotland, although the two top countries qualified, declined to go as runners-up.

The World Cup Final, 1966—England (the hosts) v. West Germany. This page, above: the teams line up before the start, facing a packed Wembley Stadium and an unseen television audience of over four hundred million, many of whom were seeing soccer for the first time. Below and, opposite page, above: dejection for Germany as England score through Martin Peters (No. 16). Opposite page, right: England's turn for despair, as Bobby Charlton kneels on the West German goal-line after a near-miss. Play during the first ninety minutes was fast and thrilling, with the West Germans levelling to 2—2 in the dying moments of normal time. Opposite page, left: the players rest before the cruel test of extra-time.

England's soccer prestige abroad was dealt a disastrous blow by this first participation in the World Cup. Having beaten Chile 2—1 at the giant new Rio Stadium, England lost 1—0 to the USA at Belo Horizonte, one of the greatest soccer shocks of all time. England's final elimination (and humiliation) followed another 1—0 defeat, this time by Spain.

Switzerland was the venue for the 1954 Final series and there were thirty-five entries. Scotland as well as England won through the qualifying rounds, but then the Scots did not score a goal in two games and were eliminated in the first round.

The 1954 tournament remains notorious because it provided one of the most unpleasant international matches ever staged, the quarter-final between Brazil and Hungary. The Hungarians won 4—2, but not

before English referee Arthur Ellis had sent off two Brazilian players and one Hungarian, as well as awarding a penalty to both sides. This game became known as the 'Battle of Berne', with unpleasant scenes at the end both on and off the field. Several players, officials and policemen were injured.

The entry for the 1958 World Cup increased to fifty-one countries but four of these withdrew without playing a game. The number increased to fifty-six for the series in Chile in 1962.

Soccer has progressed a long way from the days of the £1,000-transfer-fee—indeed it is amusing to recall that steps were taken back in 1908 to peg transfer dealings in England to £350. The biggest sum of money ever paid by one club to another for the transfer of a player is some £394,000, for Pietro Anastasi, when Juventus signed him in May 1968 from another Italian club, Varese.

The leap from Alf Common, the first £1,000-transfer player, to Sormani provides an indication of the growth of professionalism around the world, and heavily underlines the financial demands induced by the need for success. Del Sol (Real Madrid to Juventus), Peiro (Atletico Madrid to Torino), Suarez (Barcelona to Internazionale Milan), Amarildo (Botafago, Brazil to AC Milan), Denis Law (Torino to Manchester United), Sormani (Mantova to AS Roma) —these players set a trend of spiralling transfer-fees involving deals in excess of £100,000.

The second half of the 1960s produced an era of six-figure transfer fees. Chelsea paid £100,000 for Tony Hateley, a goalscorer of repute with Aston Villa and renowned for his headwork, but sold him to Liverpool some months later at a fee of around £95,000. Liverpool in turn, recouped most of that vast outlay when they transferred Hateley to Coventry City and, with the new regulations entitling players to receive five per cent of a transfer fee, his personal bank balance soared alongside the fantastic £280,000 invested in his services by three First Division clubs. England international Alan Ball moved from Black-

pool to wealthy Everton for £110,000 and Scottish international Jim Baxter went from Sunderland to Nottingham Forest for £100,000. And in the first half of the 1967-8 season Sheffield United collected two £100,000 cheques for their strikers, Mick Jones, who moved to Leeds, and Alan Birchenall, bought by Chelsea. Tottenham established a new British record fee when they paid Southampton £125,000 for England Under-23 goalscorer Martin Chivers. This record was later raised to £165,000 when Allan Clarke, who had earlier joined Leicester from Fulham for a six-figure fee and the £50,000-valued Frank Large, moved on to Leeds. The first £200,000 transfer deal in Britain was completed in 1969, and again Tottenham helped establish a record. They paid £146,000 for West Ham's World Cup star Martin Peters, and transferred former England striker Jimmy Greaves, who was valued at £54,000, as part of the deal.

The World Cup Final, 1970. This page, above: Jairzinho about to pounce as the ball rolls tantalizingly out of reach of Italian goalkeeper Albertosi and Facchetti, the captain. Below right: this time the Brazilian attack is repulsed as the Italians race back to cover against the double spearhead of Pele and Tostao. This page, top: Rivelino, one of the new stars of the Brazilian forward-line, leaves an Italian player helplessly upended after a tricky Brazilian move at a free-kick. Opposite page above: the Brazilian team line up before the Final. The players, from the left, are Carlos Alberto, Brito, Gerson, Clodoaldo, Everaldo, Tostao, Piazza, Rivelino, Pele, Jairzinho, Felix. Below: like puppies the Brazilian players clamber all over each other in celebration of winning the Jules Rimet Trophy outright.

Scotland entered the £100,000 stakes when Hibernian centre-forward Colin Stein turned down a chance to join Everton and opted to stay north of the border with Glasgow Rangers. Liverpool manager Bill Shankly created a sensation when he invested

The Transfer Market

Today, in the increasingly competitive atmosphere of national and continental club championships, transfer-fees climb ever more steeply and, in Britain, it is no longer unusual for a club to pay £100,000 for a key player who may help his team into one of the big European competitions. On these pages are just some of the players who set the big-time market in motion. This page, above: Angelo Sormani, transferred to AS Roma in 1963 for a record-breaking £220,000. Below: Alfredo di Stefano, left, Real Madrid's Argentine-born striker, and big John Charles, the Welsh international who left Leeds United for Juventus, Turin. Opposite page, left to right: Allan Clarke (transferred from Leicester to Leeds for £165,000), and Pietro Anastasi, for whom Juventus paid the all-time record fee of £394,000. Below them are Luis Suarez (Barcelona to Inter-Milan) and Amarildo (Botafogo, Brazil to Fiorentina via AC Milan).

£100,000 of his club's money on Alun Evans, a reserve with Wolves at the time and still in his teens.

Soccer, for all its sophistication and image-protection, is still the game of the working classes, a chance for the man in the street to identify himself and to rise above the humdrum of everyday work. The soccer player of the 1960s, despite his elevation in terms of high wages and show-business following, remains a symbol of the working classes.

In the years between the World Wars poverty bred the dedication to rise to eminence in the sporting world. Soccer managers and scouts (the discoverers of talent for the game) used to say, 'Whistle down a pit and you'll find a hungry footballer waiting to come up'. Those days may have gone, as has the image of a soccer spectator as a member of the lower class wearing a cloth cap and muffler, but the working-class origins remain.

Soccer in England, the birthplace of the game, maintains a healthy position as the number-one spectator sport. The Football League, according to its President, Mr Len Shipman, is the 'envy of Europe'. The Football League sent representatives to a meeting of twelve European Leagues in Paris in 1967 because so many of the other Leagues were reported to be struggling, and Mr Shipman reported afterwards, 'Our League, in fact, is probably the only League in the world doing really well'.

This is not to suggest that soccer is on the wane, rather it is to emphasize the point that the game has developed to a stage where success is of paramount importance if football is to rival the multitudinous counter-attractions of modern life.

The Football League provides the classic example. Attendances in the First Division certainly support Mr Shipman's view, and a top club such as Manchester United averages well over 50,000 spectators a game. Their opening nine League matches of the 1967–8 season were watched by an impressive total of 478,626 fans, with an average of 54,715 at home and 51,952 away.

United, under their manager Sir Matt Busby, a former Scottish international, have achieved a degree

The dream of every club in Europe—from Portugal to Siberia—is to win the European Cup. Real Madrid had a fantastic early run, winning the first five tournaments (1956–60). This page, top: di Stefano, white shirt, steers home Madrid's first goal in the 1960 Final against Eintracht, Frankfurt, which his team won 7—3. Centre: Puskas scores for Madrid in the same match. Bottom: joy in the snow at Tottenham as Bobby Smith, No. 9, scores for Spurs in their 1962 quarter-final against Dukla Prague. Opposite page, above left: Costa Pereira (Benfica) saves from Sani (AC Milan) in the 1963 Final. Above right: in the European Cup Winners' Cup Final of 1965, Alan Sealey scores for West Ham against TSV Munich. Below: captain Bobby Moore and his West Ham teammates with the Cup.

The Pools

While British clubs dream of winning the European Cup, their supporters also dream of winning the Pools. Millions each week gamble a few shillings, or more, in the hope that their forecasts will win one of the top dividends, possibly bringing them a prize of more than £300,000. This page, above: well-known sportsman Andy Capp checks his coupon. Below: a sample coupon from Vernons, one of the leading Pools' promoters, and a lucky winner—Mr Percy Harrison from Lincolnshire, seen receiving his record-breaking cheque for £338,356 from actress Glynis Johns. Opposite page, above: the industry at work, checking coupons at Littlewoods' vast premises in Liverpool. Below: a great day in the life of Norah Loftus, who became the guest of honour at the hotel where she worked after she had won a handsome first-dividend prize.

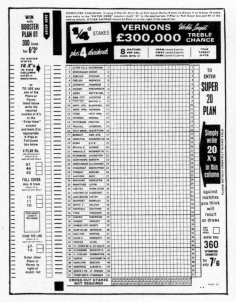

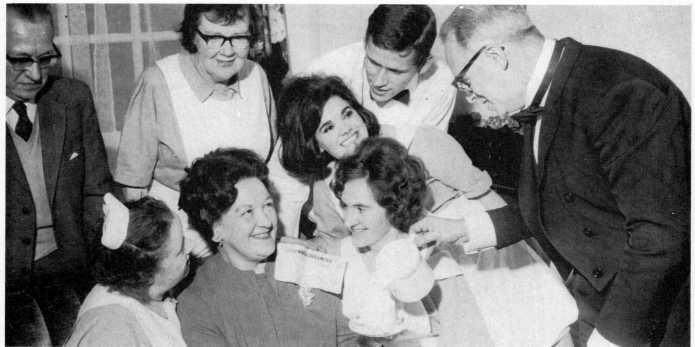

of consistency in the post-war period that is un-paralleled in England. They have been at the fore-front in both League and Cup, and were pioneers in the expanding European competitions.

What of the other end of the scale? Workington, who play in the Fourth Division, have played before less than 2,000 spectators on too many occasions for financial comfort. Workington is a soccer outpost in all senses of the word.

The fight for survival of the Workingtons of the English football world highlights a problem the game has to face in the years ahead. Soccer at Workington is on a different plane to Manchester United, yet the two clubs are bound by the same League regulations and rulings and compete in the same market for players. Yet Workington's annual takings from attend-ances would not cover the wages of a Manchester star of the calibre of George Best or Bobby Charlton.

Directors dig deep into their own pockets to keep a club like Workington on the map. Pools schemes sub-sidize the strugglers, but with most of them the only hope is for a successful, money-spinning run in the Cup, or a miracle in some unforseeable form. The little clubs inevitably lose their quota of good young players to the cheque-books of their wealthier counterparts, and the prospect of anything better than a grim battle for survival is remote.

Even in the higher Divisions the gap is widening. Few clubs in England are solvent on gate receipts, and even those with attendances in the 25–30,000 category have to struggle to keep up with the élite, to qualify for lucrative European competitions.

Leicester City, with a modestly healthy following, paid out £150,000 on new players in a bid to maintain interest and keep their First Division place. Their reward was a gate of just over 28,000.

Glasgow Celtic became the first British club to win the European Cup when they beat Inter-Milan 2—1 in Lisbon in 1967. Opposite page: two dramatic moments from this game as, above left, Celtic equalize and, below, goalkeeper Simpson jumps to catch a dangerous lob. After this win, Celtic went on to play a now infamous series of matches against Racing Club of Buenos Aires for the unofficial world club championship. Opposite, above right, and this page, below: tempers flare in the final play-off in Montevideo, which Celtic lost 1—0. This page, above: Celtic, dark shirts, on the attack against Dynamo Kiev who eliminated them in the first round of the European Cup the following season.

What is the answer? A 'Super League' has been mooted. There has been talk of a European League, pitting the best clubs of each country against one another. The major advantage would be that the top teams would no longer be hampered by the 'little fish'. The disadvantage would be that even in a competition of super-teams some would have to fail—and the problem of decreasing support would have to be faced all over again. The fanatical followings in such centres as Manchester and Liverpool might have their enthusiasm damped by following an unsuccessful team—even if the opposition was of the highest order.

The Football League jealously guards the interests of its smallest and most impoverished members and resists all talk of a change in structure which would give clubs like Manchester United the chance to break away. But it is likely that more clubs will go to the wall, after the manner of Accrington Stanley, if present trends continue.

Few clubs can exist on gate-money alone. Take Brentford of the Fourth Division. In 1969–70 they received £41,896 in gate money at home and £5,753 from away trips. Yet their players' wages cost £40,000 and their overall expenses were over £60,000.

Perhaps the Football League, with ninety-two member clubs, is unwieldy, but the basic fact remains that this competition is still the most successful in Europe. France, as a footballing nation, has in recent years faded from the top level, and through this general lack of success the famous Racing Club of Paris had to move its headquarters from the French capital. Interest and support continued to tail off and the club finally disbanded.

European participation is now a 'must' for the ambitious club. There are three major European

Opposite page: the Rattin incident in the 1966 World Cup quarter-final between England and Argentina. Rattin, the Argentina captain, sent off after fouling Jackie Charlton, refused to leave the field. When he finally went, England won the match 1—0; afterwards, England manager Alf Ramsey stepped in to prevent George Cohen exchanging shirts with Argentina's Gonzalez, and later he severely criticized the opposing team's violent methods of play.

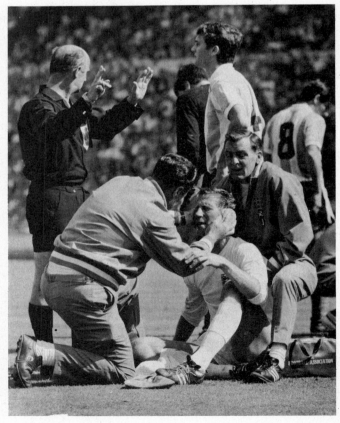

soccer tournaments: the European Cup, contested by the champion League club of each member-country of the European Union of Football Associations; the European Cup Winners' Cup, competed for by the winners of each of the national Cup competitions, and the European Fairs' Cup, a competition inaugurated in 1955—the first tournament took three years to decide—and originally between clubs representing cities which stage trade fairs.

Real Madrid, of Spain, won the first five European Cup tournaments, and repeated their success in 1966. Other winners have been Benfica, of Portugal, Milan AC and Internazionale Milan (Italy), Glasgow Celtic (Scotland), Manchester United (England), Feijenoord (Holland) and Ajax Amsterdam (Holland).

The record for the Cup Winners' Cup is: Fiorentina (Italy), Atletico Madrid (Spain), Tottenham (England), Sporting Lisbon (Portugal), West Ham (England), Borussia Dortmund and Bayern Munich (West Germany), AC Milan (Italy), Slovan Bratislava,

Goalkeepers

The most-photographed men in football, goalkeepers and their antics are a constant source of material for the lines of Press cameramen who are a regular part of the match-day scene. This page: Gordon West, of Blackpool, above, before he moved to Everton, and the great Lev Yashin of Russia twist and stretch in mid-air as they leap to stop the unstoppable. Opposite page, above: a memorable goal for Celtic, and a painful moment for Dynamo Kiev goalkeeper Bannikov, during the semi-final of the European Cup Winners' Cup in 1966. Below left: the goalkeeper's revenge, or how to punch out a corner and make a soft landing on the opposition. The goalkeeper is Mike McVittie of St Johnstone, the victim Celtic's Bobby Lennox. Below right: the other side of a goalkeeper's life, the watching and waiting, come wind, rain or sunshine, while play goes on at the other end. For Aston Villa 'keeper Withers there is the consoling thought that his team must be doing all right so long as they do not need him.

73

the first East European winners, and Manchester City and Chelsea (England).

Barcelona (Spain) have won the Fairs' Cup trophy three times, the other winners being Valencia (Spain), who have won it twice, AS Roma (Italy), Real Zaragoza (Spain), Ferencvaros (Hungary) and Dynamo Zagreb (Yugoslavia). The last four winners have been English clubs, Leeds United, Newcastle United, Arsenal and Leeds United again.

An unofficial club championship of the world was inaugurated in 1960, a contest on a home-and-away two-leg basis between the winners of the European Cup and the winners of the South American Cup. These are the world club champions: Real Madrid (Spain); Penarol (Uruguay)—twice; Santos (Brazil) —twice; Internazionale Milan (Italy)—twice; Racing

This page, above: the ins and outs of sportsmanship at international level. Uruguay's Silva, left, is sent off during the World Cup quarter-final against West Germany and, right, Germano, captain of Portugal, receives the silver salver on behalf of his team in recognition of their good sportsmanship during the 1966 Series. This page, below, and opposite page: Saturday afternoon at Sunderland's Roker Park, at White Hart Lane, Tottenham, above, and Craven Cottage, Fulham, below. Despite the violence, both on and off the pitch, and the pressing financial problems of the smaller clubs, the Football League is still the best-run and most prosperous in Europe.

Club (Argentina); Estudiantes (Argentina); AC Milan (Italy); Feijenoord (Holland).

The now infamous 1967 match between the Argentinians and Glasgow Celtic, decided by a single goal in favour of Racing during a third-match play-off, underlined the need for FIFA control of these world

games and brought into the open a real soccer problem. Six players were ordered off during the final match—one Scot was sent off in the last minute but did not, in fact, leave the field—and arguments raged afterwards over the need for sterner refereeing control, and even over the advisability of continuing matches of an international type between clubs with players of differing temperaments.

These events were an unhappy aftermath to the World Cup competition in England the year before.

In 1966 Rattin, the Argentine captain, was sent off the field during a quarter-final tie at Wembley against

This page, above: the changing fortunes of football. Since this picture was taken in 1963 at a Third Division game between Queen's Park Rangers and Northampton, QPR have won the League Cup and been in and out of the First Division, while Northampton have been twice promoted and twice relegated, going from the Third Division to the First in two seasons, and back to the Third again. Below: Lazarus, centre, wheels round after scoring the winning goal for QPR against West Bromwich Albion in the 1967 League Cup Final. Opposite above: to keep the fans happy, Birmingham laid on a half-time leg-show one Saturday in 1967, but reactions were hostile—'far too sexy', said one official—and the experiment was abandoned. Below: at Fourth Division Brentford the struggle for survival goes grimly on, take-overs are resisted and more money is borrowed; many of their supporters remember the happier days of the 1930s when Brentford played in the First Division.

Television

Four hundred million people saw the
World Cup Final in 1966, via a world-
wide TV link-up. Selected League or
Cup matches are screened on both
channels in Britain, and audience-
figures more than justify the coverage of
both week-end and mid-week games.
Opposite page, above, and below left:
the demand for soccer is such that large
crowds now turn up at the home ground
to watch their team playing away on
closed-circuit TV. They cheer and jeer,
wave scarves and rattles, and toilet-rolls
stream out on to the pitch. Although
these are still early days, and provided
the winter weather does not deter the
fans too much from going to a 'canned'
performance, closed-circuit shows may
have a big future in soccer. Opposite
page, below right: another successful
experiment was tried out recently in
Glasgow, when a brewery chain put on
soccer films in the lounge bars of some
of their pubs, and found themselves
playing to packed houses of happy,
thirsty customers.

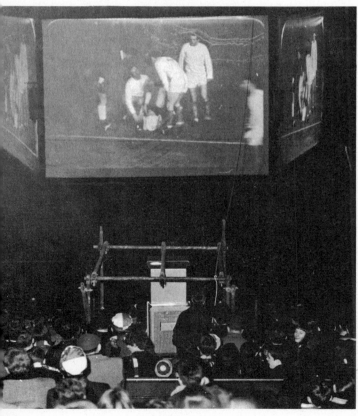

The remains at Peel Park, Accrington, pictured five years after Accrington Stanley withdrew from the Football League in 1962 in the face of ever-rising debts. The directors' entrance resembles a bomb-site, and hens parade on the pitch.

England, and South American passions were further roused by the description in an interview given after the match by the England team-manager, Alf Ramsey, in which he spoke of the Argentinians as 'animals'. Sir Alf, as he later became, apologized for his remark, but the scar remained and the unhappy conclusion was that part of the Celtic-Racing Club trouble stemmed from that moment. As a direct result of the sending-off, Rattin was suspended for four internationals and team-mates Onega and Ferreiro for three.

The passion the game arouses in South America, added to the different interpretations placed on the same set of rules by players in various countries, forms the basis for endless argument. Body-checking, for example, is an accepted fact of soccer life in South America and in many European countries as well. What constitutes a foul and a continual source of irritation to British audiences and players is regarded as no stronger than a form of gamesmanship elsewhere. Nor can the South Americans tolerate harassment of a goalkeeper, another common cause of friction.

Despite this the 1970 World Cup in Mexico was memorable as the first in which a player was not sent off—there were only four penalty kicks awarded.

Some nations have not drawn back from penalizing rough play. Belgium suspended players of Standard Liège and Anderlecht for six months in 1963-4, and three members of the West German side Munich 1860 were punished for misconduct in a League match against Borussia Dortmund. For striking a referee one of the players was banned from the game for six months and another was suspended for three.

Clubs and national associations no longer tolerate indiscipline among players. The then Chelsea manager, Tommy Docherty, attracted front-page headlines in 1965 when he sent home eight players who

broke a curfew at their hotel in Blackpool, where the team was staying before an away match, and then fielded reserve players in the game.

Ferenc Sipos, Hungary's centre-half, was suspended for a month when he had a night out on the town during pre-World Cup training, and Switzerland suspended three players during the 1966 World Cup when they returned to their Sheffield hotel an hour late; subsequently they were banned from international matches.

Despite these and other measures, however, soccer is still chiefly beset by the problem of violence, not only on the field of play but among crowds as well.

In South America every effort is made to keep fan and player apart, by the erection of wire barriers, moats and other devices; and fire hoses and tear gas are often on call. In England, where the problem has been confined to youngsters or the occasional hot-head running onto the pitch, the problem has not reached such acute proportions.

There was consternation, however, when a Second Division match at Millwall in 1967 ended with the referee being knocked down and kicked as a section of the crowd ran onto the pitch. Despite much talk of closing the ground for a period, or of putting up a wire fence, the FA's decision was to fine Millwall £1,000 and warn them of the consequences in future. Millwall then raised the level of the wall around part of the ground to prevent further trouble.

An increasing problem in the Football League in 1969 was that of crowd behaviour. The ratio of police at an English League match is one per thousand spectators, a ratio which used to be more than enough when a police-constable received due respect, but which seemed inadequate for recent times, when the special social problems of the country were being reflected at soccer matches. It became almost a common occurrence to see young fans—by far the majority were teenagers or younger—being led from the terraces with blood streaming from wounds caused by a multitude of 'offensive weapons'.

Clubs banned supporters from carrying banners,

but bottles, meat-hooks, sandbags and knives were found on louts arrested at many soccer grounds. Psychiatrists were called in to try and explain this trend towards hooliganism, but the answers applied generally to the behaviour and attitudes of the country as a whole, not merely to sport.

Railway staff reported the wrecking of compartments by vandals on excursion trains, needless damage to property that was not necessarily related to the result of a match, and railway police were detailed to travel with supporters to try and stop the hooliganism.

A spate of after-match damage as crowds streamed away from grounds was another unpleasant feature. Windows were smashed—at Tottenham they included the windows of shops owned by two of the players—and people were knocked to the ground as they got in the way of gangs of up to 200 louts. Programme-sellers were assaulted and robbed. Mobs howled for the removal of an unsuccessful manager.

England was by no means alone in Europe with the problem of crowd misbehaviour. When Chelsea

This page: jubilation on the part of spectators is one thing, violence another. Here a Rangers fan is heaved off after attacking players in the opposing Celtic side. Glasgow has a long history of bitter Rangers–Celtic battles. Opposite page, below: in Argentina, hot-blooded fans are kept off the pitch by means of a large moat twenty feet deep and filled with water up to eight feet. Above: French striker di Nallo is tackled by West Germany's Weber. For di Nallo and his teammates the problem is not how to keep out the fans, but how to bring them in; interest in France has tailed off sadly since the great days of Racing Club de Paris and Stade de Reims.

visited Roma for a Fairs' Cup-tie after a rough first leg between the two clubs in London, they were subjected to a bombardment of stones and missiles. The Italian FA fined Roma for failing to keep their spectators under control, and the Fairs' Cup committee banned the club from competing in further competitions.

Not long afterwards, two more clubs were fined following disturbances in European Cup-ties: West Germany's Werder Bremen because of a riot after

their match against Partizan Belgrade, and Dynamo Bucharest, some of whose spectators invaded the pitch and attacked players of Internazionale Milan.

It was long debated in Britain that violence off the field was related to the conduct of the players, but this was far from the case on many occasions. It extended throughout the country, from Liverpool to London and from Manchester to Glasgow, and the only real connection was that the majority of incidents were recorded by the so-called supporters of successful teams. A day out 'at football' did not seem to constitute a day out to some unless it involved damage or mischief, and from Liverpool to Tottenham came reports of stabbings in the crowd.

The symptoms of violence spread alarmingly on the field, too. The huge financial rewards made outbursts understandable in the case of top stars who were involved to the extent of hundreds of pounds on a result or a decision, but the disease spread right down the scale. Not only were international stars affected, but so were the lesser lights of minor amateur leagues and parks' football. As a result, disciplinary committees became overburdened.

To remedy the situation, the FA and the Football League announced that they would take a firm line in dealing with persistent offenders, and suspensions of up to eight weeks were awarded. The arguments that soccer was a game of passion, of continual bodily contact and emotional strain, were swept aside. Referees were given complete backing and, if this gave rise to occasional injustices, in cases where abuse or dissent received harsher punishment than a tackle that might have produced a broken limb, the overall effect was to put a brake on the disorders.

Other countries had similar problems. In Madrid, for example, a Third Division player was banned from the game for life by the Spanish Federation when he lost his temper after his side had been beaten 4—1 at home. He kicked the referee so hard that the official suffered a double fracture of the leg.

One further contributory factor towards the trend to rough play was, undoubtedly, money. The removal of the maximum wage in England—it was once £20-a-week—heralded a great future for the game, but it should be remembered that in the last season of the fixed-maximum wage only eighteen players were sent off in Football League matches. In the six seasons that followed, the number of dismissals rose at an alarming rate to a record fifty in 1966-7. The upward surge of the rough-play graph continues.

The Football League started an investigation into the relationship between cash-incentives for players and violence, which involved a survey of thousands of players' contracts. What the authorities feared was that clubs were bending the bonus rule by introducing

The Fans

From the small Scottish fan, being escorted from the pitch, below, to the howling mob on Liverpool's Spion Kop, opposite, the ardour of a true fan knows almost no bounds. A true fan goes to every home game and to most away matches as well; he will queue all night for Cup tickets, even follow his team to Poland, and his talk will be of little else but football. All the joy of supporting the winning team shines in the face of the young Nottingham Forest fan, opposite, and many will remember the happy Everton supporter, this page, above, who invaded the pitch at Wembley during the 1966 Cup Final in which his team beat Sheffield Wednesday. He gave the Wembley police one of the finest chases ever seen on television. Below him is the other type of fan: the phlegmatic 'loner' who climbs immense obstacles, the better to admire the flowing rhythms, the cut-and-thrust patterns of the game spread before him.

clauses guaranteeing players up to £30 for each League point gained. The League attitude has always been against cash incentives for individual games, and their Regulation 41 stipulates that bonuses for a win must not exceed £4, with £2 for a draw.

The League president underlined the official attitude when he said, 'We are not against talent-money for teams that win honours or high places in the table, but it appears to us that big cash-incentives, when the emphasis is placed on the individual match, can lead to violent conduct'. Yet it was an established fact that several clubs were paying bonuses, not to win honours but to avoid relegation. Newcastle, in the 1966-7 season, shared £11,000 among their players for escaping the drop to the Second Division, and then offered contracts for the following season paying each man £20-a-point once the club had passed the 'safety-margin' of thirty-five points.

Fear of defeat is, of course, not purely a club problem any more. Soccer in some countries is more an exercise in which defence comes before attack—destruction rather than construction. In this way a world-class player such as the Brazilian, Pele, can be ruled out of a competition by fierce attention from the opposition. In the 1966 World Cup Pele was injured in the first match in England, missed the second and finally limped out of the third, and Brazil's hopes of providing their eighty-million people with a third successive win dwindled to nothing.

Argentina and Uruguay often employed eight of their team in strictly defensive roles in the 1966 World Cup, and Italian League football is now so obsessed by defence that often more games are played than there are goals. This attitude is only one reason—but an important one—why success in soccer is harder than ever to achieve. Brazil spared nothing in the way of preparation for the 1966 World Cup. They were so confident of winning the trophy outright that they had another, to be known as the Winston Churchill Cup, ready to donate in its place.

Soccer is more than a game in Brazil, for many it is a reason almost for living. That is why the Brazilian authorities spent millions of dollars in 1966. They toured the world in search of experience. Players were subjected to physical examinations that, in any other context, would have been outrageous. A team of nearly fifty doctors checked everything from food-fads and feet to the blood circulation, digestion and love-life

World Cup qualifying matches for Mexico 1970: Scotland, Wales and N. Ireland bow out. Opposite page, above: Riva of Italy powers the ball past Wales' Gary Sprake for his side's third goal. Below: Dzodzuashvili makes a spectacular clearance from the head of Dougan in the match in Moscow in which Russia beat N. Ireland 2—0. This page: Scotland are defeated in Hamburg. In the top picture, West German goalkeeper Maier saves from McNeill. Below: Libuda scores the decisive goal.

of the playing squad. When television cameras peered at dentists examining players' teeth the nation looked in. Molars became compulsive viewing! That is soccer on the grand international scale in this modern age.

In 1970 the World Cup was held in Mexico, where the altitude and climate provided Europeans with many problems. Sir Alf Ramsay, team manager of England, the 1966 champions, made efforts to counter the problems by arranging a close-season tour at the end of the 1968–9 season and playing games in Mexico, Uruguay and Brazil.

What is the Everton fan saying to Manchester United players Nobby Stiles and Harry Gregg? What is Nobby Stiles saying to the Everton fan? Clue—Everton won the match.

The results were encouraging, a o—o draw against Mexico forty-eight hours after arrival being followed by a 4—o victory against a Mexican XI by what was, in essence, a second team. Sir Alf instructed two of his players, Alan Ball and Martin Peters, to 'burn them-selves out' in the first half, knowing that fresh substitutes were available to take their places.

England moved on to Uruguay for a satisfying 2—1 win, then led Brazil 1—0 until tiring in the final quarter of an hour and losing by the odd goal of three.

And it was Brazil who were to succeed England as the world champions in 1970. What was regarded as

the finest championship of the whole series ended in the Aztec Stadium in Mexico City on 21 June 1970, with the magnificent Brazilians overwhelming Italy, who were the champions of Europe, by a 4—1 margin.

The Brazilians showed skill and they had the ability to entertain and score goals. They crushed Italy after forty-five minutes of even play in the final, Pele scoring his 1,028th goal to open the scoring and the Italians equalizing through Boninsegna.

Gerson, Jairzinho and Carlos Alberto scored the second-half goals that were a prelude to a fiesta that was witnessed by millions of soccer fans all over the world. And, it must be admitted, the majority welcomed the exciting Brazilians as they returned to their role of soccer masters of the world.

Victory entitled Brazil to keep the World Cup—this was their third capture of the Jules Rimet trophy in twelve years. It was, many felt, a victory for football, a victory for attacking play and self-expression.

When the final whistle blew in the Aztec Stadium there were memorable scenes. Supporters swarmed on to the pitch and tore the shirts from the victorious Brazilians; they even took their boots and socks as mementos of a wonderful occasion. Pele was hoisted shoulder high and carried round the pitch by the swaying and chanting mob. Carlos Alberto led his side to receive the Jules Rimet trophy from the President of Mexico as the almost hysterical Brazilian supporters kept up a non-stop beat of noise.

Brazil has a special niche in international football. In 1938 the Brazilians were semi-finalists in the World Cup. In 1950 they reached the Final. Four years later Hungary, the eventual winners, beat Brazil in the quarter-finals. But then in 1958 a player named Pele arrived on the scene. And Brazil, boasting such additional assets as Garrincha, Didi and Zito, won the title. Four years later they repeated their success. England became champions playing 'at home' in 1966; but Brazil repeated the flair of earlier years to regain the world title in 1970.

Ninety-five goals were scored in the final rounds in Mexico, six more than in England in 1966. It was a well-controlled World Cup—for the first time not one player was ordered off.

West Germany, who sensationally defeated the reigning champions, England, after trailing 0–2, finished in third place in the rankings, beating Uruguay by a single goal in the play-off. Gerd Müller, the West German striker, was the competition's top scorer with ten goals.

The Brazilians were given £7,000 each as a bonus from their national FA, as well as shares in the national power and electricity industry, cars, refrigerators and television sets. The President declared a day's national holiday.

A crowd reported to be 30,000 strong greeted the Italians on their return home. Despite their defeat in the Final they were national heroes; their side gave the game in Italy a much-needed boost after previous failure at World Cup level.

So once again Brazil were world champions. But Mexico did not produce a 'giant-killer' to compare with the North Koreans of 1966. Is there an emergent soccer nation? Perhaps the United States may emerge in the seventies.

Only once has soccer in the United States leaped into the sporting spotlight. This was in the 1950

More 1970 World Cup drama. This page, top: the Moroccan goalkeeper brings off a splendid save in their 1—1 draw with Bulgaria. Below: Müller· (crouching) has just scored West Germany's third goal against Italy in the semi-final that turned out to be the most heart-stopping match of the championship. Five goals were scored in extra-time. Opposite page: the Russians in action. In the top picture, Bishovets shoots his side to a 2—0 lead over El Salvador, while, below, a Russian player is warned by the referee in the opening match against Mexico. The style of refereeing in this match was a clear warning to players in the tournament of the penalties of bad behaviour on the field.

Crowd Violence

Crowd violence is a universal problem. In Britain the police are unarmed, in South America they carry tear-gas guns and a supply of shells, often with a moat to separate them from the crowd. Damage and injury are widespread, from ripped bus-seats to a major disaster such as the one at Lima, Peru, opposite page, below left, when panic seized the crowd, the stadium gates were shut and over 300 people were crushed to death before anything resembling order was restored.

World Cup, described earlier, when America created one of the greatest shocks in the history of the game by winning 1—0 against England. The Americans did not win another game in the tournament, and since then no side from the United States has been able to qualify for the finals.

Now, however, with the advent of professionalism, the Americans are becoming aware of the emotional impact of the game, the world-wide network of soccer and the sudden need to develop their own style and players.

The public in the United States will take more readily to the game when they can identify with their own heroes. And when professionalism was introduced through the originally unaffiliated National Professional League, a vast coaching network was started in schools and colleges in a bid not only to educate youngsters but to try and unearth talent.

Players of all nationalities were recruited to America at the outset of the League and one of the major teething troubles was caused by the mixture of men of different race, colour and temperament under the same roof.

The language barrier proved surprisingly hard to crack, and European coaches and managers with limited English at their disposal had the task of moulding sides from players they could only reach at second-hand. Recruitment raised the same problem, and an interpreter was needed at more than one deal before a player could agree to uproot himself from his native land.

Phil Woosnam, player-manager of the club in Atlanta, Georgia, and London sports-journalist Clive Toye, who went to Baltimore as general manager of the local Bays' side, both hit on the idea of developing coloured soccer talent, and subsequent scouting missions to Jamaica and Africa provided them with a ready market of potential star material. In this, Woosnam and Toye were developing a pattern rather than setting a trend, since there has been player-movement on a world scale for over twenty years.

A Nigerian team toured England in the 1950s—and later Tesi Balogun, who was to become a prominent coach in Nigeria, made some impact on the Football League game as a centre-forward with Queen's Park Rangers in London.

Although the Football League frowns on foreign 'imports', players from Iceland, Sweden, Germany, Egypt, Hungary, Poland, Spain, Switzerland, Australia and South Africa have achieved recognition in the competition. The official ruling is that no foreign-born player can take part in matches under FA jurisdiction as a professional unless he has been resident for two years.

Not long ago Blackpool took on two Chinese

Opposite page: the North Koreans, undoubtedly the major sensation of the 1966 World Cup. Until the genius of Eusebio and the sheer size of Torres, below, finally combined to knock them out 5—3 in the quarter-final against Portugal, the North Koreans delighted everyone with their skill and sportsmanship. This page: a cluster of Koreans rises to keep out an Italian attack; in this match the tiny Koreans created a great stir by winning 1—0.

brothers, and although they did not make an impact in England they were quickly recruited by former Fulham and England half-back Bobby Robson, when he went to Canada as manager of Vancouver Royal Canadians in the North American League.

Italian footballers are among the highest-paid in the world, and wages are such that clubs in Italy have attracted many stars from foreign countries. Over 300 overseas players have signed for Italian clubs in the post-war period, among them some of the world's best players—from South America and all over Europe, including British stars such as John Charles, Denis Law and Joe Baker.

Many of the leading clubs in Italy are sponsored by wealthy industrialists, seemingly with unlimited supplies of money to woo the stars of all nationalities and to pay huge bonuses, which by themselves form an attractive inducement.

The case of the Hungarian Kubala, one of the finest inside-forwards of the post-war era, illustrates the point about the movement of players. He has appeared in internationals for three different countries! Kubala earned his first 'cap' for his native Hungary, and he subsequently appeared for both Czechoslovakia and Spain—another country that has dealt successfully in the importation of star players.

In recent years Spain has developed some of the greatest club sides in the history of soccer, notably Real Madrid, five times European Cup winners and once world club champions. Yet, on a national level, the Spaniards are an enigma. They undoubtedly possess some of the most talented footballers in the world, but their international record does not match

Like North Korea, the USA is an emergent soccer nation, bursting to get at the game's higher honours. Home-grown stars are few at present and teams such as Baltimore Bays and Los Angeles Toros, shown on these pages, contain players of every nation, from Haiti to West Germany.

their potential despite the fact that they have included stars in the national side irrespective of whether they were born in Spain.

Alfredo di Stefano, one of the great players of all time, was a power during the Real Madrid run of success, but this Argentine-born inside-forward did not achieve the same standard of achievement with the Spanish national side. Di Stefano was, incidentally, another triple international—with Argentine, Colombia and Spain.

Many Argentinians have made an impact on the Italian scene—Sivori and Maschio to name only two—and they too have been capped by their country of adoption as well as by their native land. Altafini led the Brazilian attack on a number of occasions when he was with Palmeiras, and, after transferring to AC Milan in 1959, he appeared for Italy. The Italians also used Schiaffino, another brilliant inside-forward, in their national side—after he had represented his native Uruguay. Santamaria, like Schiaffino a member of the Penarol side in Uruguay, was born in Montevideo, but he, too, made a number of appearances for Spain after joining Real Madrid.

Fouls

With so much at stake in soccer today, fouls occur with regrettable frequency, and it is almost accepted practice to trip a player if nothing else will stop him. Some of the old-time Corinthians would turn in their graves if they could see the goings-on, but in their day no one felt the temptations of £100-a-week pay-packets, with additional win-bonuses, position-bonuses, crowd-bonuses, etc., plus a hefty signing-on fee for joining another club. There is, in other words, much more to the push, the trip, the ankle-tap and the crafty shirt-tug than meets the eye. One of the greatest problems for referees is how to deal with the player who retaliates after he has been fouled—a feature of the game which clubs and organizers are increasingly anxious to stamp out.

Ferenc Puskas, whose name will always be linked with di Stefano as a spearhead in the advance of Real Madrid, made eighty-four appearances for his native Hungary before the 1956 revolution. Later he made four appearances for Spain.

Italy and Spain have led the way in paying huge signing-on fees to players and sending transfer-fees rocketing to unrealistic proportions. The largest reported signing-on fee was £59,000, received by Suarez, of Barcelona, on his move to Internazionale, of Milan, in 1961—for a transfer-fee of £150,000.

Holland was one of the countries to suffer from the migration of star players. With a football boom in Europe in the years after the Second World War, and with Holland's continued refusal to adopt professionalism, several of their best players left for France, Italy and Germany. The matter came to a head in 1954 when the professional game was finally admitted. Leading Dutch players were encouraged to return home and several experienced coaches were brought in to develop the game.

The two outsiders of the 1970 World Cup. El Salvador, opposite page, didn't manage any points in their group—here van Moer scores for Belgium against them. But Israel achieved draws against Sweden and the highly rated Italians. Above, an Israeli defender blocks a pile-driver from the powerful left foot of Luigi Riva.

The post-war success of the game in Australia, inspired by the mass migration of Europeans, has posed problems, notably in the matter of grounds. Very few of the leading clubs own their own grounds and few are given over chiefly to the playing of soccer. Most are owned by local councils, and clubs have to share with cricket or Australian football. (The word 'soccer' is included in the title of the senior governing body to differentiate between the Association game and the Australian-rules game.)

In 1960 the Australian Soccer Football Association was banned for three years from FIFA for poaching players from Austria. Nowadays most leading clubs employ part-time professionals and the wages offered to play, together with jobs outside the game, have attracted many professionals from Britain.

South Africa, too, offers pay for soccer, plus wages for a job outside the game, and there have been noticeable signs of a revival of interest in the post-war years. Professionalism was adopted in 1959, but there is only one club, Port Elizabeth City, that employs full-time players.

Since the Second World War politics have entered sport to a growing extent. In Bulgaria, for example, the Communist regime disbanded football clubs as such in 1946. The top teams are all from sports clubs which run football sections. The leading side, Red Banner, was formed in 1948 and was fielded by the Central House of the People's Army. The leading Bulgarians are all amateur players—they are provided with jobs outside the game—and, in 1965, there were

some 9,000 teams competing in four zonal and a further fourteen regional groups throughout the country.

Politics has also played a part in German soccer affairs. Today there are two German Football Associations, West and East, both of them members of FIFA. The West Germans have surmounted the political barrier to win the World Cup, and the East Germans, with only one-third of the clubs from which to choose players, are just as enthusiastic about the game even if they have not achieved much international success.

In this chapter so far, we have seen the enthusiasm for soccer around the world, in established centres and outposts and in emerging countries. We have also recorded trends towards violence, both on and off the field. In addition, soccer in the 'sixties, with its fabulous prizes for players and clubs, has had to face scandal in the never-ending search for success.

The twin menace of bribery and drug-taking have appeared on the scene. In July 1963, a goalkeeper with

Injuries

Amateur or professional, First or Fourth Division, soccer is a tough sport, and a severe injury can put a player out of the game for good. Injuries are an unfortunate, sometimes tragic, but largely unavoidable part of football: Derek Dooley lost a leg, Dave Mackay broke a leg twice but came back each time, and each season brings a fresh crop of broken limbs. Pele, on the other hand, the marked man of the World Cup series in 1966, was subjected to persistent, crushing tackles by his opponents until he was unable to continue—and Brazil were eliminated from the competition: one of the instances where injury was all too avoidable. For the record, the injured men shown here are: Derek Temple (Everton), top; Jimmy McLaughlin (N. Ireland), this page, centre; below him is Jimmy Gabriel (Everton). On the opposite page are Tommy Lawrence (Liverpool), left, and Eddy Brown (Leyton Orient).

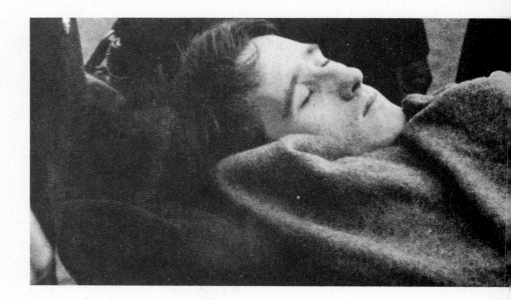

This page: President Kenneth Kaunda of Zambia spins a coin before refereeing a soccer match between his Cabinet and a team of Copperbelt mayors and town councillors. Opposite page: Stanley Matthews, now Sir Stanley, is fêted in Accra during an exhibition tour of Ghana. Africa is loaded with footballing talent—think of Eusebio, from Mozambique—but as yet no country has come forward with a strong national team, though this may just be a matter of time.

Bristol Rovers was fined £100 for his part in a bribery transaction, admitting that he had allowed two goals to be scored against his club in a match at Bradford in an effort to sway the result. Two other players were fined £50 for their part in the conspiracy and all three were subsequently banned for life by the Football Association. Two years later, ten English professional players were found guilty of conspiracy to defraud by fixing matches, and among those who received prison sentences were international players Peter Swan (Sheffield Wednesday) and Tony Kay (Everton).

Italy, France, Belgium and Greece have also had cases of corruption in recent years. And in Bulgaria, a club was found guilty in 1962 of bribing a referee to ensure victory during a promotion-campaign, and of using public money to buy players and pay win-bonuses to the team and also to pay for supporters to travel to away matches.

In Yugoslavia so many attempts have been made to corrupt referees that appointments to matches have been kept secret until just before kick-off time.

The Italian League has operated an anti-doping squad in recent years, making random tests on players. In January 1963 Naples surprisingly beat AC Milan in an away match, and tests conducted by doctors at the State's drug-detection centre in Florence showed that the team had taken drugs. Of the seven footballers nominated by the medical commission, four were found guilty and suspended for three matches.

In the 1966 World Cup, when Italy were sensationally beaten 1—0 by North Korea and eliminated from the competition, their coach, Edmundo Fabbri, accused the doctor who accompanied the party of administering the 'wrong dope'. He produced statements from ten players in support of his allegations.

The overall problem of doping may, however, be diminishing. Over 1,100 tests were made in the Italian League in 1966 and all proved negative.

What of the immediate future of soccer? In the past decade dozens of new countries have been formed, in Africa and Asia, and all are clamouring for a 'place in the sun' in international football. In the world of communications, too, satellites will soon make a match in Rio no more than a television-switch away from viewers in Moscow.

There are new areas to be explored, primarily in North America, Asia and Africa. Perhaps at this moment there is some unsuspecting youngster in New York, Accra or Pyongyang, in North Korea, who is soon to emerge as a famous name to rank alongside the Brazilian Pele or the man from Mozambique, Eusebio.

Put a rope around a pitch in Africa and there is instant enthusiasm. The Africans have instinctive skills, perhaps the equivalent of those thousands of Brazilian children who play daily on the beaches of their homeland.

The body-movements of African players underline their potential. Any dusty African village could be hiding a man with the physical attributes of a Eusebio, whose natural grace, balance and strength were channelled towards making him one of the most dangerous players soccer has ever known, once he had been transported to Portugal.

Pele, who played barefoot in his village near the bustling port of Santos in Brazil; Eusebio, from a shanty-town background—these are but two of the great names who have risen from undistinguished backgrounds to the top of the tree in football. They are wealthy men, trend-setters in the game. The 1970s will, it is certain, produce a new crop of heroes to capture the imagination of the world, as nations draw closer together.

3 Great Players and Great Teams

Back in the days before world football, even before professionalism, there were several truly great teams of amateur pioneers. The Wanderers, a side made up from the best of those who had played for public schools and universities, were the commanding team of the early years of FA competition. They won five of the first seven Cup Finals, with three consecutive wins in 1876, 1877 and 1878. This 'hat-trick' of successes made the Cup their property but, as the rules were at the time, they handed it back on condition that it was never won outright.

The dominance of the Wanderers declined after 1878 because of the growth of the public-school Old Boys' clubs. They lost many of their best players, men such as the Hon. Arthur Kinnaird. Kinnaird, who won five Cup-winners' medals and one cap for Scotland, was a dominant personality of the early game. He played in nine Cup Finals between 1873 and 1883, three for Wanderers and six for Old Etonians. He was typical of the gentlemen amateurs of his day, playing at goalkeeper, back, half-back or forward.

Kinnaird, later to be President of the FA for thirty-three years, played for Old Etonians in the last Cup Final to be won by an amateur side. With his vivid red hair and beard, and wearing an outfit of long white trousers and jersey and a blue-and-white quartered cricket cap, Kinnaird was one of the game's 'characters'.

On one occasion, C. W. Alcock, captain of the Old Harrovians, was so bruised that he said to Kinnaird in a match, 'Look here, Kinnaird, are we going to play the game or are we going to have hacking?' Kinnaird's reply was, 'Let us have hacking by all means.' Another time, as he made his way to the Oval for a Cup Final, Kinnaird was drawn one hundred yards to the pavilion by his excited supporters after they had taken the horses out of the shafts of his carriage.

Old Etonians, who were in six of the first eleven Finals, are a fine example of the great amateur sides of their time. Not even the impending approach of professionalism or the challenge from the north could prevent them from still further honours. In 1882 they met Blackburn Rovers, a side approaching greatness, in the Cup Final. Rovers had won thirty-one out of thirty-five matches that season and scored 192 goals against thirty-three. But Kinnaird and his Old Etonians beat them 1—0 at the Oval.

It was Blackburn Olympic, rather than the more illustriously known Rovers, who first took the Cup north the following season. Olympic, who spent the pre-Final week in special training at Blackpool, had three weavers in their side, a dentist's assistant, a spinner, a master plumber, a cotton operative and an iron foundry worker. They were not only well versed in the skills of the game, though—they were also fit.

Against them the Old Etonians fielded six internationals, including Kinnaird and A. T. B. Dunn, whose name is still remembered in the Arthur Dunn Cup competition. They were men of means and leisure and the contrast of the two sides reflected a changing age in England that was not limited to soccer. Olympic won 2—1 after extra-time, and the Cup went north to brass-band accompaniment.

It was to be eighteen years before it returned south. The age of the amateur was over as far as Cup-

Opposite page: the great Hungarians of 1953 gave England a terrific 6—3 pounding at Wembley. Above: Merrick tips a Hungarian shot round the post, watched by Wright, left, and Ramsey, in goal. Below: an unstoppable effort from Puskas, on ground, enters the English net.

winning was concerned, and the great names were from that day to be found in the ranks of the professionals. Blackburn Rovers, Preston, Aston Villa, these were the emerging names. Rovers won the Cup three times running in 1884, 1885, and 1886, and they won it again in 1890 and 1891.

The Football League was formed and Preston—Proud Preston, the Invincibles—came into their own. They won the first League championship in 1888–9 without losing one of their twenty-two games, and they also achieved the 'double' by winning the Cup.

Their manager Major Sudell, was the Matt Busby of his day. He picked his players with care, placing a premium on skill and great emphasis on teamwork and hard training.

Preston had great players: Nick Ross was one of the best of the early full-backs; the half-back line of Drummond, Russell and Graham was the powerful backbone of the side; the forward line was acknowledged as the best in the country. John Goodall, at

Opposite page: a gallery of early internationals. Top row, left to right: C. W. Athersmith (Aston Villa), E. C. Bambridge (Swifts), W. J. Foulke (Sheffield United). Centre: S. Bloomer (Derby County), J. Goodall (Preston and Derby), G. O. Smith (Corinthians). Bottom: E. Needham (Sheffield United), F. Spiksley (Sheffield Wednesday), W. I. Bassett (West Bromwich Albion). This page, below: the Preston side, the 'Old Invincibles', who won the Cup and League double in 1889.

centre-forward, was the brain, John Gordon and James Ross formed the right wing, and Fred Dewhurst, who also played for Corinthians, and George Drummond were the left-wing pair. Each was a star in his own right, and Preston were a revolutionary force in their time.

West Bromwich Albion were the first great side from the Midlands. They reached the Cup Final in 1886, and lost to Blackburn Rovers after a replay. They lost in the Final to Aston Villa the following year but, in 1888, they were back for a third attempt against the mighty 'Invincibles' from Preston. It was a romantic clash of the well-paid Scottish professionals against a locally-built Albion side whose wage bill was a mere £10 a week.

Preston were so sure of the outcome that they asked to be photographed with the Cup—*before* the match! The gates of The Oval were closed on a 17,000 crowd, who saw the underdogs from West Bromwich win 2—1 in one of those upsets of form that have characterized the FA Cup competition both before and since that day.

Albion had a man for the big occasion. Outside-right Billy Bassett—William Isiah Bassett, to be more formal—was chosen for England for the first time after the defeat of Preston and he was the regular choice for his country for many years. A small man,

just topping five feet five, Bassett was fast and able to centre with great accuracy without slackening his pace. His favourite trick was to stop the ball dead while sprinting at top speed, and he also enjoyed running outside the touchline. Bassett, always closely marked, was the Stanley Matthews of his generation; he also had another Matthews trait—the bigger the occasion the better he played. He won two Cup-winners' medals in his three appearances in the Final; Albion, his team, reached the Final stage five times in ten seasons.

As the nineteenth century came to a close the great club in England was Aston Villa. League Champions in 1894, 1896, 1897, 1899 and 1900, they won the Cup in 1895 and 1897—the latter being a triumphant 'double' year for them.

Derby County were the losing finalists in 1898, and starring for them was a twenty-four-year-old inside-right who was to become one of the immortals of soccer—Steve Bloomer. From the time he began his professional career in 1892 at the age of eighteen, earning 7s 6d a week, until his last appearance in 1914 when he was forty, Bloomer scored 352 League goals, a record overtaken in later years by only a handful of top marksmen—Arthur Rowley (Fulham

This page, left: an historic picture of Billy Meredith, left, the 'Welsh Wizard', and Steve Bloomer, taken at a pre-1914 benefit match—the only time the illustrious pair played together as a right wing. Right: portrait of Bob Crompton, the great Blackburn Rovers full-back who set a record of forty international appearances for England. Opposite page: Alan Morton, the Scottish international, of Queen's Park and Rangers.

and Leicester, 434), James McGrory (Celtic, 410), Hughie Gallacher (Newcastle and Chelsea, 386), Dixie Dean (Everton, 379), Hugh Ferguson (Motherwell and Cardiff, 362) and Jimmy Greaves.

Bloomer, who despite his fame never achieved a Cup-winners' medal, was one of soccer's greatest individuals. He was the complete opportunist and had an incomparable shot; although he was slight and rather pale, his physique did not hinder his progress. He was afraid of nothing and, to quote a description of the time, 'he had a blacksmith's lungs and a four-cylinder heart warranted to work in any climate'. The FA made him a presentation of his own portrait when he won a then record of twenty-one caps for England. In all he played twenty-three games in the international championship and scored twenty-eight goals.

The outstanding team of the 1900–14 era was

Newcastle United. They reached the Cup Final in 1905, 1906, 1908, 1910, and 1911, winning the trophy in 1910 but losing the other four matches. In 1909 they were semi-finalists, and in 1905, 1907 and 1909, they were League champions. Twice they were near the coveted League-Cup double; twice they failed. This famous Newcastle team was, too, the victim of an early giant-killing act when, in 1907, they were knocked out on their own ground in the first round by Crystal Palace, then a lowly Southern League side. The neat, close-passing game of this Newcastle side always seemed subsequently to flounder at the mention of Crystal Palace. They never won a Final there, and their Cup victory in 1910 was at Everton in a replay.

Meredith, to whom we have referred before, was another giant of this period. He won a Cup-winners' medal with Manchester City in 1904, and another with Manchester United in 1909. He played around one thousand first-class games in a career spanning 1894–1924, and was something of a walking record book. Apart from his forty-eight appearances for Wales, this famous Welshman scored thirty-six goals in the 1898–9 season, a Football League record for a winger, and over 200 altogether. He was a fanatic for physical fitness and was known for one particular quirk—he chewed a quill toothpick on the field throughout his entire career.

The first Cup Final at Stamford Bridge, in 1920, was won by the famous Aston Villa team, a record-breaking sixth win which the same club improved on by winning yet again at Wembley in 1957.

The great Cup teams of the 1920s were Bolton Wanderers and Huddersfield Town. Bolton won the trophy in 1923, the first Final at Wembley, with its overspilling crowd and famous scenes, and again in 1926 and 1929. A great team, they used only seventeen players in all three finals.

Huddersfield won in 1922, reached the Final in 1920 and 1928 and the semi-final in 1929. This was an especially remarkable feat since the club was practically bankrupt in 1920 and on the point of winding-up. Although Huddersfield was, and is, primarily a Rugby League town, local supporters got together on that occasion to preserve soccer—and the side justified itself by winning promotion from the Second Division that season. They then won the League Championship three times running from 1924–6, and were runners-up the next two seasons.

Who were the great names of the time? Bolton had

This page, above: Harry Hibbs, the famous Birmingham goal-keeper. Below: W. G. Richardson, centre-forward with West Bromwich Albion, seen during a pre-match kick-about in 1931. Opposite page: Sam Hardy, left, of Liverpool and Aston Villa, perhaps the greatest of the early goalkeepers. Right: Andy Ducat in 1924, wearing the claret-and-blue of Aston Villa.

David Jack, who scored the first goal at Wembley; there was also Charles Buchan, who was transferred from Sunderland to Arsenal with an unusual clause in his contract which provided for an extra £100 for every goal he scored for the Londoners in his first season with them. He scored twenty-one.

While we have dealt nostalgically with great teams and great names, it is right to pause a moment to consider the record of the greatest manager soccer has ever known, Herbert Chapman. He was the guiding genius who led Huddersfield from near-extinction to fabulous success. He achieved the same success when he moved on to Arsenal and made them into the most glamorous club of the age.

Chapman's success with the two clubs was divided by the introduction of the new offside rule in 1925. Arsenal were the first club successfully to adopt tactics to beat the post-1925 trend by introducing the third-back game. Charles Buchan suggested the

simple expedient of the centre-half dropping back to perform a purely defensive role as a stopper, with an inside-forward being used for a midfield, scheming role. The inside man supplied his fast-raiding wingmen with accurate passes, and this became a feature that made Arsenal a great side in the 1930s.

They won the Cup in 1930, and lost in the Final to Newcastle in 1932. Later, in 1936, Ted Drake scored the winning goal when they again appeared at Wembley.

Arsenal were League champions in 1931, runners-up in 1932 and champions again three times running from 1933–5. They were third in 1937 and champions again in 1938. In 1934, the year of Chapman's unexpected death, they supplied seven players to the England team that beat Italy.

Herbie Roberts was the original stopper centre-half, a giant of a man playing among some of the finest players of the time: Eddie Hapgood, a classical left-

back, Tom Parker, George Male, still on the Highbury staff today, Jack Crayston, an elegant wing-half, and Wilf Copping, 'Fearless Wilf' of the crushing tackle who did not shave on match-days so that he would look tough on the field. In the forward-line Arsenal were always a delight; one of their greatest line-ups, the Cup-winning team of 1930, included the forwards Joe Hulme, David Jack, Jack Lambert, Alex James and Cliff Bastin, each of them a memorable player in his own right.

Alex James, a ball-playing genius in baggy pants, and Cliff Bastin, 'Boy Bastin', as they called this prodigy, were two of the greatest. James joined Arsenal from Preston, home of so many gifted Scots, as an established inside-forward. The young Tom Finney saw James in his Preston days, incidentally, and modelled his own immaculate style on what he saw.

David Jack, who succeeded Buchan, was tall and

stylish; Bastin, fast and direct, scored thirty-three goals from the wing in the 1932–3 season. Yet with all this talent and an astonishing run of success, Arsenal figured in what has been accepted as the greatest giant-killing act of all time, when they lost 2—0 at Walsall in 1933. (They went on to win the championship as some slight consolation.)

Another great Arsenal star of the 1930s was Ted Drake, the epitome of wholehearted endeavour and a model centre-forward for his generation. Drake, to whom one could apply the football cliché 'he'd run through brick walls for you', had a great triumph at Villa Park, Birmingham, on 14 December 1935.

The match did not begin well for him—the crowd hooting with laughter as he raced after a ball that went out of play, tripped, fell flat on his face and grazed the skin of both arms as he sprawled on the track. Drake's answer: a hat-trick in the first nineteen

Mighty Arsenal, footballing emperors of the 1920s, 1930s, and perhaps of the 1970s. This page, above: the 1931–2 team with Herbert Chapman, seated far left, and trainer Whittaker, seated far right. Below: Alex James, the Gunners' wonderful ball-playing inside-forward. Opposite page, above: Frank McLintock holds aloft the FA Cup at the end of a remarkable week in May 1971 in which Arsenal clinched the League Championship, the FA Youth Cup, and came from behind to beat Liverpool 2—1 in extra-time at Wembley. Below: Storey of Arsenal challenges Clemence, the Liverpool goalie, early in the Final.

minutes. And, despite the fact that attention was focused on Alex Massie, Aston Villa's expensive Scottish wing-half signing, Drake scored a second hat-trick in twelve minutes of the second half. In all, he scored every one of Arsenal's seven goals that day.

Arsenal did not achieve comparable greatness in the post-war period until 1970–1 when, under the managership of Bertie Mee, they became only the second team this century to bring off the League and FA Cup double, an extraordinary feat considering they played over sixty matches that season.

Think of Wolves—think of Stan Cullis! Stan was one of the great international centre-halves of the period just before the war. He was in the Wolves side of 1939 that finished runners-up in the League and were the hottest favourites to win the Cup for years. Their opponents, Portsmouth, seemed to have little chance against the eager young Wolves, brilliantly led by Cullis. Yet Portsmouth won 4—1.

The story is told that when the autograph books went round the Wembley dressing-rooms half an hour before the kick-off, the Portsmouth players noticed that they could not recognize their opponents' signatures because of hands shaky with nerves. Portsmouth, who had a comedian in their dressing-room to take their minds off things, gained an important psychological advantage.

Cullis suffered another disappointment in his final season as a player. This was the first season after the war and the championship hung on one game— Wolves v. Liverpool, Cullis's last game in the famous old-gold shirt of his club. But Liverpool won.

Within weeks Cullis was on the staff of Wolverhampton as assistant manager; by 1949 he was manager and then he gained some measure of recompense for his previous disappointments when Wolves won the Cup. They were League champions in 1954, 1958 and 1959, and in 1960 they won the Cup.

The side that Cullis built put an emphasis on speed and helped revolutionize the post-war game in Britain. Others tried to emulate the powerful long-ball style the Wolves played, but none achieved such success.

The floodlit games at Wolves' Molineux ground

in the 1950s were a soccer feature of the period. Wolves won many converts to the game by their exciting performances, watched by countless millions on television as well as the thousands who turned up in person. The most memorable were the matches against Honved, the Hungarian champions of the time, and one of the best club sides in the world, Moscow Spartak.

Honved, who fielded players of the calibre of Puskas, Kocsis, Czibor, Budai and Bozsik, internationals all, led 2—0 at half-time. Cullis, in the words of Billy Wright, his successor at centre-half with Wolves, gave his players a 'spirited talk' at the interval, and Wolves went on to win 3—2, with wingers Johnny Hancocks and Jimmy Mullen reviving memories of Arsenal's wing-play two decades before.

In the other match Wolves, fitness personified, scored four goals in the last ten minutes against Spartak, and, to show the strength of English football, they later beat European Cup-holders Real Madrid 3—2 in 1957, and drew 2—2 in the return in Madrid.

A key man of a Newcastle side that enhanced its great Cup tradition in the 1950s was Jackie Milburn— a member of a famous footballing family, and 'Wor Jackie' to his Geordie followers.

Newcastle, whose lean seasons in the League have often been forgiven and forgotten by Cup success, have won the trophy six times, played in four other Finals and lost in the semi-final twelve times. In the 1950s they employed the speed of Milburn to good advantage: the defence pushed the ball to deep-lying wingers, whose main task was to push it through the middle for Milburn or his striker-colleague, the Chilean-born George Robledo. This Newcastle side made three appearances at Wembley in the 1950s, winning the cup three times between 1951 and 1955.

Opposite page: more scenes of the triumphant Arsenal side of the 1930s. They won the Cup in 1930 and 1936 and were runners-up in 1932, and they won the League in 1931, three seasons running from 1933–5 and again in 1938. In between they came second in 1932 and third in 1937. Above left: David Jack, left, tussles for the ball with Tommy Law of Chelsea in a match at Stamford Bridge in 1931. Above right: Eddie Hapgood, Arsenal's great left-back. Below: Cliff Bastin, looking like some Bobby Charlton of bygone days, scores for Arsenal against West Bromwich Albion at Highbury in 1932. This page, below: George Male, left, meets his match in the person of the great Dixie Dean, Everton's striker-in-chief for a generation.

Milburn scored the two goals that beat Blackpool in the 1951 Final, aided and abetted with the second by little Ernie Taylor. Taylor, who was later to collect another Cup-winners' medal with Blackpool, was a brilliant ball-playing inside-forward of the old school.

Robledo scored the winner the following year, when Newcastle became the first team to win the Cup two years in succession since Blackburn Rovers in 1891.

Milburn scored again in the 1955 Cup Final against Manchester City, a side that played to a plan built

around and named after one of their star players. Centre-forward Don Revie played a deep-lying game in the manner of the Hungarian Hidegkuti—and the Revie Plan took his side to Wembley two years in succession. They won at the second attempt.

Blackpool, whose name will forever be coupled with that of Matthews, were another great Cup team of the era. They reached the Final three times in five years, in 1948, 1951 and 1953.

Manchester United beat them in the first match, with a fine exhibition of attacking football. New-

This page, above: Dixie Dean, white shirt, duels with the N. Ireland defence in a home international played in 1928. Below left: Dean kicks off at the benefit match Everton staged for him in 1964, watched by present-day international Fred Pickering. Below right: Arsenal's powerful Ted Drake, right, challenged by Jackson of Everton. Opposite page, above: two famous Chelsea stars, Hughie Gallacher, left, and Alex Jackson. Below: the great Frank Swift, Manchester City's goalkeeper.

castle, and Jackie Milburn, beat them three years later.

And so to 1953—a game that will always be remembered as the Matthews Final. The country willed Sir Stanley to a Cup medal, just as the country willed Gordon Richards to his first-ever Derby win that same year.

Bolton provided the opposition in what was undoubtedly the most dramatic of all Wembley finals. With twenty minutes to go, Bolton led 3—1, with half-back Bell hobbling on the wing.

Matthews, then aged thirty-eight, took over the

stage. He centred for Stan Mortensen, one of the most whole-hearted players in English soccer, to make it 3—2. Mortensen scored from a free-kick three minutes from the end to level the scores and force extra-time, and finally Matthews paved the way for a winner from Bill Perry with some typical touchline trickery and inimitable ball-control.

Blackpool had several great players besides Matthews: Mortensen, 'Morty' the lion-heart, was the nearest modern-day parallel to Steve Bloomer; Ernie Taylor was a superb inside-forward, and behind

Opposite page: beside the full-length picture of Preston's majestic winger Tom Finney are, from the top, Peter Doherty (Doncaster Rovers), Billy 'Knocky' Walker (Aston Villa), and members of the historic Moscow Dynamo side, which toured England with memorable success in 1945, coming out for their match with Chelsea. This page, above: Derby County's bustling Billy Steel, left, and the acrobatic Tommy Lawton. Below: Wilf Mannion, Middlesbrough's star inside forward.

them was Harry Johnston—a classical wing-half.

When Matthews, at the age of forty, played for England against Scotland in 1955, a young left-half was making his first appearance in an England shirt, Duncan Edwards. He was one of the brightest of up-and-coming stars in a Manchester United side built up by manager Matt Busby in the 1950s and which earned admiration and respect as the 'Busby Babes'.

United have been the pride of English football in the post-war years. The 1948 Cup-winning side, led by Johnny Carey, one of the greatest all-round players of any age—he played in nine different positions for United and seven for Ireland—had great players. But in time the team had to be rebuilt.

Busby, who is the only contemporary rival to Herbert Chapman, did his rebuilding job so successfully that United won the League Championship in 1952, 1956, 1957, 1965 and 1967. They were runners-

up five times in the period from the end of the war until the end of the 1950s, and again in 1964. They were Cup-finalists in the same two seasons. They won the FA Youth Cup for five years in succession, from 1953–7.

And success continued despite the crippling blow of the Munich air crash of 1958, when eight star players lost their lives. Edwards, a powerhouse player who seemed destined to reach fresh heights in international and club achievement, was one. Roger Byrne and Tommy Taylor, a centre-forward of exceptional promise, were others. Again Busby had to rebuild.

There were three survivors of the crash, Billy Foulkes, a reliable centre-half, Irish international goalkeeper Harry Gregg and young Bobby Charlton, who found real maturity in his new responsibilities following the crash.

United went on to the Cup Final with a hastily-assembled team months after the crash, but lost 2—0 to Bolton, the goals coming from Nat Lofthouse, one of the most eminent of post-war centre-forwards in England.

Tottenham Hotspur, like Manchester United, have been tremendously consistent in recent years, and the Tottenham side of 1950 must also rank as one of the great sides. Ron Burgess, the complete half-back, led a team that pursued manager Arthur Rowe's simple push-and-run style to perfection and collected championship medals. The team was: Ted Ditchburn; Alf Ramsey, Arthur Willis; Bill Nicholson, Harry Clarke, Burgess; Sonny Walters, Les Bennett, Len Duquemin, Eddie Baily, Les Medley.

Later, Ramsey went on to manage Ipswich and England, while Nicholson stayed to lead Spurs into the club's most golden days. He became the club

Opposite page, above: Stoke City's classic centre-half Neil Franklin, who later joined a breakaway league in Bogota, Colombia. Below left: inside-forward Jimmy Delaney, playing for Aberdeen in 1951. Below right: centre-forward Trevor Ford, whose £30,000-transfer from Aston Villa to Sunderland in 1950 created quite a stir. This page, above: the dynamic Jackie Milburn of Newcastle fires in a typical goal against Arsenal at Highbury in 1953. Below: Johnny Carey, Manchester United's rock-steady full-back and team captain. Since his playing days, Irishman Carey has been manager of Nottingham Forest and general manager of Blackburn.

coach after his playing career ended, and rose to be manager in 1958.

Key man in the fabulously successful Spurs side that conquered the League-and-Cup Everest for the first time this century was the extrovert Irishman Danny Blanchflower. This was the team: Bill Brown; Peter Baker, Ron Henry; Blanchflower, Maurice Norman, Dave Mackay; Cliff Jones, John White, Bobby Smith, Les Allen, Terry Dyson.

They won the League championship in 1961, scoring 115 goals and conceding only fifty-five to finish eight points ahead of the runners-up. Then they beat Leicester 2—0 to win the Cup, but failed in that match to live up to their reputation as the 'team of the century'.

The following season, with Jimmy Greaves, the greatest goalscorer English football has ever known, and Terry Medwin in the side, Spurs repeated their Wembley success, beating Burnley 3—1. They returned again in 1967 with a rebuilt side to beat Chelsea. Three Cup Final appearances—three wins. It was a great achievement for manager Nicholson and two great Spurs sides.

Turning now from the domestic scene in Britain, one side above all others compels attention—the Hungarian national team of the 1950s. For these 'Mighty Magyars' made a mark on football that will be hard to erase. They were without question the finest side to represent a country in the history of soccer.

The Hungarians went thirteen years without a defeat at home in international matches, from their 7—2 defeat by Sweden in 1943 to their 4—2 defeat by Czechoslovakia in 1956.

Their most outstanding team played twenty-nine games without loss at home or away over a period of more than four years during the 1950s. The match which ended that impressive run was the 3—2 defeat by West Germany in the 1954 World Cup Final.

England 3, Hungary 6. That result, at Wembley in November 1953, is the one that lifted the Hungarians

This page, top: Stan Mortensen scores Blackpool's second goal against Bolton in the 'Matthews Final' of 1953, when everyone barring avid Bolton supporters seemed to will Matthews to his first FA Cup victory. Blackpool finally won 4—3, with a goal in the last minute. This page, centre: at the age of fifty Sir Stanley, as he had become, retired from active football, and to mark the occasion a farewell match was played at Stoke, where Matthews began his career thirty-three years before, between his XI and an all-star team. In our picture Sir Stanley is applauded on to the pitch in the wake of a Dagenham Girl Piper. Below: a typical effort by Sir Stanley—scourge of full-backs the world over. Here he leaves Eddie McCreadie on the floor during a Chelsea—Stoke League match. Opposite page: defenders twist and turn to cover one of Matthews' bewildering advances on goal.

into the category of memorable sides and helped revolutionize soccer thinking the world over.

England had never before been beaten on her home soil by a foreign international side, and the Hungarians showed their hosts just how they had improved on lessons learned from the 'masters'.

At right-back in the England side beaten at Wembley—they were further humiliated 7—1 in Budapest a year later, England's heaviest-ever defeat—was Alf Ramsey. He scored from a penalty at Wembley. At right-half in front of Ramsey was sturdy, fair-haired Billy Wright. At outside-right in front of him was Stanley Matthews.

These men were three of England's greatest players, in the team that played second fiddle to this magnificent Hungarian side: Grosics; Buzansky, Lantos; Bozsik, Lorant, Zakarias; Budai, Kocsis, Hidegkuti, Puskas, Czibor.

Ramsey (now Sir Alfred) went on to achieve managerial success with modest Ipswich Town, guiding them from the Third to the First Division, and then to world-wide acclaim as team manager of the England side which won the World Cup in 1966.

Wright, who made 490 appearances for Wolves in their heyday in the early post-war period and the 1950s, achieved immortality by setting up a world record with a run of seventy consecutive appearances—and by representing England 105 times in his illustrious career. He was the first player to top the century-mark in international appearances.

Matthews, who later received a knighthood and was awarded the CBE, played twenty-nine times for England in war-time and victory internationals—which do not rank as full internationals—and fifty-seven times in peacetime matches. Matthews, a legend in his time, played over 700 League games for

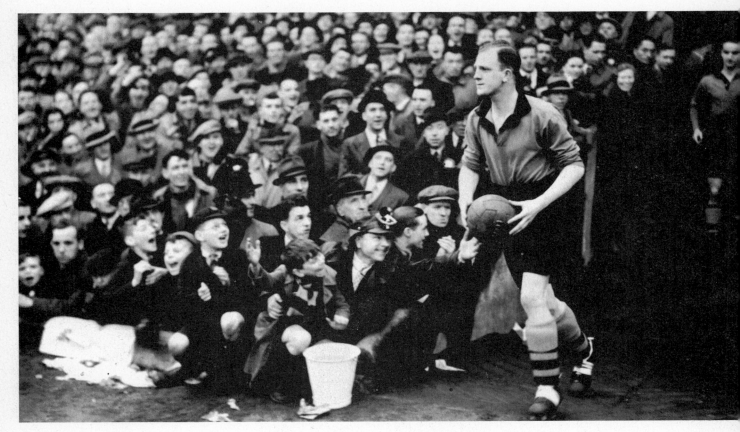

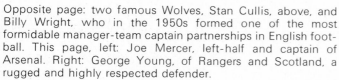

Opposite page: two famous Wolves, Stan Cullis, above, and Billy Wright, who in the 1950s formed one of the most formidable manager-team captain partnerships in English football. This page, left: Joe Mercer, left-half and captain of Arsenal. Right: George Young, of Rangers and Scotland, a rugged and highly respected defender.

Stoke and Blackpool in a career spanning the years 1932–64. He was twice awarded the silver statuette awarded by England's soccer-writers to the 'Footballer of the Year'.

Nowhere, perhaps, did that crushing 6—3 defeat by the Hungarians make a bigger impact than in the mind of full-back Ramsey, a stylish player who was a member of the fine Tottenham side of 1951.

Long after England had won the World Cup, Sir Alf looked back to that November day in 1953 to say, 'I have had one great ambition hanging over me for years, to replace the image of that great Hungarian side by the image of an even greater England team. From that time everybody has judged football by those wonderful Hungarians. I think this team (England) could do it. No, I don't just think. I believe.'

Ramsey, derided by many for his out-of-character prediction, 'England will win the 1966 World Cup', is a man of tenacity and careful thought. The England team he inspired to Wembley success, the 'wingless

wonders' they were called because Ramsey did not employ orthodox wingmen, qualified in their own right for a place among the great teams of all time.

Yet, over a year after England's victory, Ramsey was still looking ahead, saying, 'This side can be the greatest that football has ever had, the greatest football will ever know'. Sir Alf, the perfectionist, seeks fresh fields to conquer in the soccer world. But he pays apt tribute to the Hungarians in trying to emulate their memory.

Take a look at the England side that won the 1966 World Cup: Banks; Cohen, Wilson; Stiles, Charlton (J), Moore; Ball, Hunt, Charlton (R), Hurst, Peters.

More great players. But none greater than Charlton (R)—Bobby, the younger of the Charlton brothers, capped a record 106 times by England and a star of two Manchester United sides that have played their way into soccer records.

Bobby Charlton, first capped in 1958 under the leadership of Billy Wright, and a 'Footballer of the Year' in England and Europe, emulated his former captain's record number of international appearances during the 1970 World Cup. He had scored forty-nine goals for England at the end of that year, which is also a record number, five more than Jimmy Greaves and nineteen more than Tom Finney and Nat Lofthouse. In his career he has trodden the famous

Munich 1958

Few disasters have hit football so hard as the Manchester United tragedy of 1958, when eight of the club's players were killed in a 'plane crash at Munich. The team was returning from a match with Red Star of Belgrade; the ill-fated side, one of the greatest in post-war football, is seen lining up before the start of the game in Belgrade, opposite page, above. Below are Duncan Edwards, left, a truly great player who was killed in the crash, and manager Matt Busby, seen lying in an oxygen tent in Munich Hospital. This page: the wreckage of the aircraft, above, and two pictures of Matt Busby; on the left he is arriving in Munich for a friendly match staged six months after the crash. On the right, nine years after, England's most celebrated club manager waves to his fans after Manchester United had won the 1966–7 League championship.

Spurs Go Marching On

Famous Tottenham sides. Opposite page, above: Ron Burgess, captain of the 1950–1 team, battles with Stanley Matthews and, right, leads his team during training at White Hart Lane. Below: Danny Blanchflower, captain in 1961 when Spurs again won the League, addresses the crowd after the presentation. This page, above: Dyson's goal in the 1961 Cup Final, when Spurs completed a Cup and League double. Below: the 1961 side with their trophies. The players are, back row, left to right: Bill Brown, Peter Baker, Ron Henry, Danny Blanchflower, Maurice Norman, Dave Mackay. Front row: Cliff Jones, John White, Bobby Smith, Les Allen, Terry Dyson.

English soccer suffered a major setback in 1953 when the Hungarians beat England 6—3 at Wembley, the first home defeat by a foreign international side. On the opposite page, and above, we see how the game looked from goalkeeper Merrick's end of the field—an almost ceaseless onslaught. This page, centre: Hungarian goalkeeper Grosics leaps to save. Below: the great Hidegkuti hammers in No. 6 for Hungary.

Wembley turf as a schoolboy star, a Cup Finalist, an international, and a European Cup Finalist.

One interesting fact emerges from this survey of the 'all-time greats' of the soccer scene. Charlton is acknowledged by referees as the most sporting professional player of today. Like Matthews in his time, he is not provoked and uses skill to counter brute force and the close-marking attentions of opponents.

As internationals are more numerous today than at any time in history, it may be unfair to elevate into the ranks of the great players those who through cir-

Opposite page, above: Billy Wright, left, leads the England team onto the field for his last international and, right, thirteen years after the Hungarian match in which he played, England manager Alf Ramsey celebrates his team's World Cup victory.

Below: Ramsey joins in an England practice game in 1964. This page, above: the England squad limbers up shortly after Ramsey's appointment as team manager. Below: members of the England team, still dazed by their World Cup win.

Opposite page: England's only goals in their World Cup group matches in Mexico. Hurst finds the Rumanian net, top, while, below, Clarke coolly takes the penalty that defeats Czechoslovakia. This page: three of the England players who took part in both the 1966 and 1970 World Cups—Bobby Charlton, Alan Ball and captain Bobby Moore.

cumstance and age have won more caps, but for the record the Englishmen behind Wright and Charlton are Bobby Moore (over 80), Tom Finney (76 caps and again, a thorough sportsman and credit to the game), left-back Ray Wilson (62), marksman Jimmy Greaves (57), former England captain Johnny Haynes (56), and Matthews. England goalkeeper Gordon Banks, adjudged the best in the world in recent years, has topped the half-century mark.

Danny Blanchflower, the Spurs captain in the famous 'double' side of 1961, holds the record for the highest number of consecutive appearances in the home international championship. Starting with the game against Wales at Swansea in 1952, he played in every one of Northern Ireland's championship games to the end of 1962—an uninterrupted run of thirty-three consecutive matches.

Hanappi, Austria's right-half in almost a hundred post-war internationals, included a run of fifty-five consecutive appearances for his country, while the Belgian players Carré and Mermans each made fifty-

England v. Brazil, Mexico 1970. A closely contested game in the heat of the midday sun saw the Brazilians come off the winners by a single goal. The scorer was the fast and elusive Jairzinho, seen, above, escaping the attentions of Cooper. This page, below: Banks takes care of a high ball in the England goal area as Pele threatens. In the same game, Banks made one save from Pele that many believed to be the finest they had ever seen. Opposite page, above: one of England's best chances fell to Lee, but his header was parried by Felix. Below: Colin Bell sandwiched between two Brazilian defenders.

six consecutive appearances for their country between 1949-56.

A great player of another era was Bob Crompton, the Blackburn Rovers full-back before the First World War, who set a record of forty international appearances, thirty-four of them in the home championship and eight against foreign opposition. Crompton, unequalled in his time, did not have the benefit of the regular number of international matches of the moderns, a fact that underlines his achievement the more.

George Young, steady, rock-like George who was never happier than when in the thick of the fray against England, 'the Auld Enemy', topped the half-century mark in appearances for Scotland. For Wales, the most-capped men of all time are present-day players Ivor Allchurch and Cliff Jones, but the most revered in the valleys is still the Wizard, Billy Meredith.

Opposite page: Svensson, the Swedish goalkeeper, tussles with Pele during the World Cup Final of 1958. This page, above: the 1966 Brazil team lines up before the start of a warm-up match in Madrid against the local Atletico side. From the left they are: Jair, Amarildo, Servilio, Altair, Zito, Pele, Gerson, Fidelis, Brito, Gilmar and Enrique. Brazil spared no expense in their World Cup preparations, investing £285,000 in the most comprehensive campaign ever mounted for a football tournament. In the end, despite all the planning and the brilliance of individual players, Brazil were eliminated in the final qualifying rounds. Below: Pele, Brazil's greatest and most celebrated player.

Scotland have triumphed at Wembley five times starting, of course, with the 5—1 triumph of the never-to-be-forgotten 'Wembley Wizards' of 1928. Another result that will live long in the memory is the 3—2 win by the little-fancied Northern Ireland team at Wembley in 1957.

A look at the multi-capped players of other nations discloses an impressive list of stars, including the Austrian Ocwirk, who played an attacking centre-half role long after the rest of the world had submitted to

This page: Lev Yashin, Russia's famous and popular goalkeeper, diving to save a free-kick by West Germany in the 1966 World Cup semi-final, in which the Russians were defeated 2—1. Opposite page, above: a big day for Jimmy Greaves—his last appearance for Chelsea before his departure in 1961 for Milan. To mark the occasion he scored four goals. Below: England international wing-half Jimmy Dickinson, who set a record of 764 peace-time appearances for his club, Portsmouth.

defensive duty for the No. 5; the Brazilians Pele, Didi, Gilmar, Santos D. and Santos N; the Czechs Novak

and Planicka; Johnny Carey, twenty-nine games for Eire and seven for Ireland; the Finn, Mynti; Marché and Jonquet, of France; the Germans, Janes, Lehner and Fritz Walter, hero of the 1954 World Cup success; the Dutchman Van Heel; Caligaria of Italy; Bergmark and Svensson, of Sweden; the Uruguayan Martinez, and Zebec, Bobek and Beara, of Yugoslavia.

Bozsik, of the Hungarian team of the 1950s, achieved a century of caps, while Grosics, his colleague with the Honved team, reached eighty-nine.

Ferenc Puskas, the 'Galloping Major' with the lethal left foot, played eighty-four times for Hungary, then added caps for Spain to his collection when he joined Real Madrid.

Russia's most-capped player—and, probably, her most popular—is Lev Yashin, the goalkeeper who has won seventy-eight caps and has played over 500 first-class matches. Yashin has played twice as many times for the USSR in the past fifteen years as all the other Soviet goalkeepers put together.

He succeeded the legendary Tiger Khomich in the Moscow Dynamo goal in 1953, was elected the Soviet Union's first 'Goalkeeper of the Year' in 1960 and was chosen again in 1965 and 1966. In 1963 Yashin was European 'Footballer of the Year' and played for the FIFA XI against England at Wembley.

The visit of Moscow Dynamo to Britain just over two decades ago made a lasting impression. Having beaten Norrkoping in Sweden 5—0, they drew with Chelsea 3—3, beat Cardiff 10—1, Arsenal 4—3 and drew 2—2 with Glasgow Rangers.

Crowds totalling 271,000 watched their four games in Britain, games that cemented sporting relations

This page: George Best, of Manchester United and N. Ireland, one of the most exciting players in the world. Opposite page: Denis Law, Best's flamboyant colleague at Manchester United and a Scottish international. Law is famed for his tremendous spring-heeled jumps and rocket-like headers.

between the two countries and encouraged the Soviets to enlarge their soccer horizons. It is not solely nostalgia that makes those who remember the visit of the Dynamo side rate them as one of the great teams.

Igor Netto, one of Russia's greatest post-war players, moved to Cyprus to take a coaching appointment after a distinguished soccer career in which he was capped fifty-six times. Netto, an outstanding

wing-half played in the Helsinki Olympics and captained the victorious side in Melbourne four years later. He played in the 1958 World Cup, won a European Nations' Cup Medal in 1960 and led the national side again in Chile in 1962. Netto captained Moscow Spartak and played over 300 championship matches for them.

Valentin Ivanov, who succeeded Netto as captain of Russia, went better, with fifty-nine caps for his country. Ivanov, who has received a diploma as a registered coach from the Moscow Institute of Physical Culture, played in the 1958, 1962 and qualifying stages of the 1966 World Cup competitions. He won a European Nations' Cup medal in 1960 and also appeared in the 1964 Final. Ivanov tops the list of Russian goalscorers in international matches.

Ricardo Zamora, the legendary Spanish goalkeeper, has won more caps than any other player for his country. He collected forty-six caps between 1920 and 1936. Zamora helped to make soccer history, for he played in the Spanish side in 1929 when they became the first foreign country to beat England in a full international. A 4—3 victory electrified Spain and elevated Zamora and his colleagues to national heroes.

England gained a 7—1 revenge at Highbury two years later—and goalkeeper Zamora was on the receiving end. Some tribute to his durability is that a crowd of 50,000 watched a 1967 match played in Madrid in his honour. Great players of the modern era saluted a giant of the past that day, as a side labelled a 'Foreign XI' beat Spain 3—0. Centre forward Mazzola scored the three goals, leading a forward line comprising Hamrin, Rivera, Mazzola, Eusebio and Corso.

Argentina, despite losing numbers of her most talented players to Italy for many years, has produced great players and great teams. The first appearance of the Argentinians at Wembley in 1951—England won 2—1 with goals in the last ten minutes from Jackie Milburn and Stan Mortensen—left the crowd revelling at the speed and skill of the South Americans and the wonderful goalkeeping of the acrobatic Rugilio.

Pele, Didi and Garrincha, the 'Little Bird' whose skill on the ball was likened to Matthews, are among the finest products of the fabulous era of Brazilian dominance in world soccer affairs in the past decade.

Uruguay, considering her late conversion to professionalism, has made a magnificent impact from the winning of the 1924 and 1928 Olympics and the 1930 World Cup to the present day. The great figure of those early days was a Negro, Jose Andrade, who was known as the 'Black Star'. He died in 1958, but his nephew, Rodriguez Andrade emerged as one of the principal Uruguayan players in the World Cup

This page: Uwe Seeler, the West German striker, seen in action against France. Opposite page: Eusebio, the Mozambique-born Portuguese international whose deadly shooting in the 1966 World Cup tournament earned him the lasting admiration of millions of fans. Eusebio is a living example to thousands of would-be players of how a man can rise to fame and fortune through soccer.

campaigns of 1954 (Switzerland) and 1958 (Sweden).

Over the years many great players come to mind. Here there is space to mention just the names: goalkeepers such as Sam Hardy, Harry Hibbs, Vic Woodley and big Frank Swift; full-backs Laurie Scott and George Hardwick, successors to Male and Hapgood; Britton, Cullis, Mercer—England's greatest half-back line—and Neil Franklin, the best footballing centre-half of recent years. In the forward

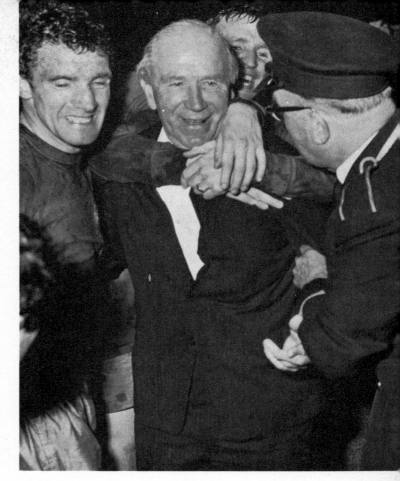

Benfica v. Manchester United

The greatest day in Manchester United's history happened in May 1968 when they defeated Benfica 4—1 after extra-time to win the European Cup—the first English club to do so. Played at Wembley Stadium, the match was watched on television by an estimated 250 million fans. After ninety minutes the scores were level 1—1, then three superb goals from Best, Kidd and Charlton won the day for Manchester. Opposite page: Kidd scores the third goal, above, and Charlton, below left, bangs in No. 4. Below right: Manchester United players rest on the field before the start of extra-time, urged on by manager Matt Busby to overcome their exhaustion and the notorious 'Wembley cramp'. This page, above: Matt Busby is embraced after the match by Bill Foulkes and Pat Crerand. Below: Bobby Charlton shows the European Cup to the ecstatic crowd.

The people of Western Europe are the most unfortunate of all in terms of climate and its effect on football. In Britain, Germany, Holland, Belgium and France the players plough their way through mud, slip around on ice and then end their season on grounds almost completely shorn of grass and baked hard by the spring sun.

Inevitably, the varying conditions have had a marked effect on the type of game developed in each region. Forty years ago there were more sub-regions but today there are three major schools within the framework of the European game—the Latin, the Mitropa (Mittel Europa) and the Nordic.

The Latins, led by Italy, Spain and Portugal, evolved a game in which agility and individual skill predominated. Being warm-blooded and easily roused, the Latins' game is marked by frequent clashes when physical contact unbalances a skilful but fiery player.

Further north the colder, more phlegmatic Britons, Germans and Scandinavians accepted physical contact more readily, even relished it. Since the last war the Russians have joined this school together with the Dutch and Belgians, although the last two countries followed less willingly and still appear reluctant whole-heartedly to go for the physical challenge. It should, of course, be understood that strength rather than skill is required to kick a heavy ball in thick mud, which means that the northern game must differ radically from that of the Latins.

Austria, Hungary, Czechoslovakia, Yugoslavia and Switzerland all conform to the Mitropa style of play based on short-passing along the ground. Here the physical challenge is barred, discouraged by coaches, jeered by spectators and penalized by referees.

Increasing contact with teams from other countries, following the improvement of air travel and the

The European Cup 1969. This page: AC Milan, winners for the second time. Opposite page, top: Sir Matt Busby protests as Fitzpatrick is sent off during Manchester United's semi-final in Milan. Centre: Prati heads Milan's fourth goal in the final against Ajax. Bottom: snow-bound quarter-final in Amsterdam. Eusebio leads a Benfica attack on the Ajax goal.

commencement of regular international competitions at club and national level, have tended to blur the lines which once clearly marked these regional styles of play. Although they are still evident, there are slow but perceptible changes being made, and continued contact at all levels will finally produce a truly European game.

In the final analysis this European game will not be the skilful game of the Latins nor the 'man's game' developed by the British and the Germans. Neither will it be the intelligent, chess-like contest so loved by mid-Europeans but, rather, a polyglot style for artistic and intelligent men.

The status of the European player varies from country to country according to the degree to which the national game has been developed as a business. Socially the top-class player is as well-known in his own country as any Hollywood film-star, but at international level it is the professionals who dominate.

Like any other business, football flourishes in heavily populated areas and it follows that the best-paid players are with clubs in the big industrial cities. In this pattern it is the Italian and British clubs who lead, with Spain and Portugal close behind. Milan, Turin and Rome each have two big clubs which almost control the Italian game, while in Britain the giants of the game are to be found in Manchester, London, Liverpool and Glasgow. To pay high salaries the clubs must draw big crowds and only in the heavily populated areas can clubs expect crowds

The pictures on these pages feature teams from Czechoslovakia, one of the Mitropa group of countries, where the season begins in the early autumn, stops for about three and a half months to avoid the worst of the winter, and continues until June. Opposite page, top: Dukla Prague, dark shirts, attacking against Esbjerg, Denmark, in a European Cup match. Centre: Dukla v. Anderlecht, Belgium. Bottom: the Czech national side, white shirts, playing the Netherlands. This page, above left: another incident from the same match, which the Czechs won 2—1. Above right: Czechoslovakia's Pluskal stretches to beat Suarez, Spain, during the 1962 World Cup tournament in Chile, in which the Czechs finished second, losing 3—1 to Brazil in the Final. Below: members of the Sparta Prague team.

Many countries scorn professionalism on moral grounds. Russia, Hungary, Czechoslovakia, Poland, Bulgaria and Rumania are the leaders in this group. Nevertheless, sport is encouraged at every level from the tiniest children to the most aged, male and female alike. In these countries a Ministry of Sport controls football as it does all other aspects of sport and culture, spending millions of pounds to develop sports grounds, gymnasia and training areas, but refusing to allow the players to be paid. Officially, they all have a job outside the game but, in fact, these jobs are only nominal. Thus, although they train like professionals, they are paid like amateurs.

Some European countries have no moral objections to professional football but in small countries like Sweden, Norway, Finland, Denmark and Luxembourg, the clubs could not afford to adopt professionalism. Many do pay their players unofficially, but the payments are comparatively small—proportionate to the size of the crowds which watch them play. Inevitably the best players from these countries drift abroad to join clubs in professional countries.

Finally, there are two countries, Belgium and Switzerland, where the status of a player is best described as non-amateur. According to the Swiss FA all players are amateurs though, in reality, they are poorly-paid professionals; the FA is content to ensure that all players have a job outside the game, while newspapers openly report on transfer-fees, signing-on payments and win-bonuses.

In Belgium the players are officially regarded as *indépendants*—neither amateur nor professional. Paid openly, though not lavishly by Italian and British standards, they can be prevented from joining other clubs unless a transfer-fee is paid, yet they are not officially recognized as professionals.

Whatever the official attitude towards paid players, it is an inescapable fact that the big clubs in the big cities pay their players. This applies equally in Moscow, Budapest and Prague, but the rewards a player can earn are related not so much to his ability as to the crowd-drawing capacity of the club and the total population in its locality.

Across the whole of Europe nothing varies quite so much as the internal structure of the clubs. In Britain every professional club, with only one

This page, above: the Dynamo Zagreb team, Yugoslav League champions in 1966–7. Centre: Yugoslav goalkeeper Beara, a veteran of sixty international matches, seen during training. Bottom: Asparouhov, Bulgaria's chief striker in the 1966 World Cup series. Opposite page, above: members of the Dosza, Hungary, team which played in the 1965–6 Inter-Cities Fairs' Cup. Below: Grosics, goalkeeper in the dynamic Hungarian national side which beat England 6—3 at Wembley.

exception, is controlled by a handful of shareholders. Shares cannot be bought and sold freely, though they cost comparatively little when they change hands, and, in general, the clubs have rules which allow the directors to approve potential buyers. This provides stability for the club but generally retards progress because most shareholders retain their shares for life. On average, therefore, the shareholder is probably an elderly man with old ideas. Between them, shareholders elect the club directors on the basis of one share–one vote.

In Spain and Portugal the clubs are run on far more democratic lines. In keeping with the general continental approach, football clubs are usually just one section of a giant sports club catering for every field of activity from athletics to water-polo. For a small monthly subscription anyone can join the club of his choice, receive a membership card which entitles him to vote at all meetings and enables him to obtain match-tickets at reduced rates.

The biggest club in Portugal is Sport Lisboa e Benfica, twice winners of the European Champions' Cup. The club usually has around 60,000 members. The Spanish giants are Real Madrid and CF Barcelona, each with more than 50,000 *socios*, or members. In addition to winning the European Champions' Cup six times, Real Madrid have also won the European Basketball Championship and together with CF Barcelona usually provide the

backbone of the Spanish athletic teams which take part in the Olympic Games. Apart from the football sections, the other groups are predominantly amateur and, in the big multi-sport clubs, the profits which accrue from football are often used to subsidize the less popular sports.

In Italy there are several big clubs which have been 'adopted' and helped financially by a major company. The best example of this is the Juventus club of Turin (Torino), which was controlled for years by the Agnelli family which runs the huge FIAT Motor Corporation. Successive heads of the Agnelli family have donated large sums of money to the club, affectionately known throughout Italy as 'the old lady'. Although most Italian clubs are run for football only, Juventus provides another exception by being multi-sport. The tennis section has such lavish premises that Italy often stages Davis Cup games there.

The majority of Italian clubs, however, exist purely for football and have no real assets of their own. With local authorities providing most of the grounds and maintaining them, the clubs hire their stadia in exchange for a percentage of the gate-receipts. The real power in the clubs is wielded by a President who is elected annually, normally on the strength of his bank-balance and his willingness to sign a bank-guarantee covering the club's overdraft!

This practice has led to a series of crises within the

More players from Eastern Europe. Opposite page, above: the Albanian national side which held West Germany to a 0—0 draw in Tirana in 1967. Below: Albert, of Hungary, leaps over the Portuguese goalkeeper in a 1966 World Cup match. This page: Turkish players help clear the snow at Brno, Czechoslovakia; snow is one of the main reasons why several countries in Central Europe interrupt their season during the mid-winter months.

Italian game, for at the last estimate several clubs were close on £750,000 in the red. At one time the Roma debts totalled almost £1 million. If the big banks were ever to demand payment the Italian League could collapse overnight since, without real assets, the clubs could sell only their players' contracts.

In Eastern Europe—Czechoslovakia, Hungary, Rumania, Bulgaria and Russia—several new clubs have been formed since 1945, sponsored by various government departments. Very largely these new clubs were backed by the Army; by offering promising players a good salary and a commission, they were able to capture many of their country's best players. This advantageous situation began to swing away from army clubs such as Honved (Hungary), Dukla (Czechoslovakia), Legia (Poland), CDNA (Bulgaria) and CCA (Rumania) when the other clubs began to acquire more influence and objected to having

their best players tempted away in times of success.

At that time certain clubs had been adopted by other government departments: Lokomotive Sofia was sponsored by the Bulgarian Railways, the Dynamo clubs were subsidized by the various electrical industries and others were backed by police, universities and state-owned factories.

More and more clubs in Eastern Europe are now demanding and obtaining autonomy and, in addition, they are slowly regaining their pre-war names. Kiniszi (Hungary) was among the first to revert to its old name, Ferencvaros, while Red Banner soon followed suit to become MTK once more. In Czechoslovakia Dynamo Prague regained its proud old name, Slavia, while Spartak Stalingrad was again known as Bohemians. Control in these clubs rests with committees made up from local dignitaries and officials whose influence can often be wielded in the clubs' interests.

Yugoslavia recently became the first communist country to recognize professionalism. Although the government was not easily persuaded, it had little choice. So many players were leaving Yugoslavia, where they were officially amateurs but, in fact, poorly-paid part-timers, that the flood had to be stopped. Eight of the Partizan Belgrade team which reached the European Champions' Cup Final in 1966 left the country a few weeks later, together with the coach and the manager.

Within a twelve-month period around the time of the Partizan success, more than 100 First Division players left Yugoslavia to play as professionals in Austria, Switzerland (paid-amateurs), France, West Germany, Holland and Belgium. Finally the government agreed to professionalism and now, if players leave their clubs, it can at least demand compensation in the form of transfer-fees.

Holland was one of the first of the smaller countries to opt for professionalism but the old-fashioned Royal Dutch Football Association tried for years to hold back the tide. Finally in 1954 a group of the top clubs broke away from the KNVB to form its own professional league, and when peace was made between the two bodies, payments were permitted. Fortuna Geleen was one of the leading clubs in this campaign, and later took the name Fortuna 54 to mark its part in the affair. However, Fortuna has never been successful as a professional club; coming from a small town, it cannot match the giants in the two big cities, Amsterdam and Rotterdam.

Since the introduction of professionalism Ajax (Amsterdam) and Feijenoord (Rotterdam) have dominated the championship with only token resistance from PSV Eindhoven. PSV is the Phillips Sport Verein, the sports' club of the internationally

The All-Weather Game

Snow, mud, fog, floods—these are just some of the hazards which regularly confront players and clubs and, some say, add spice to the game. Certainly the modern player has to adapt quickly to some startling changes of climate as he is catapulted by jet from the snow and rain of Manchester or Glasgow to the torrid heat of Madrid or Buenos Aires. The pictures on these pages show a few of the variations available in England alone. Top: Arsenal v. Sheffield United at Highbury. Below, left to right: Charlie Hurley, risen from the mud at Roker Park, Sunderland; Ernie Pythian of Wrexham peering through the fog, and that great warrior Tom Finney, Preston North End, scything up a huge shower of spray which almost completely obscures his Chelsea opponent.

known electrical manufacturers. Not surprisingly, PSV has what is claimed to be the best floodlights in the world, but though the club offers good jobs to all its players it is unable to compete with the big two.

As in all small countries the Dutch population is insufficient to support a fully professional league and only half-a-dozen clubs can command regular crowds of more than 10,000; for the rest, life is a constant struggle against rising costs. One of the big problems in Holland stems from the fact that football is not played in schools and youngsters must, therefore, join a senior club if they are to play. Only the biggest clubs can afford to maintain as many as forty players, as Feijenoord do, and naturally the youngsters tend to go where the facilities are.

The French provide a striking example of a nation that has lost interest in football. Between the wars the game developed steadily and with the introduction

of professionalism in the 1930s the French game grew in stature, comparing favourably with any other. From 1950-60 the famous Stade de Reims led the way, backed by a millionaire champagne-producer, M. Henri Germain. For years he poured in millions of francs and twice Reims reached the final of the European Champions' Cup, only to lose each time to Real Madrid. In 1958 this fabulous Reims squad provided seven of the French team—and the coach, Albert Batteux—which earned third place in the World Cup.

That was probably France's grand finale, for soon afterwards M. Henri Germain withdrew his support and Reims are now in Division II. Other clubs have already begun to cut their costs for, quite inexplicably, the French people started to lose interest in watching football. Attendances tumbled and now, after years of struggle, many clubs exist solely through the

generosity of local authorities which hand over thousands of pounds every year to keep the clubs going. AS Monaco, champions five years ago, have a ground which can hold only 4,000 people, balanced on the edge of the sea. They carry on with the support of Prince Rainier and the elected government of the Principality, and if ever this support was to be withdrawn the club would collapse.

Paris provides the biggest surprise of all, for with several million inhabitants the city should be able to support at least one thriving professional club. Racing Club was perhaps the best-known club in

Opposite page: Nordic meets Mitropa in this European Cup match between Celtic and Dukla Prague. On the night the Nordic style of the Scots proved superior; here Wallace scores one of his two goals. This page: a Nordic v. Latin encounter, Chelsea against AC Milan.

France, even though after the war the team bounced up and down between the First and Second Divisions. The Racing Club of Buenos Aires, 1967 winners of the world club champions' Cup, took its name and colours from the French team many years ago—but the Racing Club de Paris no longer exists.

There are two clubs left in Paris, Stade de Paris, formerly Stade Français until the disappearance of

With the increase in European club competitions, the various regional styles are slowly beginning to merge. This page, top: Haller, a German, in play for his Italian club, Bologna. Centre and bottom: Liverpool lose 2—1 to Borussia Dortmund in the 1966 European Cup Winners' Cup Final; St John just fails to score, centre, and Yeats strives in vain to keep out the deciding goal. Opposite page: Spurs score against Feijenoord through Dyson in 1961, above, and against OFK Belgrade in 1963, below, with Mackay (No. 10) the scorer.

Racing, and Red Star, who actually play in the suburb of Saint-Ouen. Stade are currently losing £1,000 a month while Red Star carry on with considerable help from Saint-Ouen Town Council.

In Switzerland, as in West Germany, Sweden, Norway and Austria, the game exists very largely through the support of wealthy businessmen. The Swiss refer to these club angels as *donateurs*, and they regularly hand over hefty donations to club funds.

In Britain, Spain and Portugal, clubs are organized on a more substantial basis but in Italy, Switzerland, Austria, France, Holland, Belgium, Norway, Sweden and Denmark, the financial problems grow heavier each year.

If it is clear that only big clubs, in big cities, can really afford to stage highly professional entertainment, then the future of the game, it is argued in some quarters, might be assured by the creation of a European League. This would almost certainly guarantee big attendances for those clubs lucky enough to obtain a 'place in the sun', but those who were left outside would inevitably be forced to revert to a system of part-timers.

In Britain, where the game began in its modern form, many clubs are more than 100 years old. Many countries which took up the game later have managed to avoid the pitfalls which the early English and

The rough-and-tumble of League and FA Cup are still the bread-and-butter of British clubs, with Europe an attractive extra for which only a few clubs in the big cities can really expect to qualify. The pictures on these pages show two of the most successful English teams, Leeds and Everton, both in action, opposite, against Crystal Palace, 1969 newcomers to the First Division. This page: Clarke scores for Leeds against Sheffield Wednesday.

Scottish clubs encountered; and one of the most important problems has been that of space.

In the early days it was the working classes who made football successful and naturally it was in the heavily populated industrial areas that the first big clubs emerged. In those areas building-space was limited in or near the town centres, and today clubs eager to expand are thwarted by factories and houses pressing in on all sides. Some very fortunate clubs were able to buy adjoining sites, but for the majority it has proved impossible either to extend the available accommodation for spectators or to develop training areas beside the stadium.

The Goodison Park ground in Liverpool illustrates this problem. With stands on three sides, the unbroken array of seating suddenly ends where the rear of a church juts into the ground. It was in this church that the present football club was formed over 100 years ago.

Training is much better organized today, and

Cup Final Day

Up for the Cup! Each year 100,000 fans descend on Wembley Stadium for the FA Cup Final, and millions at home follow the match on television. The Cup Final is perhaps the most popular event in the English soccer calendar—the climax to a competition which starts many months before when the smaller, non-League clubs battle to decide who shall qualify for the first round, and a chance to knock out one of the top sides. For these Liverpool fans, right, gathered in Trafalgar Square before the 1965 Final, it was to prove a happy day—their team beat Leeds United 2—1 after extra time.

where clubs called their players for training maybe once a week fifty years ago, training is now a daily routine. Unable to extend their ground and knowing that to use the main playing pitch every day would soon leave it bare of grass, the majority of British clubs have been forced to acquire land for training purposes at considerable distances from the stadia.

Opposite page: Les Allen of Queen's Park Rangers walks to the trainer's bench after having his shirt ripped in the heat of the game. This page: star players like Bobby Charlton can expect to be tightly marked throughout the ninety minutes when precious League points are at stake. Here he is closely shadowed by Keith Weller of Spurs (now with Chelsea).

Some now travel as much as twenty miles each way in order to train.

Although the game was exported to Denmark, Germany and Austria in the nineteenth century, it was not in most cases until the 1920s that clubs in these countries were well enough established to want to build big grounds. Until then the few hundred who watched could be accommodated behind a rope or fence a yard or two from the touch-line, but as crowds grew bigger so terraces and stands were needed.

Having noted the expansion problems which already faced the older British clubs at this time, most Continental clubs moved to new, larger premises

before building began. In Belgium, Spain, Italy, Holland and Switzerland training pitches have been developed alongside the stadia and there the players can go to warm up before matches. In the more cramped British grounds, warming-up is limited to muscular exercises, stretching and so on, in the changing-rooms.

With the absence of adequate pre-match facilities, one might expect the British to experience a great many muscular injuries, but surprisingly this is not so. It may well be that the need for warming-up is largely psychological, but whatever the real facts, it is a distinct disadvantage not to have proper training premises next to the main stadium.

Since the Second World War, several countries have followed the British lead and introduced football pools. Making a small weekly bet on the results of the week-end's football results, winners in Britain have often received more than £200,000. In Holland, Norway and Sweden, home-based companies operate several pools, using the names of British trend-setters, but in these countries the proceeds remain in the hands of the promoters.

Switzerland and West Germany took a big step in the right direction when their governments each granted a monopoly to a State-sponsored pools firm. This operates precisely as in Britain except that the

profits are turned over to local authorities who use the capital to buy land and build training areas, playing pitches, gymnasia and swimming pools, etc. In both Switzerland (Macolin) and Germany (Cologne) these funds have also been used to develop what can accurately be described as 'sports towns'. Here, with superb facilities for living and sleeping accommodation for large groups, every type of sports team can practise for weeks on end.

Italy and, more recently, Spain have also set up government-sponsored pools with the aim of developing more and more sports grounds. In Italy local authorities have helped considerably by using public funds to construct modern stadia which are used for a variety of sports and leased to the clubs. In Spain one problem is that there are more than two clubs affiliated to the Spanish FA for every football pitch in the country, and many amateur clubs use grounds that are played on two or three times every week.

The West Germans, hard and consistent players, are always somewhere near the top in European competitions. Opposite page, above: national team trainer Helmut Schön talks to star players Overath, centre, and Beckenbauer. Below: Fortuna Düsseldorf's goalkeeper, Sepp Maier, saves an almost certain goal against Bayern Munich in a German League match. Maier has since moved to Bayern Munich for whom Müller, this page below, plays. Right: Overath in training.

West German Stars

Opposite page, above: West Germany's Lothar Emmerich (No. 11) goes for the ball with Ponomarev of Russia in the 1966 World Cup semi-final. Below: veteran striker Uwe Seeler is foiled by Russian goalkeeper Lev Yashin, another seasoned campaigner, in a scene from the same match. This page, above: in the World Cup Final Haller eludes England's Alan Ball. Below: Franz Beckenbauer, one of West Germany's finest players, a commanding defender who also scores a lot of goals with thumping, long-range drives.

In Turkey this problem is even greater, for while the shortage of grounds is limited to the amateurs in Spain and Italy, the Turkish situation is so acute that even in the First Division three or four clubs have to share one ground.

In the last twenty years several countries have developed big, modern stadia, but before that time there were only two grounds in Europe which could accommodate crowds of 100,000. These were both in Britain—100,000 at Wembley Stadium, which is privately owned and limited to international matches and FA Cup Finals, and Hampden Park, Glasgow,

where 134,000 have been packed in. Internationals are staged at the latter ground, which is also the home of amateur club Queen's Park.

With the post-war boom which spread across Europe, huge concrete palaces rose everywhere. The Prater Stadium in Vienna was extended from 60,000-capacity to 90,000; Real Madrid built the 104,000-capacity Estadio Santiago Bernabeu and their rivals CF Barcelona promptly followed suit with Nou Camp, which houses 90,000.

The Italians have been active, too, in this field. Rome's Olympic Stadium matched the 100,000-capacity Olympic bowl in Berlin, and San Siro in Milan (90,000) and the Stadio Communale in Turin (80,000) were developed and improved.

In Eastern Europe many new stadia have been built since the war but the biggest are in Poland and Russia, where there is room at Chorzow and at the Lenin Stadion in Moscow for 104,000. Pride of place

Opposite page, above: Benny Muller scores for the Netherlands against Belgium. Below left: English referee Jim Finney abandons a Scotland v. Austria international in 1963 after persistent fouling by both sides. Below right: Lev Yashin in goal for the Rest of the World against England, also in 1963. This page: Dynamo Kiev, the Russian League champions who eliminated Celtic from the European Cup in 1968.

The Prizes

Europe's two major prizes—the European Cup and the Cup Winners' Cup. This page: holders of the latter trophy include Tottenham, above, and Bayern Munich, below. Opposite page: jubilant Celtic players seen with the European Cup in their Lisbon dressing-room in 1967 and later, on their return to Glasgow, performing a lap of honour at the Parkhead ground. Below: members of the Celtic team after they had beaten Dukla Prague on the way to the Final.

This page, above: dance of the Magyars in the Hungarian goalmouth during a Liverpool v. Ferencvaros Fairs' Cup match in 1968. Below: three of the world's most expensive players in action for their Italian League clubs—left to right, Amarildo, Facchetti and Mazzola. Opposite page: a World Cup linesman with a handful of horns thrown on to the pitch by dejected Italian fans during the Italy v. Russia match in 1966.

in the region, however, must surely go to the enormous Nep Stadion in Budapest, where 100,000 can be accommodated and everyone has a seat.

Elsewhere 65,000 is about the limit, and while some clubs occasionally may have to turn customers away this happens only at the really big games—Finals of the European Champions' Cup and the like. Indeed, grounds holding more than 100,000 have rarely been needed.

With the advent of rapid air-travel the European game has progressed more quickly in the last fifteen years than ever before. Where once it took three or four days to travel by rail from London to Budapest the journey can now be accomplished in two-and-a-half hours. This led first to more frequent matches against foreign clubs and finally to the development of regular competitions for club teams at international level. Such matches now provide the highlights in the European game, with some lucky clubs collecting as much as £90,000 in gate-receipts.

Frequent meetings with teams from abroad have tended to level off the game as a whole, for clubs and coaches are now more aware of their deficiencies. By comparing their players with those of other countries, clubs have come to appreciate that some players are better prepared physically, some are quicker and others are more highly skilled with the ball. Beaten teams have become aware they must work harder in training and prepare themselves more conscientiously for a wider variety of opposition.

Although air travel has brought tremendous advantages to the game it has also led to several disasters. The first major accident involving a football team occurred near Turin in May 1949, when the aircraft carrying AC Torino back from a friendly match in Portugal crashed. The entire team and reserves on board were killed, and the only player to survive was Carapellese who, because he suffered from air-sickness, had travelled home by train.

A similar disaster took place nine years later when English champions Manchester United were returning from a European Champions' Cup match in Yugoslavia. Their 'plane landed at Munich and failed after take-off, with the result that more than half the team was killed.

The big international tournaments have given the European game a great impetus, however, and despite an apparent decline in public interest, it is clear that the future is assured. A place has to be found for television; the international calendar must be extended and many clubs will have to learn to live within their incomes, but, indisputably, the game has travelled a long way in the last fifty years. With the aid of new technical achievements it will go forward even more quickly in the next fifty.

5

South America

Football in the New World south of Panama is a vast international complex. Spread across thousands of miles of dramatically changing land is a fantastic footballing network, nourished in many places by enormous wealth.

It is the living, growing product of a loose alliance of nations for which the game has become almost a religion, a blessed escape for many from poverty and privation. It is a promised land dangling fame and fortune under the noses of millions of lithe, dark-eyed youngsters, who play at being Pele on the streets and beaches of Rio and Buenos Aires.

Soccer came to South America in the 1890s. The seeds were sown by European pioneers—railway builders, merchant seamen and businessmen—who christened clubs with names like Liverpool of Uruguay, Everton of Chile and Barcelona of Ecuador.

A pastime rapidly became a passion. Uruguay transformed this enthusiasm into delirious dedication by beating Argentina in the Final of the World Cup in Montevideo in 1930 (though it should be pointed out that only six countries outside South America took part—the USA, Yugoslavia, Belgium, Rumania, Mexico and France). However, twenty years later, Uruguay won again. Then Brazil took up the torch, carrying off the trophy in 1958 and 1962 to become undisputed rulers of the global soccer kingdom.

For most people South American football symbolizes inspired attacking play—a kind of eleven-man circus act in which players with musical-sounding names and rubbery limbs seem to possess hypnotic powers over the ball. Yet, just as there is no such thing as European, or even British soccer, South American soccer, as a style, is a myth.

The Argentine, Bolivia, Brazil, Chile, Columbia, Ecuador, Paraguay, Peru, Uruguay and Venezuela—each of the sub-continent's nations serves up its own blend. Each is fiercely proud of its traditions, its organizations, its stadia and, above all, its stars, and rivalry between rival nations' fans can be frightening and even fatal.

Vicious on-the-field brawling in the 1967 world club championship clash, in which Racing Club of Buenos Aires beat Celtic of Glasgow 1—0 after six players had been ordered off, was an example of the terrifying product of inflamed passions.

The match, a play-off a few days after Racing had beaten the Scottish side before their own fans to wipe out Celtic's home-win, was staged in neutral Montevideo. But the Uruguayans, who have little love for their Argentinian neighbours, made it plain that they were pro-Celtic in the turbulent scenes which followed.

Ironically, the Argentinians had earlier earned a reputation as villains and provocateurs in the World Cup at Wembley in 1966, when their captain Antonio Rattin refused to go after being sent off in a violent match against England.

It was the latest in a chapter of incidents involving Argentina, who refused to enter the World Cups of 1934, 1938 and 1950 and had an application to stage the 1970 championships turned down, despite having superior claims to those of Mexico. Furthermore, the Argentinians make no secret of the fact that they feel themselves grievously wronged by the absence of FIFA-intervention to prevent stars like Monti, di Stefano and Sivori being lured by European clubs.

Opposite page: Pele, idol of a generation in South America and undoubtedly Brazil's most famous player. Above: Brazil's first female professional referee, Leia Capos, the natural product, perhaps, of a land where the men would rather play than referee.

Matches involving European and South American teams have repeatedly caused violence both on and off the field. In 1954 Brazil and Hungary figured in the 'Battle of Berne'. Eight years later open 'war' broke out between Italians and Chileans in Chile.

Such incidents serve only to bolster the case of those who would pigeon-hole all South American soccer players and fans as 'a bunch of hot-heads in a hot climate'; and they open a chasm of mistrust and misunderstanding between nations with vastly different backgrounds of tradition and temperament.

Four countries have dominated the South American soccer scene—Brazil, Uruguay, Argentina and Chile. None has ruled it more forcibly in recent times than Brazil, scene of strife, revolution and booming wealth, of soccer stadia like Rio's 250,000-capacity Estadio Maria Filbo, formerly Maracana, where 200,000 spectators paid £125,000 to see the 1950 World Cup Final between Brazil and Uruguay.

And no one has dominated Brazilian football more sensationally than Edson Arantes Do Nascimento—

This page: how to preserve the peace at a South American soccer match—put the crowd behind wire netting or a moat, or both, and arm the police with tear-gas guns. Opposite page: members of Brazil's 1954 World Cup squad with, below, the forward line of Julinho, Humberto, Baltasar, Pinga and Maurinho.

Brazil in Sweden 1958

After losing to Uruguay in the 1950 Final, Brazil first became world champions in 1958. Opposite page: two scenes from the 1958 semi-final in Stockholm, in which Brazil overcame France 5—2; Garrincha, above, wearing white socks, falls during an attack on the French goal and, below, Vava and Pele join forces in an aerial battle. In this match Pele scored three goals and overnight became the star of the tournament. In the Final he scored twice against Sweden, when Brazil again won by 5—2. This page, above: Zagallo scores Brazil's fourth goal in the Final. Below: after the match the Brazilian team carry the flag of their Swedish hosts round the ground on the traditional lap of honour.

the man the world knows simply as Pele. At the beginning of 1958 he was seventeen and an unknown so far as the soccer world was concerned. Brazil included him in the World Cup squad 'just for the ride', with the 1962 Championship in mind.

Then, after a dismal attacking display in a goalless draw against England, the Brazilians called him in against Russia and strode into the semi-finals with a 2—0 victory. That was the signal for the young Negro to unleash an avalanche of goals, which today stands at over 1,000 for club and country. He netted three times against France, then banged in two more to give Brazil victory over Sweden in the Final.

This page, above: Bangu winger Paulo Borges leaps over a Vasco da Gama opponent during a match in Rio. This page, below: the Bangu team, Rio de Janeiro soccer champions in 1966, pose for the cameras in Rio's 250,000-capacity Maracana Stadium, now known as the Estadio Maria Filbo. Opposite page, above: Pele scores for Santos, his home club. Below: veteran goalkeeper Gilmar saves for Brazil against England in 1963.

This page: scenes from Brazil v. Russia, played in Rio in 1965. Opposite page, above: the Minas Gerais Stadium in Belo Horizonte, a magnificent covered bowl capable of holding up to 130,000 spectators. Below: the multi-tiered benches and seats, and the electric scoreboard at the Estadio Maria Filbo.

Eye-witnesses still talk about his second goal against the bewildered Scandinavians. Here is how one described it: 'Pele leapt like a jack-rabbit to cushion a swooping pass from winger Zagalo on his chest. A big defender swept in for the tackle but Pele left him floundering like a babe by bouncing the ball on his outstretched knee, up and over the astonished Swede's blond head. Pele, as though launched from starting blocks, flashed round him to catch the ball on his thigh, and repeated the trick to round another dazed Swede. Then he arched his body like a bow and crashed a full-blooded volley high into the net. A deafening roar threatened to lift the stand roof as this fantastic athlete danced and whooped his delight.' The other goal, by the way, was just as majestic—a header, struck with the lethal swiftness of an attacking cobra.

Brazil won 5—2, before the King of Sweden, and poignant pictures of the new soccer-monarch Pele, openly weeping after the presentation, touched the world.

Pele, whose club, Santos, turned down a £300,000 transfer-bid by Inter-Milan, is reputed to be soccer's first millionaire. Brazil's supremacy, however, did not stem from one man alone.

There is no shortage of raw material. Tourists stand spellbound at the sight of endless sets of goalposts on Rio's Copacabana beach, each surrounded by seemingly identical clusters of youngsters displaying their mastery over ball and man in marathon matches.

As a boy, Waldyr Pereira—another inside-forward star of 1958, better known as Didi, which means Cobra—would spend six hours a day practising. In this way he is typical, and on the basis of 'practice makes perfect' it is easy to understand why Europeans rarely match the South Americans in ball-artistry.

In 1970 the Brazilians again became world champions. They beat Italy 4—1 in a magnificent final match and, it was reported, three people had heart attacks and died in Italy during the match. In Brazil it was recorded that the number of people admitted to hospital with cardiac disorders on the day increased by forty per cent.

The Brazilians were fit—they moulded their strength on the lessons learned during their ill-fated trip to England for the 1966 World Cup—and showed an attacking flair that no other country could match.

The qualifiers for the 1970 tournament contained five countries from the Latin-American world—Mexico, the host nation, Brazil, Uruguay, El Salvador and Peru; four from Western Europe—England, West Germany, Sweden and Belgium; four from the 'Iron Curtain' countries—Russia, Bulgaria, Rumania and Czechoslovakia; plus Italy from Latin Europe, Israel and Morocco. In a poll conducted by the Soviet news agency Tass in May 1970 the managers of the sixteen finalists named Brazil as the favourites.

Brazil were the only finalists to have competed in all the finals since the Cup began in 1930. They were third in 1938, second in 1950, quarter-finalists in 1954, winners in 1958 and 1962, and eliminated in the preliminary rounds in England in 1966 when Pele was injured.

In the qualifying rounds for 1970 Brazil swept through as if by right, completing six victories against Paraguay, Colombia and Venezuela and scoring twenty-three goals against two.

The intensity of Brazilian preparations for the World Cup is only exceeded by the intensity of their celebrations afterwards. Below: the team training in Guadalajara, Mexico. Right: Pele and Clodoaldo leap for joy after the latter had equalized against Uruguay in the semi-final. Opposite page: back in Rio de Janeiro there is no doubt who won the Jules Rimet Trophy.

Pele, who had said that he would never again compete in the World Cup after his experiences in 1966, was again a star of the side and a national hope for success. The one blot on the Brazilian horizon as the World Cup approached was an eye injury which threatened their talented centre-forward Tostao.

Then, just two months before the competition, the Brazilians removed their controversial manager, Joao Saldanha, who claimed that he had been dismissed because he had wanted to rest Pele. Mario Zagallo, outside-left in the two successful finals, was appointed as Saldanha's successor, but it seemed to the watching world that any change of manager at this late stage

must be a handicap to Brazil's chances. In fact, it was no such thing. Zagallo introduced a 4–3–3 formation and any doubts concerning his side were swept aside by their victory over Czechoslovakia in the first match of the preliminary round in Guadalajara, the centre for Group Three four hundred miles north-west of Mexico City. Brazil won 4—1, and their astonishing display of flair and attacking elegance captured the headlines and won them countless admirers on television screens all over the world.

The Czechs scored first, the blond Petras silencing the Jalisco Stadium when he burst through on the left to beat goalkeeper Felix. Rivelino equalized, Pele

Opposite page, above: star players from Brazil and Argentina pose with two film starlets after a screening of the 1966 World Cup film *Goal*. Below: a near miss for Brazil in their match against Hungary in 1966. This page, above: the flamboyant players of Independiente salute spectators before the start of a game. Below: Independiente are awarded a much-disputed goal against Inter-Milan (striped shirts) in the 1964 Final of the world club championship. Inter-Milan finally won the trophy after a third-match play-off.

scored a remarkable goal to put Brazil ahead and Jairzinho added two more late in the game. The Mexican crowd, who adopted Brazil as the favourites next to their own team, erupted at each goal from a devastating forward line.

Then it was the confrontation of the champions, Brazil, of 1958 and 1962, versus England, the 1966 winners. Brazil won 1—0, a victory they accepted later as their best of the series. It was an outstanding match by any standards. The crowd had plenty to cheer and applaud, for beaten England squandered enough chances to have reversed the victory. The goal came when Pele sent a short pass to Jairzinho.

Brazilian manager Zagallo commented after the match: 'English football is not on the decline. At no moment did I think our victory was certain until the final whistle.'

Three days later Brazil beat Rumania 3—2, despite

the absence of Rivelino and Gerson. They began with a display of attacking soccer that matched their hey-day of a decade before. The Brazilians were two ahead through Pele and Jairzinho before faltering. Pele scored their third.

In the quarter-finals Brazil beat Peru, another attacking side, 4—2 at Guadalajara. Tostao scored twice against a side stunned by a disaster at home when an earthquake killed up to 50,000 people. The Brazilians were the brighter of two sides that scorned defence though they were perhaps, in the words of their manager, 'too cocky'.

And to reach the Final Brazil beat Uruguay 3—1 at Guadalajara, where they had played all their matches. Uruguay, twice winners of the Jules Rimet trophy and, like Brazil, in line to win it outright, protested at the venue. They scored first, but had three players cautioned before half-time and lost to goals from Clodoaldo, Jairzinho and Rivelino.

So Brazil became permanent holders of the Jules Rimet trophy. Winger Jairzinho scored seven of their goals and Pele four, but the attack of these two, plus Tostao, Rivelino and Gerson captured the imagina-tion of all football followers and restored South American supremacy. This was the Brazilian side that beat Italy in the Final: Felix; Carlos Alberto, Brito, Piazza, Everaldo; Gerson, Clodoaldo, Rivelino; Jairzinho, Tostao, Pele.

In neighbouring Argentina, one word sums up the nation's recent approach to international soccer—defence. The Argentinians earned the reputation of being the world's most defensively effective football power with a string of 1—0 and 2—0 wins in the build-up to the 1966 World Cup.

In the 'Little World Cup' of 1964, for instance, they beat England 1—0, Portugal 2—0 and Spain 3—0. A single goal seems to be the most they are prepared to concede. In the World Cup qualifying rounds they defeated Paraguay 3—0, 0—0, and Bolivia 4—1, 2—1. In the finals in England they beat Spain 2—1, drew 0—0 with West Germany and beat Switzerland 2—0, and, of course, they went down 1—0 to England in that incident-scarred Wembley quarter-final.

An England official's recollection of the 'Little World Cup' clash between Argentina and Brazil vividly illustrates their defence-in-depth strategy: 'A long punt from the Argentine half finished as a corner after glancing off a defender, yet only three Argentine players moved into the Brazilian half for the kick,

Fear of losing, clashes of style and temperament—all were factors in the Celtic-Racing Club battles for the world club championship in 1967 (this page), in the Manchester United-Estudiantes tussles for the same crown in 1968 (opposite page, above), and, worst of all, in the 1969 battle between Estudiantes and AC Milan (opposite page, below).

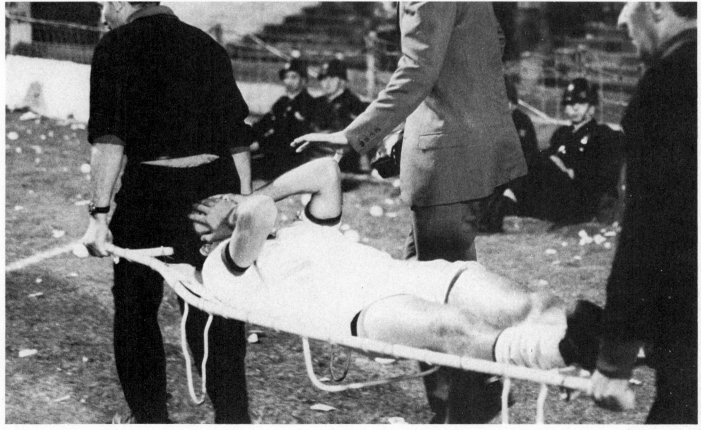

including the winger who took it. One stood in the penalty-box and one just over the halfway-line and as soon as the kick came over all three sprinted back to their own lines as fast as they could.' In that match Argentinian destroyer Delgado, a full-back in winger's clothing, so stifled Pele that, in desperation, the great man uncharacteristically butted his relentless shadow in the face.

Also in 1964, a sudden solitary breakaway, when the opposition's eight-man attack was battering away in growing frustration at the Argentinian defensive

This page, above: Argentina's Onega slips through the Swiss defence in a 1966 World Cup match. Below: police protect the Boca Juniors goalkeeper during a First Division match in Buenos Aires. Opposite page, top: Argentina v. Italy in 1966, a warm-up match for the World Cup series; Italy won 3—0. Centre: Argentina's World Cup forwards, left to right, Pianetti, Gonzalez, Lallana, Onega and Mas. Bottom: the scene at a special training camp near Buenos Aires where the national squad prepared for its assault on the Jules Rimet trophy.

wall, was enough to knock England out of the competition.

The blanket-defence method spread to club level and Boca Juniors once won the championship by scoring fewer goals than they played matches. But Argentina's march to the World Cup quarter-finals in England was no surprise to many who knew all about their class players—half-backs like skipper Rattin and Jorge Albrecht, and forwards like Oscar Mas, Ermindo Onega and Luis Artime—and of the mouth-watering £2,000-a-man bonus for reaching the last sixteen, with £5,000-a-man offered for landing the trophy itself.

This page, above: Racing Club of Buenos Aires, a major force in South American soccer. Below: police escort two players from the pitch during a match between Racing Club and Atlanta. Opposite page, above: Russia score through a dramatic bicycle-kick in their match against Argentina in Buenos Aires in 1961; in the centre of our picture is Delgado, a celebrated defence expert. Below: England centre-half Neil Franklin, white shirt, who joined the Colombian gold rush in 1950, when a breakaway league was started offering huge sums to lure players from all over the world.

Little purpose is served by raking over the ashes of ugly clashes like the Rattin match at Wembley, and Celtic's club-championship battle with Racing Club at Montevideo. But a closer look behind the scenes in Argentinian soccer helps shed some light on such unhappy affairs.

In 1930 the Argentinians reached the final of the first World Cup, and they later evolved a team that would very probably have beaten the world. Sadly, under the regime of President Peron, Argentinian sides were forbidden between 1943 and 1955 to travel to Europe.

Their great side, labelled 'El Machina', was at its peak in the early '40s. Its success was founded on the River Plate forward line: Munoz, Moreno, Pedernera, Labruna and Loustau—reputedly as scintillating an attacking combination as the game has seen. A handful, like 'El Eterno', Angel Labruna—he played in the 1958 World Cup at the ripe old age of forty-two —lived on.

As Peron's reign neared its end Argentina plunged

This page, above: in the 1966 World Cup defence-conscious Uruguay pack their penalty-area against Mexico. Below: West German goalkeeper Tilkowski punches out as Uruguay's Silva charges in. Opposite page, above: Jimmy Greaves on the run from two hefty Uruguayans. Below: a close shave for Uruguay but their defensive tactics paid off against England and they gained a 0—0 draw.

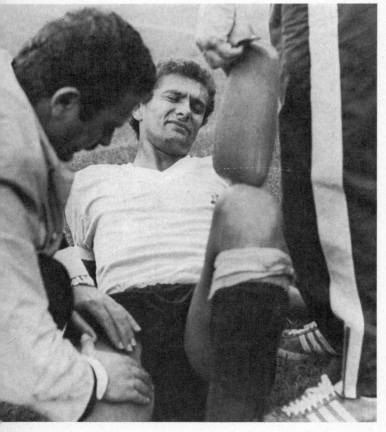

This page, above: South American delight as Mujica (far right) finds the net for Uruguay's second goal in their 2—0 victory over Israel at Puebla, Mexico. This was somewhat tempered, however, by the injury to Rocha, their star player, below, in the same match. He took no further part in the tournament. Opposite page, top: Uruguayan goalkeeper Mazurkiewicz just gets his fingertips to a dangerous Russian cross in their quarter-final. Below: a brief vision of glory for the Uruguayans as Cubilla puts them ahead in their semi-final against Brazil.

into economic crisis, and professional footballers joined in open revolt. Simultaneously, in Bogota, capital of Colombia, a breakaway league came into being, outside the authority of FIFA, and agents throughout the world tempted stars to fly there to 'make their fortune'. Among their captures was England centre-half Neil Franklin.

Well over 100 top Argentinian footballers joined the Colombian gold rush in the space of two months —almost an entire generation. And, to add insult to injury, stars such as Alfredo di Stefano (Real Madrid, Spain) and Enrico Sivori (Juventus, Italy) were later sold for fabulous sums.

A golden era had passed. Argentine slumped by 3—1 to West Germany and 6—1 to Czechoslovakia in the 1958 World Cup. They failed to qualify in 1962 and in 1963 crashed to their first home defeat, going down 2—0 to Russia in Buenos Aires.

Rebuilding was started, and foreign stars were brought in to reverse the process of the 1950s, but despite a succession of South American Championship victories, Argentine soccer continued to be beset by domestic problems.

In the seven years before 1966 the country had no fewer than fourteen national team-managers, three of whom left during immediate World Cup preparations. Eventually the strict disciplinarian, Juan Lorenzo, answered an SOS to take command. Earlier, a dozen stars had gone on strike in protest at losing money by training with the international squad when they could have been collecting fat bonuses from Cup matches in South America.

The World Cup ended as it had began—in upset. Rattin was banned from the next four internationals and the Argentinian FA fined—merely a nominal £100. Unfamiliarity with rugged European soccer

methods, and the language barrier, contributed greatly to the affair.

But Argentinian soccer, despite the failure to qualify for the 1970 World Cup Finals, is certain to regain its health. The country has more than 2,500 clubs, over 1,000 professionals and 320,000 amateurs. And stadia like those of River Plate (capacity 110,000), Racing Club (105,000) and Boca Juniors (100,000) are regularly jammed with wildly enthusiastic fans. In short, interest is higher than ever.

Uruguay, who won the Olympic title in 1924 and 1928 and the World Cup in 1930 and 1950, can also explain away a subsequent lean international run through the loss of many star players to rich European clubs.

Yet they went down only 2—1 to England at Wembley in 1964, when they had just one player from the two leading clubs, Penarol and Nacional;

they returned to London for the World Cup after handing out defeats of 5—0 and 3—1 to Venezuela and beating Peru 2—1 and 1—0 in the qualifying rounds.

Under their manager-coach Ondion Viera, then aged sixty-four, they had been baulked by the early refusal of premier clubs to release stars for international practice, but then they underwent rigorous toughening-up training, which even involved English-style rugby, and fulfilled a heavy programme of international warm-ups in Europe.

Viera, who has been player, coach and administrator in his fifty years in soccer, managing ten league sides, six of them top Brazilian clubs, must have been delighted with their opening performance when they held England to a goalless draw at Wembley.

Possession, Uruguay showed, was nine points of the law. 'We have got good ball-players, but they must have the ball. At Wembley we shall be the owners of the ball,' he warned. They went on to beat France 2—1 and draw 0—0 with Mexico, accom-

This page: hundreds of coloured balloons are released in the vast Aztec Stadium in Mexico City to signal the opening of the ninth World Cup. Opposite page, below: a goal for Mexico in the 1966 tournament. Borja scores against France at Wembley. Above: a goal against Mexico in 1970. Riva of Italy boots his country's fourth and last goal past goalkeeper Calderon in their quarter-final at Puebla.

panied England into the quarter-finals but went down 4—0 to West Germany at Hillsborough, blotting their copybook by having two men, full-back Horacio Troche and forward Hector Silva, sent off and suspended. Troche, thirty-two-year-old veteran of

Opposite page, above: Chile v. Russia. The Chileans fared badly in the 1966 World Cup against the physically larger, more powerful European sides. Below: Marcos of Chile and the North Korean goalkeeper battle for possession; in this match Chile picked up their solitary World Cup point, with a 1—1 draw. This page, above: a moment from the Chile v. Italy game, and a group photo of the Chilean team.

forty-eight internationals, who later, ironically, moved to West German club Alemannia Aachen, was fined £300. Silva had to pay £75 and manager Viera £133.

Yet little Uruguay, a country of two-and-a-half million people compared with Brazil's seventy million and Argentina's twenty-two million, had done enough to banish once and for all any doubts about the quality of its soccer compared with its mighty neighbours. And for further proof of their comeback as an international power, they snapped up their eleventh South American Championship title in 1967, beating Argentina in the final. Hero of the hour was Uruguay's number-one player, Pedro Rocha.

Rocha towers over the Uruguayan soccer scene in the same way that Pele reigns in Brazil. Yet he cost a paltry £15 transfer fee when he was discovered as a sixteen-year-old playing with his father's old team, Salto, by Penarol of Montevideo in 1959. At seventeen he was playing for his country, displaying an uncanny ability to make and score goals with nonchalant ease. He bagged eight of Uruguay's eleven World Cup qualifying goals. Today this curly-haired six-footer is the country's highest paid star. The price on his head is £150,000, just 10,000 times what Penarol paid for him! An admirer once said of Rocha, 'He makes more goals than he scores, yet scores more than anybody else'.

But Uruguayan fans long for the good old days

when sides boasted more than one player of Rocha's brilliance. They did well in Mexico in 1970 to underline their 1967 South American success, but they suffered through losing the services of Rocha. He injured a calf after a quarter of an hour in the opening preliminary-round match in which Uruguay beat Israel 2—0 and he took no further part in the competition.

Uruguay then played a predictable goalless draw with Italy—both sides are acknowledged as the archpriests of defensive football—but they qualified from their group because the standard of the other opposition was weak.

Sweden, in fact, were the only side to score against Uruguay in the preliminary round. They beat them 1—0. There was a pre-match breath of scandal when FIFA switched the Brazilian referee nominated for the match because of 'malicious rumours' about a bribery attempt.

In the quarter-finals Uruguay beat Russia with a goal late in extra-time scored by Esparrago. But the side failed to win many friends and incurred the displeasure of the referee. Brazil beat Uruguay 3—1 in the semi-final, and West Germany beat them 1—0 in the third-place final. Uruguay are masters of defence—but their ideas on the game were exposed by the attacking Brazilians in Mexico in 1970.

All ten Uruguayan clubs have their headquarters in Montevideo. Not surprisingly the weaker brethren go to the wall—or pretty near to it. Penarol and Nacional rule the roost, while sides like Liverpool and Wanderers face an interminable struggle for survival.

Penarol, despite the loss of many stars to wealthier

foreign clubs, have a dazzling record. They reached the world club championship final in 1960, losing to Real Madrid, but avenged that defeat by beating the Spanish stars in 1961. And in 1966 they took the trophy again, beating the same Real Madrid 2—0 home and away.

Chile finished with the most unenviable record among the South American qualifiers for the 1966 World Cup. They ended up bottom of a group including Russia, North Korea and Italy, having gained a solitary point. They lost 2—0 to Italy, 2—1 to Russia—sides they had beaten in 1962—and could only draw 1—1 with North Korea.

The clash with Italy revived memories of one of international soccer's blackest days—the 'Battle of Santiago' in 1962—in which two Italians and a Chilean were ordered off amid violent scenes. One man who stayed on-field was the brilliant winger Leon Sanchez, and he was seen all over the world, via television, applying a model left-hook to the chin of

This page: the start of the riot in Lima, Peru, in 1964, which began when the referee disallowed a goal by the home side against Argentina. Opposite page: police fired tear-gas into the crowd, the gates were shut and more than 300 spectators were crushed to death in the massive panic which broke loose. Below: bodies laid out in Lima Hospital after soccer's biggest-ever disaster.

Italy's Argentinian-born inside-right, Maschio.

Chileans, however, prefer to remember 1962 as the year they staged the World Cup and finished in third place behind Brazil and Czechoslovakia.

Every victory inspired wild rejoicing among hundreds of thousands of fans, none more so than the 2—0 defeat of Russia, after which Santiago airport had to be closed when the team arrived home to an incredible welcome.

The 1962 World Cup bred so much interest in the game in Chile that attendances at league games immediately soared, and what is more they stayed up. At a friendly club tournament in Santiago in 1966, with Santos of Brazil, Penarol of Uruguay and Vasas

of Budapest among the participants, gates averaged 60,000.

But Chile's international stock had fallen. They qualified for the 1966 World Cup only after a play-off with Ecuador at Lima. Their party included 1962 heroes like skipper Sanchez, full-back Eyzaguirre, centre-forward Campos and left-half Cruz, and talented newcomers like linkman Prieto and centre-half Figuerola.

But they were without the dedication and experience of their 1962 coach Fernando Riera, manager of

This page: some pretty jumping but no ball! Actually it is already in the East German net, put there by Guadalajaran striker Cisneros during a match in the six-day tournament held in Mexico in 1966. Opposite page: Paraguay, striped shirts, defend against Colombia in a South American championship match in 1963, played at Cochabamba high up in the mountains of Bolivia.

the Rest of the World team against England at Wembley in 1963, and, for a spell, of Portugal's Benfica. Riera, who had spent four painstaking years moulding the 1962 side into shape, was committed to work with his club side, Universidad de Santiago.

They did have Riera's former assistant, Professor Luis Alamos, but it was not enough. Lacking also the priceless emotional support of vast numbers of fellow-Chileans, they slumped to thirteenth place in the last sixteen.

Dr Wainer, head of the Chilean delegation to England, explained that they had been surprised at the pace of the game and the degree of physical contact. Their small forwards had fared dismally against big defenders, managing to score only two goals in three games.

These, then, are faults that must be remedied if Chile is to return to more successful days. The side failed to qualify for Mexico in 1970, missing out when Peru got through to the last stages to qualify with Brazil and Uruguay.

Nevertheless, Chile is the most successful of the South American nations which live in the shadow of their big brothers.

One estimate puts the number of soccer players in Ecuador at half a million, which is roughly equal to the male working population. Yet standards are low

The Peruvians won many admirers in the Mexico World Cup with their vivid style of attacking play and their unquenchable zest for the game. They surprised the world, but obviously not their fans, below, by beating Bulgaria 3—2 in their opening match. In the picture opposite, the ball hangs in the net behind the upended Bulgarian goalkeeper for Peru's equalizing goal. This page, above: Rubinos saves from Müller of West Germany. Peru lost this group match but still qualified for the quarter-finals.

and rival attractions such as basketball, baseball, hockey and rugby command thousands of adherents. Some 60,000 play basketball, which draws crowds of eight to ten thousand for big games.

Paraguay astonished the soccer world with her impressive 1958 World Cup side—and paid dearly, losing more than half the team to wealthy foreign clubs in no time at all.

Peru and Bolivia have also lagged behind on the soccer field. Chiefly Peru has gone down in the game's history books as the scene of football's greatest tragedy.

Some 300 fans were killed and more than 500 injured at Lima on 26 May 1964, when the crowd at the National Stadium rioted over a disallowed goal in an Olympic Games qualifying match against Argentina. Most of those killed were trampled by the

marauding mob, who smashed and burned everything they could lay their hands on. And today stories of police and troops, armed with firehoses and tear gas to cool down rioting fans, are commonplace.

Bolivia, like Peru, is sadly short of wealthy fairy godfathers eager to invest in the game, and has a peculiar problem all its own—altitude.

The thinness of the air in the capital, La Paz, and other cities perched at a height of around 10,000 feet above sea level, can reduce footballers to breathless wrecks. Visiting sides frequently include masks and cylinders of oxygen with their team equipment—for reviving exhausted players in mid-battle.

Peru, of course, created something of a stir in 1970 when the national side eliminated mighty Argentina. Peru won 1—0 at home and drew 2—2 away. This was the first time that Peru had qualified, although they were one of the original World Cup entrants (by invitation) in 1930.

Manager of Peru was the great Didi, of the World-Cup-winning Brazilian side of a decade before, and he instilled discipline and the methods of his native country. Peru played a 4–2–4 formation.

Bulgaria led them 2—0 in a preliminary-round match—but Peru won 3—2 and signalled a warning to the European sides of their attacking challenge. They beat Morocco 3—0 (three goals in fifteen minutes) and, despite defeat by West Germany, they qualified for the quarter-finals. There they had the misfortune to face Brazil, but they justified themselves in a match of all-out attack.

Peru, inspired by Didi and with the 1970 success behind them, could help rewrite the South American scene in the 1970s.

6

North America

A few years ago you could read this sign on the fence of a playground on Manhattan's West Side: 'Soccer playing not permitted'.

Baseball, presumably, or basketball, or softball, or American football you could play, but not soccer. Today it is different. The Americans have lifted the barriers of indifference and prejudice towards the most popular game in the world.

The American Soccer Football Association has been running for fifty-five years, but it had achieved little in attracting the attention of a large sports-conscious population. One event, the 1966 World Cup Final, shown on coast-to-coast television, did more to boost soccer in the United States than any other promotion in recent years.

England's 4—2 victory over West Germany was watched by a world television audience of four-hundred million people. Superb football was shown to the Americans via the Early Bird satellite. The high skills and excitement appealed to the chance viewer, and a sport which had previously been scorned from Boston to Houston, and from Miami to Forest Hills, suddenly won thousands of new admirers.

Americans talked about the World Cup matches for weeks. On cable cars, in the subway, the barber's saloon, at cocktail parties, and in the bars you could pick up snippets of fascinating 'soccer chat'.

'That soccer is some game. I never realized it could be played like that. Those guys have a heck of a lot of stamina and real skill.' Such were the comments of one New York commuter to another.

The United States, apart, perhaps, from China, remains the largest inhabited land mass where soccer has had minimal impact. Everyone asks why the North American people have not taken to soccer.

A major reason—physique—has held back the game's development. Two of the country's principal sports, American football and basketball, demand fairly rigid physical proportions. Few men under 200 lb achieve any real success at football. In the professional game, players in defensive positions weigh anything from 240–280lb. In basketball, it is a matter of height rather than weight. For a start nobody can expect to reach the top unless he stands a minimum of 6ft 6in. Some of America's outstanding basketball players have measured 6ft 10in, and a number have stood around the 7ft mark. Thus the American schoolboy discovers at a very early age whether he is going to make the grade in either sport.

Soccer, on the other hand, lends itself more readily to the schoolboy. Whereas size can kill an American boy's ambitions in basketball and football, only a shortage of skill can prevent him from reaching the highest levels in soccer.

Gradually the game is spreading among schools and colleges. Some teachers and coaches say they are turning away from their own football because it has become 'too much of a ritual and bears too much violence'.

It might be a slightly unkind and carping remark to accuse Americans of wanting to do everything in a bigger and better way than everyone else. But they do feel they have been left off the world's soccer band-wagon, and they would certainly like to make up for lost time.

Sir George Graham, former secretary of the Scottish FA, and now—well in his seventies—acting·executive director of the US National Professional Soccer League, summed up the new American outlook on the game:

Opposite page: the elaborate designs of soccer in the USA, with numbers and names for all to see—in a match between Baltimore Bays and Los Angeles Toros in the National Professional Soccer League which began operations in 1967.

'When England gave soccer to the world, the United States was somehow missed out. Now, a hundred years on, that gap can be filled with a world-beating demonstration of how it should be done.

The Americans have always been very quick and extremely smart at putting things right. They are not slow to learn from original mistakes.'

Before elaborating on the birth of professional soccer in North America in recent years, it is necessary to trace the erratic history of the game in this vast country.

Soccer was first played in the USA as early as 1830, and towards the end of the nineteenth century a number of colleges, mostly in the East, had introduced Association Football to their sporting curriculum.

They experimented with it. Instead of forty-five minutes each way they tried playing four quarters of twenty minutes duration, and they altered the markings on the pitch.

Steady European immigration in the early 1900s preserved the game as the rest of the world knew it. These groups stuck together in a close community and rarely integrated with the young college men going through their variations on the game.

In the midst of the game's patchy advance there have been isolated moments of glory such as in 1930, and twenty years later when the United States actually defeated England. In 1930, the first world soccer championship was held, and the Americans entered, bidding for the Jules Rimet Trophy, popularly called the World Cup. At that time the United States team was composed almost entirely of immigrant British players, most of them former professionals.

A glance at the team told of the British influence. Douglas was in goal, Wood and Moorhouse were the full-backs, Gallacher, Tracey and Brown the half-

Opposite page above: US soccer in 1918, featuring the Bethlehem Steel Company XI. Below: the British Navy helps to spread the soccer gospel in the USA. This page, above: the Philadelphia Nationals goalkeeper in action against the New York Brookhattan club in 1945. Below left: Passon v. German Americans, played in Philadelphia in 1939. Below right: dangerous play by a USA defender against Turkey in 1950. The Turk was knocked out cold but his team won 5—0.

backs. Auld and McGhee formed a left-flank partnership in attack. The three other forwards, Gonsalez, Florie and Patenaude were, so-to-speak, the only 'outsiders'.

This extraordinary team surprised the critics by qualifying for the semi-finals. On the way they beat Belgium 3—0 and Paraguay 3—0. It took the Argentine with six goals to check their impertinent advance to the last four.

Since their achievements in Uruguay, however, the United States has had precious little to recall in seven World Cup tournaments. In 1934 the only US result was a humiliating defeat by seven goals to one at the hands of the Italians. Four years later, Cuba and the Dutch East Indies managed to qualify for the finals but the USA never even emerged from the qualifying rounds.

But the Americans will let no one forget their

finest soccer hour, the day when eleven unknowns humbled the pride of English football.

On 27 June 1950, the score of a football match was relayed out of Belo Horizonte in Brazil, which stunned the sports world: United States 1 England 0.

There must have been a mistake on the tapes, said startled sports editors as they picked up the news from Bombay to Belfast. Probably the scoreline should have read 'England 10'. However, the confirmation followed quickly as a mass of queries were cabled back to the Brazilian mining town.

Yes, England the founders of the game, acknowledged everywhere as the 'masters', and joint favourites to win the World Cup at the first attempt, had been completely humbled by the unknown USA.

It is worth recalling the names in one of the strongest and most skilful sides in the world. The England team that day read: Williams (Wolverhamp-

ton Wanderers); Ramsey (Tottenham Hotspur), Aston (Manchester United), Wright (Wolverhampton Wanderers), Hughes (Liverpool), Dickinson (Portsmouth), Finney (Preston North End), Mannion (Middlesbrough), Bentley (Chelsea), Mortensen (Blackpool), Mullen (Wolverhampton Wanderers).

Names in the USA team meant nothing to the world's football fans. The England team had moved sixteen miles north of Belo Horizonte to a quiet mining town, Morrovelho. The English gold-mining

community were betting heavily on England but were given the tightest odds by local bookmakers.

Everyone agreed England would walk it. The only thing in doubt was how many goals they would run up, and some members of the England team who had previously played against the Americans expressed doubts about their opponents' defence.

Their comments turned out to be ill-chosen on a day which English fans would like to have deleted from the history books. The English players, sure of success, were over-confident; the Americans, facing certain defeat, were not exactly devoted in their training. They admitted to being out at a party on the eve of the match. Whatever they consumed, however, turned out to be the ideal tonic.

At the start England played cautiously. This was a bad mistake. The Americans, conscious of having nothing to lose, produced a daring brand of adven-

Opposite page, top: fun and games at the 61st annual Scottish Picnic in Massachusetts, 1950; a Clan Sutherland player bangs the ball at the cameraman. Centre: the goalkeeper plays for safety. Bottom: the Franklin and Marshall College soccer team, 1952. This page, above: team group from the 1950s, when migrants from Europe kept soccer alive in the USA. Below: an angry fan is restrained from punching the referee during Manchester United's US tour in 1952.

turous football. They sensed they were in with a chance and after thirty-seven minutes scored a legendary goal.

Centre-forward Gaetjens, from Haiti, turned in a cross from left-half Bahr. England were suddenly committed to a policy of all-out attack, but they found their opponents both courageous and cool around their penalty-area.

Among the unknowns were Borghi in goal, quite unbeatable that afternoon; in front of him Colombo, playing the game of his life at centre-half; the captain McIlvenny, a Scot who only eighteen months earlier had been playing Third Division football for Wrexham, in England; and among the forwards, the tireless Souza brothers caused no end of despair to England's vaunted defence.

Time ran out for England, who claimed Mullen had scored through a header, although the Americans scrambled the ball away. The referee maintained the ball had not gone into the goal and the USA had

flabbergasted the world, beating England's best 1—0.

Jubilant Brazilians rushed onto the field, carrying the Americans off. The few Pressmen then gathered their thoughts before sending away their dramatic cables. The Americans won on merit and Sir Stanley Rous, then secretary of the English Football Association said, 'They were fitter, they were faster, and they were the better fighters'.

It remained the greatest shock in World Cup history until the summer of 1966, when North Korea beat Italy.

American team-manager Bill Jeffrey exclaimed of that Belo Horizonte victory, 'This is what we need to make the game go in the States'. It should have been; unhappily it wasn't. Here was the incentive for soccer to catch on, but nobody reacted with much spirit.

In later World Cup tournaments, the United States failed to emerge even from the lesser qualifying pools of Central and North America and the Caribbean. In the Olympic Games too, the Americans fell down badly, rarely surviving the regional qualifying rounds.

Literally nothing of real moment occurred in soccer in the USA until the end of the 1950s when an American named Bill Cox started an international soccer league in New York. Cox imported reputable teams from around the world to play in four- or

Opposite page, above right: a goalmouth scramble in the 1958 National Open Soccer Championship game in which Baltimore beat Los Angeles 2—1. Above left: a heading duel in the 1954 tournament. Below: the Lighthouse of Philadelphia boys' team. This page, above: the Los Angeles goalkeeper saves from an attack by the Ukrainian Nationals of Philadelphia in 1960. Below: soccer at New York's Downing Stadium.

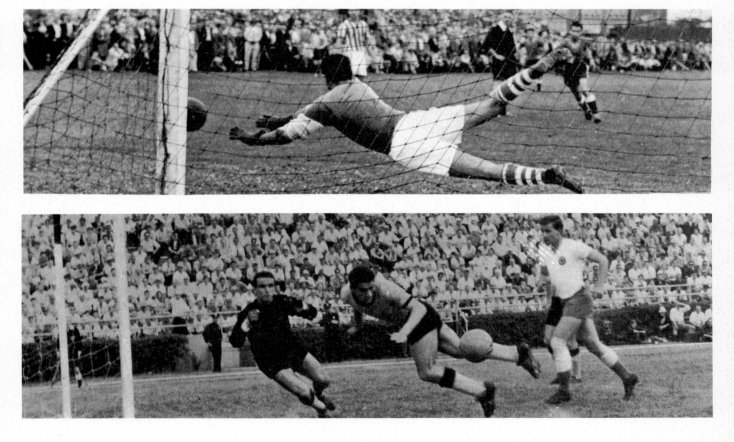

five-week competitions. He was a burly man, a banker, timber merchant, and owner of a basketball team, and he had played soccer at Yale.

However, he ran into difficulties. Officials of the US Soccer Football Association hindered his professional promotion, wary that some promoter might be out to make a 'quick buck'.

Cox wanted to break up the previous pattern of matches played by leading European sides in the States. Famous teams had been there before, but always regarded the venture as a close-season perk, a touring holiday, in which weak sides were beaten at half-pace. Quite rightly Cox felt these tours did the game no good. He wanted them to produce tough, competitive football demonstrating the virtues of first-class professional football to the Americans.

He succeeded in drawing good teams for his summer tournaments. Dukla, champions of Czechoslovakia, and West Ham, at the start of a palmy spell of success, were grateful to Cox and his competition. So were Kilmarnock, Scotland's perennial runners-up to Celtic and Rangers.

West Ham's manager Ron Greenwood, looking back, considered that their later triumphs in the FA Cup and the European Cup Winners' Cup had much to do with the pressure and serious intensive rivalry in New York.

Cox's promotion moved up the pages of national newspapers and magazines. Matches won television coverage, attendances were reasonable considering the enormous rival attraction of the country's greatest love, baseball, and in 1961 he was encouraged to forecast: 'One day we shall have a nationwide major soccer league in this country'.

After his experience with the International Soccer League, Cox thought it was time to push soccer on a national level. He gathered the help of wealthy friends and business associates, and they started to form the National Professional Soccer League, the one originally outlawed by FIFA.

A lack of finance and drive had previously blocked the game's progress. There was an interesting comparison with the income of the poorer clubs in the English Football League. The smallest of the ninety-two clubs earned £40,000, the equivalent of roughly 100,000 dollars. Yet a typical year's revenue for the entire USSFA was a trifling 32,900 dollars (1963-4).

The Little Report on the state of the game in

This page, above: an agile Mexican outleaps his Vancouver opponent during the Pacific Coast International Championship of 1963. Below: one young American finds that heading can be a tough business. Opposite page, above: former All Stars of the American Soccer League. Below: the New York Hungaria goalkeeper saves from the San Francisco Scots.

America had drawn pointed conclusions. It said, 'The USSFA needs greater financial backing to conduct a programme which could make soccer a significant sport in the United States'. It called for top-level coaching, more support for US representative teams in international competitions, a different approach to publicity, an education programme on the game, and sponsors.

Cox was also the leading spirit behind the launching of an unofficial £1,500,000, ten-city professional league. Ten clubs, Atlanta Chiefs, Baltimore Bays, Chicago Spurs, Los Angeles Toros, New York Generals, Philadelphia Spartans, Pittsburgh Phan-toms, St Louis Stars, California Clippers, plus the Toronto Falcons, the only Canadian club, started the rebel league programme in April 1967.

The adventurous Cox was ready to sell the game hard. He flew into London in October 1966, at the start of his campaign. He wanted to recruit English players and coaches to help his massive sales drive. He admitted, 'Our aim is to market soccer like the English would market soap-suds. We will probably dress the game up a little and add a few of the fanfares and the kind of trimmings we have in American football, but we want the activity on the pitch to be just as it is known in England.'

Cox was on the look-out for twenty top coaches and 200 players. According to the system operated by his organization, one man or group bought the exclusive right to a team in a particular city in a certain league, and Cox owned the rights to promote soccer in New York.

Bitterness was rife as the NPSL, the breakaway group, and the North American Professional Soccer League all sought affiliation with the US Soccer Football Association and, thereby, affiliation with FIFA.

The North American League were willing to pay 25,000 dollars a club for affiliation. The money, they claimed, would be for the proper promotion of soccer. They got it, while the NPSL, explaining that a high FIFA official had advised them against it, were unwilling to pay that kind of money.

Branded as outlaws, the NPSL jumped the gun and started the season right away. The most expensive

Opposite page: one of Baltimore Bays' demonstration clinics, above, and some of the hopefuls, below, who came to their first trial session. This page, top: Englishman Ray Bloomfield, left, is welcomed to the USA by Atlanta Chiefs' manager Jack Carlin, watched by the club's Welsh international coach Phil Woosnam. Centre: Woosnam scores for Atlanta against Los Angeles Toros. Bottom: another scoring attempt by Woosnam is blocked in the same match, which ended in a 1—1 draw.

shop-window football had known was prepared by this League. There were ten modern, lavishly-appointed stadia, a ten-million-dollar contract for colour TV, wages of £3,000 a year for English Third and Fourth Division players, and a 250,000-dollar cash-down guarantee by each club.

The NPSL vowed to raid the world for players. Britain became the number-one target, and the best British players were offered up to £160 a week to desert to America when their contracts expired.

Soccer players dreaming of a football fortune in America were given a stern warning by Cliff Lloyd, secretary of the English Professional Footballers'

This page, above: the North American glamour treatment, provided here by Baltimore Bays cheerleaders. Below left: Baltimore Bays player-coach Denis Viollet conducts a dressing-room press conference. Below right: Baltimore Bays, light shorts, versus California Clippers. Opposite page: Viollet attacks the Clippers goal and, below, he is besieged by team-mates after scoring.

Association. Lloyd pointed out that any player going outside FIFA faced a ban from playing elsewhere. With this in mind British players were wary about being lured across the Atlantic, and although the footballers' 'brain-drain' started promisingly enough with the signing of veteran Welsh international Phil

Woosnam by Atlanta, it was soon down to a trickle.

Two other experienced internationals followed Woosnam. They were Vic Crowe (Wales), who had been more concerned with coaching than playing at Peterborough, and Peter McParland (Northern Ireland) who had failed a month's trial period with the same club and was playing in non-League football.

Even with its rebounding problems, the NPSL still attracted a few weighty names. Horst Szymaniak and Joe Haverty (ex-Arsenal) were at Chicago; Brazil's Zemaria (Jose Maria dos Santos) and ex-Real Madrid star Santisteban went to Baltimore; ex-Sparta centre-half Theo Laseroms was at Pittsburgh

and Nigel Sims (ex-Wolves and Aston Villa) joined Toronto.

Despite its outlaw status, the League signed players from all over the world. The average roster of an NPSL club contained seventeen players of four or five different nationalities. The coaching problems were formidable, and St Louis Stars went to the extent of sending players to language school to learn English!

In support of the better-known players were others who formed an unknown quantity, coming from such places as Jamaica, Trinidad, Malta, Zambia, Ghana, Costa Rica, El Salvador and Israel. And when the

238

Baltimore v. Atlanta

On these pages are four scenes from Baltimore's opening NPSL match with Atlanta in 1967, televised coast-to-coast in colour. Opposite page, above: a picture which throws into focus how many different nationalities were involved in the first US professional soccer season; the players here, from left to right, come from Brazil, Spain, Ghana, England and Jamaica. Below: Art Welch of Baltimore races away from Atlanta's Willie Evans. This page, above: a scramble in the Atlanta goal-area; in the background is a baseball scoreboard, and underfoot the pitch changes suddenly from grass to hard earth. Below: Guy St Vil scores for Baltimore and is mobbed in the Atlanta net.

total list of 170 players was broken down according to birthplace it showed a heavy European bias: Europe, 101; Latin America, 40; Caribbean, 17; America, 6; Africa, 4; others, 2. Of the Europeans, 27 were British, 16 were German and there were 15 Yugoslavs; and about 30 others, although born in Europe, had played at least some of their soccer in the US or Canada.

Among the coaches, the Old-World emphasis was even more pronounced, with nine Europeans to one South American. The European coaches included four Britons: Atlanta's Woosnam, Baltimore's Doug Millward (St Mirren), New York's Freddie Goodwin (Scunthorpe) and Chicago's Alan Rogers (FIFA coach). Of the referees four were British including Peter Rhodes (York), Walter Crossley (Lancaster) and Ken Stokes (Newark), and there was one Israeli; all the linesmen were American.

Ken Macker, the league's commissioner, regarded the large congregation of foreign players as unavoidable in the early days of the league. He commented, 'Our ultimate goal is to develop our own soccer players and to make every team completely American.'

At the same time the league's president, Robert Hermann, stated, 'We want all our players to coach, to teach, to educate, just as much as we want them to play first-class football'. He emphasized that the hunt for world-class scouts was just as intense as the hunt for quality players.

The league imposed certain restrictions on its clubs. Each was allowed to spend up to 75,000 dollars on transfer fees; each could employ between fifteen and twenty players, and the wage bill was not to exceed 150,000 dollars for the season.

'Back the Bays'. . .'Get Your Kick with the Spartans'. . .'Soccer, the Go Game'. . .'I'm a Phantoms Fan'. These were a few of the slogans put out by the clubs in an effort to draw Americans and Canadians to a new sport.

The big kick-off unhappily coincided with a tornado forecast which warned off potential customers at the Chicago Spurs v. St Louis Stars game. Nevertheless, just eight months after formation, the league got under way on 17 April 1967.

Five games drew 45,210 fans. In Philadelphia,

This page: scenes from a summer tournament organized by the United Soccer Association, in which foreign club sides represented American and Canadian cities. Above: Cleveland Stokers (Stoke City) in the striped shirts v. San Francisco (Ado, Holland). Below: Dallas Tornados (Dundee United) in the dark shirts v. Toronto City (Hibernian). Opposite page, above: Los Angeles Toros (dark shirts) v. St Louis Stars. Below left: Trapattoni of Inter-Milan, left, challenges Arlindo dos Santos, America of Mexico City, in a 1965 exhibition match in Los Angeles. Below right: Los Angeles Toros v. New York Generals.

soccer outdrew by 5,000 a major-league baseball game in the city between Philadelphia Phillies and New York Mets. Philadelphia Spartans beat Toronto Falcons 2—0 before a crowd of 14,163. Baltimore Bays beat Atlanta Chiefs 1—0 before a crowd of 8,434, and the game there was televised in colour from coast to coast.

The Columbia Broadcasting System, backing the league with £350,000 for television rights, claimed this game was seen by thirteen-and-a-half million viewers, without counting another potential million in Canada.

Viewers said afterwards that the ten sixty-second beer commercials during the play did not disturb them. There were typical American comments such as, 'We are used to it here', and, 'We just use the time to go to the ice-box for another beer.'

The first judgment suggested that the standard of play throughout was on a par with the better Fourth Division clubs. Baltimore lost twelve balls during their game because of the baseball custom whereby the fans keep any ball they catch!

The US critics reacted favourably. They described professional soccer as fluid, yet rugged and skilful, requiring maximum fitness and endurance. They were surprised by the attendances.

Graham Newton, No. 10 for Atlanta Chiefs, tries to lever his way past two St Louis players.

Danny Blanchflower, the former Northern Ireland and Spurs wing-half, was given the job of explaining soccer to the American public. He was signed by CBS to provide summaries during full broadcasts on matches, giving background and analysis to the American commentator, Jack Whitacker.

Spectators were paying between one and six dollars for the privilege of watching from an assortment of positions. In many cases, the field was one of the many diamond-shaped baseball stadia, with the soccer pitch as close as it could be to the stands.

All kinds of stories emerged from the early matches. Peter Rhodes, the York referee, who once sent off the great Denis Law, became the first British soccer official to carry a revolver while taking charge of a match. Rhodes wrote home about the habit of a cannon being fired two minutes before half-time and again near the finish to warn spectators. At first he refused to use a gun on the pitch. Then he asked for a holster, but officials said they preferred him to carry the gun in his pocket. So out he went for his first 'armed match' between Los Angeles Toros and the Atlanta Braves.

Television was an important medium for selling the game. The response to coverage was heartening. CBS broadcast a game, live and in colour, every Sunday afternoon during the twenty-one-week season. League officials claimed that these transmissions did the job of introducing soccer to the millions of Americans who knew it only as a word.

In this direction they were optimistic about the game. American sports promoters have always been most conscious of being in the entertainment business, and they never hesitate to make use of

This page: USA defend against a Mexican attack in Mexico City in 1965. Opposite page: a battle of the giants in New York's Yankee Stadium in 1966, as Inter-Milan (striped shirts) play Santos in an exhibition game that pulled in a crowd of over 40,000—large numbers in a country where soccer was relatively unknown until a few months before, when the World Cup tournament, televised from England, put the game squarely in the public eye.

'showbiz' gimmicks. The sport and TV, in fact, have become close friends. There has been healthy competition among the many networks for the right to cover the major events, and the standard of coverage is extraordinarily high. The Americans regard the English methods of televising a match as primitive. They have gone far beyond sticking one camera high up in the stand, and take the view that following the ball about that way is simply dull.

For each televised game, seven cameras are used. Two give basic play-by-play coverage from midfield, one is set up on the touchline near each penalty-area to cover goalmouth action, one on the touchline for crowd-shots and close-ups of players, and one behind each goal taking in the action in the goalmouths. All are videotaped for instant replay.

Such carefully planned filming has succeeded in drawing away some of the vast baseball viewing audience on Sunday afternoons. The World Cup film 'Goal', too, showed what could be done by the imaginative use of many cameras.

In their first season the NPSL underlined their willingness to try out ideas which would make the game appeal to the public. They experimented with a bonus-points scheme, one that attracted considerable interest among European clubs. The idea was to

encourage attacking play, awarding extra points for goals scored.

Teams were awarded six points for a win, three for a draw, and none for losing; in addition, one extra point was given for each goal scored (by both winning and losing teams) up to a maximum of three. A team winning 2—0 (or 2—1) thus collected eight points; while a team winning by scoring three or more goals (e.g. 3—0, 7—0, 4—2) obtained the maximum of nine points. In the last example, the team losing 4—2 collected two points for its two goals.

Each of the NPSL teams played thirty-two games, meeting all other teams in the league (seven of them four times, two of them twice). For classification the league was divided into East and West sections, with the winners of the two sections meeting at the end of the season in early September. This two-game championship play-off was won by California Clippers, who beat Baltimore Bays.

If we apply this system to the 1966–7 season's top two English Divisions, some interesting statistics are revealed. For instance Newcastle and not Aston Villa would have been relegated from the First Division, Spurs and not Nottingham Forest would have been runners-up to Manchester United, and Wolves and not Coventry would have been Second Division champions. In each of these instances the team which benefits on the American system, scored the more goals, and also, to a purely neutral observer, each in fact seemed the more attractive side.

The NPSL's rivals in the meantime had been laying their plans to prevent the 'rebels' getting too much of a head-start. The North American Soccer League, or United Soccer Association as it became known, had the full sanction of the USSFA.

They were not ready to launch their own sides in a league. Despite their official backing they did not have a television network promoting them, and so they made do with exhibition games played by visiting foreign teams, who represented American cities.

They paid 750,000 dollars to stage a series involving some of the world's top clubs. They called on Red Star (Yugoslavia), Atletico Bilbao (Spain). Real Madrid (Spain), Leeds United (England), Vasas (Hungary), West Ham (England), Frankfurt Eintracht (West Germany), Cruzeiro (Brazil), Glasgow Rangers (Scotland), Liverpool (England) and Benfica (Portugal).

The clubs tied up in this league, with plans to open in the spring of 1968, were based in Boston, Chicago, Cleveland, Dallas, Detroit, Houston, Los Angeles, New York, San Francisco and Washington DC in the States, with Toronto and Vancouver from Canada.

The United Soccer Association's principal aim was still to persuade the rebel American body to join them. They met unsuccessfully to try and sort out a merger. Jim Maguire, president of the affiliated body, said at the beginning of the 1967 summer, 'The last thing we want is a war. It would be much better for professional soccer in the States if we do not cut each other's throats.'

FIFA's president Sir Stanley Rous met representatives from both leagues, and was equally anxious that they should merge. He commented, 'It would be pleasing to us if these two leagues determined that it would be in their best interests to consolidate'. The exploratory talks on amalgamation led nowhere, however, and both leagues ran into spots of trouble.

British referee Ken Stokes abandoned an NPSL match between Philadelphia Spartans and St Louis Stars when two St Louis men were sent off, and they and their manager Rudi Gutendorf refused to leave the pitch.

In the other league Tony Allen (Stoke) and Danny Trainor (Glentoran) were sent off for fighting. Stoke City represented Cleveland, and Glentoran played for Detroit in the competition. Glentoran were also involved in a turbulent game against Bangu (Brazil), and American referee Ed Clements abandoned play seventeen minutes from the end of a match played in a temperature of 92 degrees in Detroit. Six Bangu reserves invaded the pitch. One of them grabbed a corner flag and wagged it menacingly at the referee.

The United Soccer Association divided their twelve teams into Western and Eastern sections. They comprised Cagliari of Italy (Chicago), Bangu, Brazil (Houston), Ado, Holland (San Francisco), Sunderland, England (Vancouver), Wolverhampton Wanderers, England (Los Angeles), and Dundee United, Scotland (Dallas) in the West. In the east were Stoke City, England (Cleveland), Aberdeen, Scotland (Washington), Glentoran, Ireland (Detroit), Hibernian, Scotland (Toronto), Cerro, Uruguay (New York), and Shamrock Rovers, Ireland (Boston). Wolves, the most skilful and consistent side, won the overall competition.

The visiting clubs were financially well off. They had their air fares, hotel bills and meals paid for. Players were entitled to pick up £3 10s in pocket money per day, and after the twelve-match series the clubs returned home richer by £15,000.

Everyone outside the leagues cried out for an amalgamation and the inter-league rivalry took on an increasingly phoney character. A typical example occurred in New York where one team, the Generals, was controlled by RKO, the other, the Skyliners, was run by Madison Square Garden. Yet both companies combined with one another to present sport on television. Here was a farcical point showing up the need for one strong league.

In the outlaw league crowds were stuttering around the 5,000 and 6,000 mark, and often fell below these figures. However, in Oakland, Baltimore, and Atlanta, clubs drawing crowds of about this size were not over-despondent.

It costs some 10,000 dollars to hire the Yankee Stadium, with its 65,000 capacity, and the break-even attendance figure can hardly be short of 10,000. Cerro and Hibernian (alias Toronto City) drew an alleged 21,000 for their opening game; a publicity man, asked whether some 7,500 tickets had not been given away, replied with a wry grin on his face, 'That would be just about right, sure.'

So the teething problems flowed on. Baltimore's player-coach Denis Viollet, the former Stoke City player, voiced strong feelings after a dreadful goalless draw between the Bays and New York Generals. A Generals official said afterwards, 'We played it defensively, 5-2-3. Our attack wasn't good enough, and so we kept it tight.' Said Viollet, 'It's so stupid because this is a game we're trying to sell here. To me, this is what's killing the game in Europe.'

So there was no flying start to the American soccer experiment. Instead there was too much dull football, fluctuating attendances, violence on the pitch, erratic refereeing, internal squabbles, and unbearable heat even for the South American players.

One hopeful factor was the Americans' acknowledged ability to learn quickly from their mistakes. Talks on a merger grew easier towards the end of 1967. Clearly, in those cities where there was a team in each league, it had to come. There were rumours from reliable sources that FIFA would have liked the NPSL to be given recognition.

In San Francisco, where the Golden Gate Gales—with Ferenc Puskas as their player-coach—confronted the Oakland California Clippers, declared bitterness existed. Across the Bay George Fleharty, the Gales' owner, warned he would not enter into a fifty-fifty partnership. 'That's husband-and-wife stuff,' he declared. In Toronto both clubs wanted fifty-one per cent of the stock, and one did not have to be the brightest mathematician to realize that this was stubborn deadlock.

In Los Angeles, the owners of the two clubs, the LA Wolves and the LA Toros, had suffered a number of disagreements. They had gone through a hectic quarrel over the city's ice-hockey franchise. Jack Kent Cooke, the owner of Los Angeles Wolves, officially recognized, got the franchise. But he was forced to build his own rink.

The NPSL rebels had the advantage, in many cases, of being powerfully run. Clubs such as Atlanta and Baltimore had behind them immensely wealthy and highly organized baseball clubs. And in St Louis, a city kindly disposed towards football, there was already a great deal of soccer played in the schools. A future National League could not ignore such clubs.

In between the amalgamation discussions other difficulties arose, one confined to the NPSL, the other shared by both leagues. The first was the problem of non-communication between Briton and Argentine, German and Pole; and there was further conflict both in styles of play and in approaches to the game.

The South Americans played at a graceful jog-trot, the Germans and English players were more involved in physical commitment; the Latin players throve on pace, and its changes, as well as perfect control. Trying to integrate the various nationalities so quickly brought the managers endless worries.

And when it came to buying new players, the NPSL were unable to affiliate to FIFA, and any player joining them risked his future in the game.

Both leagues complained about the humidity and excessive heat in which they had to play. Afternoon matches fought out in temperatures around the 85-95 degree mark became a penance for some players, and even the Uruguayans regarded one or two stifling afternoons as an ordeal.

Manlio Scopigno, the manager of Cagliari, complained bitterly about the difficulties. He became so depressed by conditions in the league, and in Chicago where his side played, that he fell out with the directors and was the first manager in either league to be sacked.

Lamar Hunt, the owner of the Dallas Tornado club, wanted the season to last eight months instead of five. This suggestion would have brought the added problems of the cold winter and also a clash with America's other favourite sport, American football.

This page: Gordon Banks of Stoke and England saves for Cleveland Stokers against Washington Whips (Aberdeen) in the United Soccer Association tournament of 1967. Opposite page: a goal for the Chiefs. Atlanta forward Emment Kapengwe (14) poised to strike the equaliser in the National Professional Soccer League game against the Toronto Falcons.

Hunt, too, was a stern advocate of strictly limiting transfer fees. He wanted to peg them back to the amazingly low total of 100,000 dollars. In the end they were restricted in 1967 to 200,000 dollars.

During that first summer the Americans realized that soccer came to them very much as an uncharacteristic American activity. The game is by nature foreign to the American temperament, and only through an enormous increase in the amount of soccer played in schools can a lasting attachment to the game be developed.

The most important step towards a united front came in the middle of December 1967, when the rivals announced a merger in Chicago.

Under the merger a new National League was formed consisting of twenty teams playing in two Divisions. A FIFA meeting in Zurich, Switzerland, gave its blessing, and so did the Canadian Soccer Football Association.

In the new League were teams from Atlanta, Baltimore, Boston, Chicago, Cleveland, Dallas, Detroit, Houston, Kansas City, Los Angeles, New York, Oakland, St Louis, San Diego, Toronto, Vancouver and Washington.

The two New York teams announced an immediate merger, and the owners of the Toronto club (USA League) sold their franchise, leaving the city to the NPSL team. Boston's USA team and the NPSL clubs of Chicago and Los Angeles moved to new cities, and the San Francisco and Vancouver teams merged, agreeing to play in Vancouver.

So professional football in the highly competitive world of the USA entered 1968 optimistic about its prospects.

But, by the start of 1969, the situation looked different, if not gloomy and unsettled. After the initial counting of the Great Soccer Experiment had finished it was estimated to have cost the clubs involved somewhere in the region of £3 million. Backers were uncertain whether or not to throw good money after bad.

Gordon Jago, the coach who left Fulham to join Baltimore Bays, expressed these views on what must be considered an ill-fated venture when he admitted: 'You could not begin to realize the enormity of the mistakes that were made and the money that was wasted over the last two years.

'After the magnificent TV coverage of the 1966 World Cup, the sponsors and promoters thought they could just pick it up from there, so to speak. It was like a pyramid—they had a top, but not a base.

'Now we see things in their proper perspective and must build from the bottom. We must consolidate and extend the already considerable foothold that soccer has gained in the States these last few years'.

Jago, who stayed in America to help Phil Woosnam guide the national side in their World Cup qualifying bid, outlined the likely plans for the future of the game in the States.

1. To develop and nurture soccer in the various centres, particularly schools and colleges, possibly with the aid of city, state and national championships.
2. To introduce top teams from all over the world to compete against each other in the various centres.

New York returned to the soccer fold in 1971 and 'pioneers' such as Woosnam, who is executive director of the North American Soccer League, believe that the battle for survival and impact can be won.

Woosnam flew to England at Christmas 1970, looking for top-class coaches to travel the Atlantic to help soccer.

It would seem then that the game still has a future in the States.

7 World Soccer Organization

The world of soccer is governed by the Fédération Internationale de Football Association, which abbreviates comfortably to FIFA (pronounced Feefa) in football jargon.

Without the sanction of FIFA no national association can function on an official basis, although soccer is open to any nation which will agree to abide by the laws, rules and articles of the game as laid down by the world governing body. Together with the International Olympic Committee, FIFA is the largest and most successful sporting organization in the world.

Beginning with seven members in 1904, FIFA has grown to a present-day membership of some 130 nations. And, inevitably, since England is where the game sprang from, the history of FIFA has been closely linked with England—though not, as three English presidents out of a total of six would seem to suggest, as closely as it might have been.

The current President is Sir Stanley Rous, an imposing figure whose sagacity, judgment, experience and leadership have done much to guide the fortunes first of the Football Association, of which he was secretary for twenty-seven years, and then of FIFA.

Sir Stanley, now in his seventies, travels hundreds of thousands of miles each year around his 'parish' and once admitted, 'I am often asked exactly how many miles, but I cannot even guess'.

Inevitably, Sir Stanley has been dubbed 'Mr Soccer', because of his important role in the expanding world game, and he himself treads firmly along football's corridors of power, exuding English bonhomie, in diplomatic style, and a great deal of experienced guidance.

'Mr Soccer' is a guest at four or five dinners a week and has to decline three invitations for every one he attends. He has little time for private social life and claims his major relaxation is obtained in the air, while travelling to and from his 130 member-nations.

Sir Stanley became President of FIFA in 1961 and has, through his capacity for hard work and his desire to encourage the emerging nations, seen more of the world than most. He sprang from an amateur background to the forefront of world soccer politics. He played village football in Suffolk, was an assistant master at Watford Grammar School and then became a first-class referee. This led him to become secretary of the FA in 1934, a job he held continuously until his FIFA appointment.

Sir Stanley is also chairman of the Central Council of Physical Recreation and chairman of the Arts Educational Trust. He is a Rotarian in London, a company director and a Chevalier de l'Ordre Grand Ducal de la Couronne de Chêne de Luxembourg. He is, of course, one of the busiest speakers on the affairs of the game. Wherever he goes he has, in his own words, 'to sing for my supper'.

The best achievement he can remember was the adoption of the diagonal-control system of refereeing, now used all over the world. This method—the referee covering the midfield, and moving from corner to corner, with his linesmen taking one half of the field each, on the touchline farthest from him—was taken up by the Football League in the 1930s; though it had, in effect, been in use since about 1900.

The diagonal system is in use in Britain and most other countries, but the Russian method—the other

Opposite page, above: Sir Stanley Rous, left, President of soccer's governing body FIFA, at a reception in the USA. Below: Jules Rimet, after whom the World Cup trophy is named, is introduced to the England team in 1951 by captain Billy Wright. M. Rimet was President of FIFA from 1921–54.

Opposite page, above left: Sir Stanley Rous on his appointment in 1934 as Secretary of the FA, seen with the retiring Secretary Sir Frederick Wall. Above right: a first-class referee, Sir Stanley teaches a group of schoolmasters at an Easter vacation course, also in 1934. Below: the presentation of the trophies after the United Soccer Association's summer tournament in 1967, won by Wolverhampton Wanderers. This page: Manchester City forwards on the rampage against Leicester during the 1969 FA Cup Final—the most celebrated annual event in English soccer.

officially accepted system—entails the referee acting as his own touch judge along one side, with the linesmen, on the other side, taking one half each. Both systems meet with general approval; both depend on the efficiency of the officials.

One of Sir Stanley's pet 'hobby horses' has been the reorganization of the World Cup tournament in time for West Germany in 1974. Sixteen clubs will again take part in four groups. The first and second in these groups will go forward into further groups of four. The first of these go through to the Final. That means that the quarter-finals and semi-finals are no longer on a knock-out basis.

Sir Stanley would also like uniformity of procedure on disciplinary matters for, as he rightly points out, the troubles of the 1970s are those of procedure rather than interpretation.

Most countries, notably in South America, suspend a player for a certain number of matches and then only from the competition in which he offended. In England offending players are suspended from *all* matches for a specified length of time, a legacy from the days when one match a week was normal. Sir Stanley has urged the British associations to revise their thinking on the matter, and moves have recently been started through his initiative.

One controversial incident occurred in the 1967 world club championship finals when Glasgow Celtic chose their winger, Jimmy Johnstone, to play in Argentina during a period of suspension—because of the South American interpretation of this ruling. (The Racing Club side had included a suspended player in the first-leg match in Glasgow.)

Ironically, Johnstone, whose suspension was lifted for the visit to the Argentine by the Scottish FA, was one of the Celtic players sent off in the bitter play-off match for the championship in Montevideo.

The world club championship, an inter-continental battle that has grown fiercer since its inception in 1960, has posed increasing problems for the world governing body and the attendant national associations. At the start it was peaceful enough—until 1964, when fighting began between the players of Internazionale (Italy) and Independiente (Argentina) in Buenos Aires. The Internazionale manager, Hellenio Herrera, said after this match, 'We dared not score from the penalty awarded to us. We should never have left alive.'

The Union of European Football Associations (UEFA) and the South American Confederation had authority for these annual matches and a member of the UEFA executive committee presented a cup for the winners.

FIFA has now stepped in to try and establish regulations for these matches and would also prefer to appoint the referees.

Sir Stanley Rous has advocated a wider tournament between the club champions of the five confederations of Europe, South America, Central and North America, Africa and Asia, all of whom are classified as decentralized limbs of FIFA.

For years FIFA has introduced courses for international referees in a bid to stamp out problems of

Camera Eye

On the lighter side, here are some of the amusing moments which happen or seem to happen wherever soccer is played, from Scotland to Australia. This page, above: Burnley's Willie Irvine swings in the rigging after scoring against Blackpool. Below: Hakoah teammates go up for the ball and one clonks the other on the nose during a game against Northside United in Sydney. Opposite page, above left: West Bromwich Albion striker Jeff Astle nearly bursts the ball with this header against Fulham. Above right: referee George McCabe shares the players' agony after a collision during a Birmingham v. Spurs game. Below: a swan invades the pitch at Shawfield, Glasgow, in a match between Clyde and Heart of Midlothian.

language and interpretation of the rules. The organizing body has issued films, literature and guides all over the world. Lecturers have visited all parts of the globe, spending a week or ten days in each country, visiting all centres and talking to referees in their own languages. There have also been mixed courses for referees and coaches.

Referees, in the main, do interpret the laws in a uniform way, contends Sir Stanley. In 1964 FIFA laid down a code of disciplinary measures and a scale of punishment for offenders. Sir Stanley argues that troubles begin because players and coaches do not interpret uniformly—what is needed mostly is greater courage by referees in dealing with offenders. 'As for physical styles and matters of temperament and climate', he says, 'those, I am afraid, are beyond our control.'

In his twenty-seven years as secretary of the FA

This page: the draw for the final rounds of the 1966 World Cup. Sir Stanley Rous is seated in the centre. Opposite page, above left: French film star Claudine Auger, looking beautiful in her World Cup T-shirt. Above right: a poster for the World Cup film *Goal*, made by Columbia Pictures. Below: the victorious England team and manager Alf Ramsey with their wives at a celebration lunch.

Sir Stanley helped to bring England out of the isolation in which the country had become ensnared, enabling her to regain her leadership of the game.

He gave clear evidence of his strength when, as secretary of the FA, he clashed with Ernest Thommen, a member of FIFA and the boss of the Swiss football pools. Thommen came out with an attack on growing inter-European and inter-continental tournaments—this was in 1960—but Sir Stanley, as an advocate of world contact in sport, travelled to Zurich to convince him of the need for progress. As a result the first world club championship final between Penarol, Uruguay, and Benfica of Portugal, which had earlier been in jeopardy, went ahead.

Before he became secretary of the FA, Sir Stanley achieved notable success as an international referee. This has stood him in good stead.

Paradoxically, Sir Stanley has never favoured a European League. He has stated that he does not believe that it lies within the realms of possibility because home tournaments would take precedence over any international tournament. He argues that there would be difficulties in compiling and completing fixtures because seasons do not overlap and that, in any case, Spurs playing Manchester United at Tottenham in a League fixture would have the advantage over Arsenal meeting, say Munich, at Highbury.

On one occasion Sir Stanley did come out strongly with a suggestion for a 'Super League' in Britain, which had a mixed reception from the clubs, the Press, and his fellow administrators.

The Football League jealously guards its own. When it was founded, no one could have imagined that it would have grown into such a powerful organization as it is today, with a membership of ninety-two clubs. Nor could it have been believed

that the competition would meet with such world-wide acceptance.

The agreement of a dozen clubs to form themselves into a league competition in the 1880s led not only to the prosperity of soccer as it developed in the United Kingdom but to the development of other Leagues. In Great Britain, on the Continent and all over the world, the League system of inter-club matches prevails.

The Football League is a self-contained organization. Like all other Leagues, it plays the game under the rules laid down by the International Football Association Board, and is bound by the rules, regulations and bye-laws of the FA. But in matters concerning its internal management it has complete autonomy.

The League system is a national asset. The Chancellor of the Exchequer is grateful for the large contributions received from soccer in England, the Postmaster General accepts the fillip to the income of his department through the game, and British Rail and other transport concerns all benefit. Indirectly, the Football League gives employment to thousands, supplies the Press with a never-ceasing flow of sporting topics and brings pleasure into the lives of millions.

For, despite talk a few years ago of 'missing millions' from soccer grounds, the game in England has had a healthy revival of spectator-interest. And the Football League is doing well.

Returning to the proposal for a 'Super League', the pros and cons are complex. The major argument in favour of such a scheme is that the cream of footballing talent already inevitably finds its way to the relatively few wealthy clubs able to spend the astronomically high transfer-fees of today.

This page, above: Minister of Sport Denis Howell meets Argentina's captain Antonio Rattin at a Government reception for the defeated quarter-finalists in the 1966 World Cup. Below: a Hungarian player with his team's 'instruction pitch' arrives in London. Opposite page, above: Denis Law congratulates Eusebio on becoming European Footballer of the Year in 1966. Below left: Eusebio shaking hands with the Prime Minister after being awarded the £1,000 prize for being the highest goal-scorer in the World Cup. Below right: Eusebio scores the first of his four goals against North Korea.

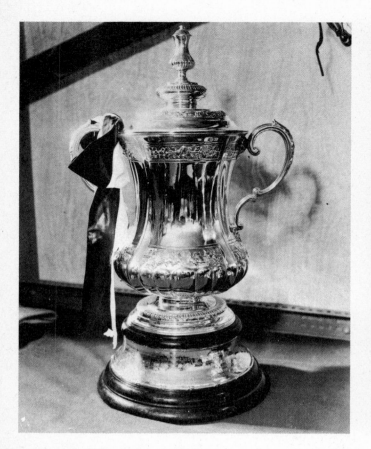

In England, the two Manchester clubs, United and City, also the two Merseyside clubs, Liverpool and Everton, and two or three from London, Tottenham, Arsenal and possibly Chelsea, would qualify for membership by virtue of their crowd-pulling power and wealth.

Manchester United have long stated that the major part of their ambition is directed towards bringing the European Cup to England for the first time.

But the argument against the top sides breaking away is solid. Not only would a Super League isolate vast areas of the British Isles, but it would prejudice a healthy network of clubs which operate on the basis

that an overall average attendance of around 14,000 is better for the game than a few 50,000 crowds in one or two city centres.

It is true that the League does carry too many passengers among its ninety-two members and that, at times, the competition is unwieldy. And starting a Fifth Division to incorporate a few up-and-coming non-League sides would only make it more so.

Regional soccer has been suggested, but this would only serve to reduce expense rather than create new interest. The amateur game has floundered because the same clubs played the same fixtures year-in year-out without the benefit of promotion or relegation.

Opposite page, above: the FA Cup, left, and the Jules Rimet trophy. Below: the World Cup referees with Sir Stanley Rous at a reception; each received a silver whistle and badge for his services in the tournament. This page: life at the top means tough tackling and massed defence when things go wrong; Manchester United, above, pack their goalmouth but, below, the fruits of victory are sweet; Joe Mercer and Malcolm Allison celebrate Manchester City's FA Cup win.

The FA has experimented with the introduction of a Northern League, to link up with the long-established Southern League (which, despite its name, extends well into the Midlands), and become a 'feeder' organization for the Football League.

Soccer certainly needs more incentives, such as four-up, four-down promotion and relegation throughout the League, to enliven the competition and thus to counter the arguments for a Super League.

As with a Super League, the suggestion of an international European League is also impractical, maintain its critics, because of the effect it would have on the game as a whole in the various countries.

One of the advantages favouring football fanaticism in England, is that fans are able to travel to away games and follow a favourite side. Few journeys are too far or too expensive to be beyond the reach of keen supporters.

If Tottenham, for example, became part of a

European League, their away games would be out of reach of all but a few—and crowd-support would definitely favour the home side and, possibly, influence results.

A Super League would push once-famous soccer centres such as Bradford and Cardiff further off the map by making their competitions purely subsidiary. In the 1960s the trend was towards the 'big games', and any introduction of an alternative to the Football League, involving all the top sides, could only prove detrimental.

Perhaps certain Leagues in Europe, none of which does as well as the Football League, would welcome an injection of fresh enthusiasm by the setting-up of a European League, but they would be advised to study the general attendance figures when clubs from other lands visit them.

Some European teams have attracted crowds of under 10,000 for matches played in top competitions, even though there was the possibility for the home club of advancement to a further round. What response could they expect from their public when the team was doing poorly in a European League competition, even if the opposition was attractive and doing well?

Before steps such as a European League can be seriously considered, however, the game's administrators will have to overcome many problems of interpretation. Although there are only seventeen Laws for soccer, and they have altered little over the years, the administrators run into problems of application at national, international and world-wide levels.

Upholding the Laws, the international maintenance of discipline, the administration of finance and the organization of international fixtures and tournaments are the responsibility of FIFA.

The oldest-known soccer association outside Britain is the Boldspil Union of Denmark, formed in 1889, but before the turn of the century the game had spread far from England. In 1902 a Dutch banker named Hirschman approached the FA for help in the formation of an international body and the staging of an international championship—the first seed of the World Cup.

Opposite page, above: England captain Bobby Moore, aided by West Ham colleague John Charles, keeps out Jimmy Greaves in a League match. Below: Chelsea players train hard for a new season. This page, above: Leeds goalkeeper Sprake is injured and colleague Bremner protests to the referee during a violent Cup-tie against Sunderland. Below: Chelsea substitute Murray waits by the touch-line after the new law permitting one substitute per side per match was introduced in 1965 by the Football League.

At a time when no real response was forthcoming from England, Robert Guérin, of the French Sports Union, also asked the FA in 1903 if it would help found a European Federation.

And so it was that, despairing of co-operation from Britain, Hirschman and Guérin joined forces and, on 21 May 1904, at a meeting in Paris, delegates from Belgium, France, Denmark, Holland, Spain, Sweden and Switzerland founded FIFA.

That was the beginning. A year later the FA had second thoughts and a four-man delegation attended a FIFA conference in Berne and helped to clarify their regulations. D. B. Woolfall (England) was elected President of FIFA in 1906 in succession to Guérin, and he held the post until his death in 1918. In 1913 two FIFA members were elected to the International Board.

After the First World War came the first of two splits between Britain and FIFA. In 1920 Britain and other countries resolved not to renew relations with Germany and her neighbours, but France and Belgium backed out of the agreement and the British associations then withdrew from FIFA. They also terminated FIFA's membership of the International Board.

Jules Rimet, a Frenchman, was elected President of FIFA and he remained in office until 1954.

Britain relented and returned to FIFA in 1924, only to depart again four years later for another reason.

On the second occasion it was because FIFA informed the International Olympic Committee that it had approved the reimbursement to amateurs of money lost through absence from work—'broken-time' payments—and that unless the IOC stepped into line, there would be no soccer tournament sponsored by FIFA in the 1928 Games at Amsterdam.

The IOC reluctantly agreed. Britain, who anyway disapproved of the FIFA decision, refused to send a team to Amsterdam and withdrew from membership of FIFA in February 1928.

This was only a formal separation. Relations on the International Board remained unchanged, and for nearly twenty years British countries played matches against other member-countries of FIFA, although this was technically against the regulations. Both parties seemed happy with this gentlemanly bending of the rules.

Britain returned to FIFA after the Second World War and, in celebration, a match was played between Britain and the Rest of Europe at Hampden Park, Glasgow, in 1947. A crowd of 130,000 saw Britain win 6—1, and the money from this game helped to place FIFA on a sound financial footing for the first time in its existence.

That event had been preceded in the years before the war by others less noticeable at the time but, in their way, equally significant. In 1934 Sir Frederick Wall retired from the position of secretary of the FA after thirty-nine years, and he was succeeded by Stanley Rous.

Within four years of taking office, Rous, with the authority of the International Board, had rewritten the laws to clarify and modernize them, a substantial but overdue task. It was probably as a result of his persuasion that Britain rejoined FIFA after the war, and in 1949 he was knighted for his services to sport.

Over the next ten years Sir Stanley's authority grew to almost unprecedented proportions, both in England and abroad, a fact which was welcomed by foreign officials who recognized his statesmanship. For years Sir Stanley's motto was 'there is no substitute for skill' and it was under his care that the FA put into operation, through their Director of Coaching, Walter Winterbottom, a wider system of coaching throughout the country. This slowly put England back on the international map even though, on the way, humiliating defeats were suffered by the national team at the hands of the United States and Hungary.

Sir Stanley, as befits a leader in his field, was able to acknowledge a good lieutenant. He 'discovered' Winterbottom, a little known pre-war professional player, working at the Air Ministry during the war on the RAF's physical fitness programme. Winterbottom did fine work developing the FA coaching scheme and won international repute as the England team-manager.

Another example of Sir Stanley's value as a mentor was provided by George Raynor, another footballer whose career rarely hit the headlines. Sir Stanley recommended him for a coaching post in Iraq and, after the war, he gave him his backing for the position of chief coach and national team-manager in Sweden. Raynor became one of the most respected team-managers of his day, and took Sweden into the Final of the 1958 World Cup in Stockholm.

In 1954 Jules Rimet was succeeded as FIFA President by R. W. Seeldrayers, a Belgian sporting pioneer. He was shortly succeeded by Arthur Drewry in 1956, who held office until his death in 1961. The presidency carries a four-year period of office, and anyone taking over an uncompleted period has to be re-elected at the end of that period. In the autumn of 1961 it was imperative to elect a new President to

Policemen are everywhere on match days—keeping order, picking up debris, marshalling the crowds, chasing unruly fans, or just taking the weight off their feet.

direct the administration of the forthcoming 1962 World Cup in Chile.

The candidates at an extraordinary general meeting in London were Ernest Thommen, deputy president since Drewry's death, Ottorino Barassi, of Italy, Dr Anrejeveic of Yugoslavia and Sir Stanley Rous. Despite some opposition from some Iron Curtain countries and the Asian group, Sir Stanley Rous was elected—and returned unopposed at the World Cup congresses of 1962 and 1966. But there were troubled times ahead.

The first indications came at the 1962 World Cup in Chile. It was soon made clear that in the four years since the competition was last held, in Sweden, the game had become more defensive and, with national prestige valued even more highly than before, teams and managers were prepared to go to greater lengths for victory.

This page, above left: Pegasus win the FA Amateur Cup in 1951. Below: Bishop Auckland's captain with the trophy in 1955. Above right: non-Leaguers Bedford Town prepare for their FA Cup-tie with Everton in 1966. Opposite page, above left: Walthamstowe Avenue v. Leyton. Above right: Sir Stanley Rous meets 1967 Amateur Cup finalists Skelmersdale United. Below: Enfield attack the Skelmersdale goal.

The preliminary-round matches, in which groups of teams play on a league basis, were conspicuously tough. Yugoslavia, Uruguay, Chile and Italy each had players sent off; the Chileans and the Italians freely exchanged punches. By the quarter-finals things had settled down, but it was obvious that something was necessary to reduce the tension of the early matches. Because these were not on a knockout basis, it was thought to be more important not to lose than to go all out for victory. But the system remained unaltered for 1966.

Without Europe paying too much heed, the South American countries had formed themselves into a Federation in 1916 and, although in 1928 that Federation was granted a permanent vice-presidency with FIFA, and although Uruguay won the World Cup in 1930 and 1950, FIFA continued to be dominated by European influence.

The last two Presidents have been English and, in addition, Britain is given a permanent vice-presidency, as is Russia. However, all this European influence could do no good when, in 1963, with the FA celebrating its centenary, Brazil refused to release her players for a match at Wembley between England and a FIFA Rest of the World XI.

Both sides were obviously anxious for Pele, as the top box-office attraction in soccer, to take part in the match, but the San Paulo League dug in its toes and there was no Pele. However, Djalmar Santos, the famous Brazilian full-back star of two World Cup Finals, simply told his club that this was an honour he did not intend to miss. He played—and no disciplinary action followed.

Incidents on the field can cause considerable embarrassment to FIFA. One occasion was when Pele, provoked during the 'Little World Cup' competition in Rio, held to mark Brazil's half-centenary, butted an Argentinian opponent in the face—and escaped with a caution.

During the 1964-5 season FIFA held a number of experimental matches to consider changing the offside law. The object was to try and find a way to increase the number of goals scored in soccer. But the experiment was held without real conviction and the teams involved were inadequately prepared and briefed; it proved little and was allowed to slide into the background. The 1966 World Cup arrived

without a change in either the laws or the form of the competition.

It did not take long for two facts to emerge, that this was to be the most defensive competition of them all and that some teams were determined to pursue a win-at-all-costs policy. The different interpretation of the laws by the Latins and the Western Europeans, together with the failings of some referees, led to more trouble. Uruguay and Argentina had players sent off in early matches and, in spite of a stiff warning, the Argentines rose to a new pitch of violence in the quarter-final tie against England, as a result of which they were threatened with expulsion from the next World Cup.

There quickly followed a protest meeting of the South American Federation, which sent to FIFA a demand that Britain be only allowed to enter one and not four countries for the qualifying competition for the 1970 World Cup in Mexico.

This seemed an impossible demand, for England, Scotland, Ireland and Wales were separate associations long before the Argentinians appeared on the soccer scene. The demand did, however, underline the point that unless FIFA does find more common understanding and a mutual acceptance of the interpretation of the rules, a split is likely.

This is one of the issues Sir Stanley Rous and FIFA face at the present time. The South American continent is not the only one from which Sir Stanley faces hostility. The Asians and Africans, the emerging soccer nations, are setting up a hue and cry for greater representations on FIFA and a larger allocation of places in the Finals. In 1966 they had to be content with one place, won by North Korea, and their argument was strengthened when the Koreans reached the quarter-finals at their first attempt.

FIFA, in almost all respects, has had a marvellous record in developing, expanding and organizing the world's biggest spectator-sport, but its path in recent times has been strewn with increasingly difficult hurdles. Gone are the days when the English, as acknowledged masters of soccer, could look indulgently on the behaviour of other nations and shrug it off as 'not like us'.

It might even be true to say that England took until 1966 to appreciate fully the passionately partisan attitude of other soccer nations. International Jimmy Greaves once said he found difficulty in getting 'fire in the belly' when he pulled on an England jersey— and it was certainly true that more emotion was engendered by the crowd on Liverpool's Spion Kop than by the spectators at an international match at Wembley.

England has a sporting history as 'good losers'. In football this did not apply while the English remained indisputable masters of the game which they, after all, gave to the world. But once the mastery was gone, national prestige quickly became a pressing issue.

The Football Association has always insisted that its players maintain a standard of manners and sportsmanship and adhere strictly to a referee's decision. In England a referee is given 100 per cent backing, sometimes seemingly to the detriment of justice. But the reputation of British referees is still unparalleled in the world. They receive invitations from Europe and South America and some of them are as well-known as the top players, Arthur Ellis, Ken Aston, Bill Ling, Reg Leafe, George Reader, Jim Finney, Mervyn Griffiths and 'Tiny' Wharton to name but a few.

Ling had the distinction of refereeing an Amateur Cup Final, an FA Cup Final, an Olympic Games Final and a World Cup Final. Like Sir Stanley Rous, Ling was a school-teacher and fitted refereeing into

his spare time. In latter years referees such as Leo Horn of Holland, Latychev of Russia and Istvan Zsolt, Hungary, have emerged to compare favourably with the English.

Referees' problems are FIFA's problems. After the 1966 World Cup, the FIFA committee issued a recommendation: 'In order to limit the practice of feigning injuries and to reduce consequent interruptions of the game, players should not be treated for injuries on the field except in serious cases like broken legs. The game should only be interrupted while the players are taken off the field for treatment.'

The organization of world soccer, despite its problems, is well controlled by FIFA from its Swiss headquarters. And with air travel making intercontinental travel easier, so that barriers may be broken down by regular meetings and discussions, the way ahead is not too bleak.

The efforts of Sir Stanley Rous in his ambassador's role help clear the way for greater enlightenment in the nooks and crannies of world football. Perhaps his dreams of a Super League will materialize in the not-too-distant future. It is not much over a decade ago, after all, that Chelsea were advised by the Football League not to participate in the European Cup. Nowadays the League uses Europe as a bait to attract clubs into its own once-maligned League Cup competition.

The organization of soccer in Britain is in capable hands, even if the amateur-professional rift appears occasionally to cause difficulties in the dealings of the FA and the League. In the 1960s there was go-ahead thinking at all levels of the game. England, once the land of missionaries, has learned to accept that the rest of the world has something to offer in football. The vision of men such as Sir Stanley Rous is bearing fruit. He foresees an era in which supersonic jets

On these pages are some of soccer's outposts—all of which come under the watchful eye of Sir Stanley Rous and his FIFA colleagues. Opposite page and this page, above: football in the parks—where the scouts from the big clubs go to look for talent. Below: a bit young for League football but moving in the right direction—under their team-coach Sister Gabriel.

will enable teams from Britain to play frequent games in countries such as the United States: an era that would enrich the progress of football in new lands as well as the clubs—who could travel there and back in twenty-four hours.

Pipe dreams? Not entirely. And they are a far cry from the complacent English attitude of days gone by. The English, by virtue of their World Cup success at Wembley, were again among the masters on the field. Their League system is the envy of many and the model for most. And their contribution to world

affairs through such administrators as 'Mr Soccer', Sir Stanley Rous, helps them keep well abreast of the mounting problems.

One very important issue concerns the high bonus payments paid to players. Many administrators have asked whether incentive money was not a contributory factor to violence in the game? The Football League is one body that has investigated and found that the rising price of winning (or, in some instances, avoiding defeat) *is* a major cause of violence.

Since the abolition of the maximum wage in England—a move favoured by the clubs—there has been a trend towards making payments in incentive form over and above the basic wage of the player. A former England captain, Johnny Haynes, was England's first £100-a-week footballer—yet the only immediate incentive he had after the removal of the £20-a-week ceiling on wages was to earn an extra £4 each time his side won a match, or £2 for a draw.

The question soon arose: How could a player already assured of £100 in his pay packet take much heed of a mere £4 bonus? Haynes, as a dedicated professional, could argue that he would not consider a question of finance once he was actively involved in a game, but the fact remained that clubs had to find an attractive alternative 'bait'.

Signing-on fees, now regulated in England so that a player receives ten per cent of his transfer-fee valuation, proved one answer. Players were tempted by handsome signing-on bonuses; clubs could invest £50,000 on a star player and hand over another £5,000

as a signing-on fee, the cash being paid before the player had kicked a ball for the club. This, though, was an unsatisfactory arrangement for many clubs, and a source of irritation to management and players.

Study the case of two brothers with one English First Division club. Brother A was a loyal servant to the club and a first-team regular for several years. His reward: a steady basic wage, plus the authorized bonus 'perks'.

This page: England won the European Youth Cup in 1963 and 1964. Ron Harris, above, captain in 1963, carries the trophy surrounded by his team; Howard Kendall, below, receives the Cup in 1964 from the President of the Dutch FA. Opposite page, above left: Rivera (No. 10) scores for Italy v. Mexico in a warm-up match for the World Cup in 1966. Above right: Bobby Charlton hits the post with a header against Brazil in 1963, the year the FA celebrated its centenary. Below: a scene from the centenary match organized between England and a FIFA Rest of the World XI.

Brother B also graduated through the junior ranks of the club and made his mark in the first team. He was transferred—and received a signing-on fee from his new club. Eventually, he returned to his first club, and was then transferred again. So Brother B, who moved at the wish of his club each time, benefited financially by a healthy five-figure sum. Brother A did not, in fact, moan about his brother's good fortune, but the fact was that his loyalty went unrewarded.

The payment of signing-on fees, and the inevitable gossip linking players with other clubs, breeds dissatisfaction. A player with a lowly Fourth Division club, reading that a glamorous First Division side was interested in him, would be flattered—but then upset if the move and the financial inducement faded into thin air.

Clubs looked for other means of giving incentives.

Some offered extra money for European success. Others for League success, the championship, promotion or a leading position. Some even offered lump-sum bonuses to avoid relegation.

The stage was reached where some players had as many as *eight* different bonuses to aim for at each match. These might include: crowd bonus; points bonus; periodic talent money; first-team appearances; an incentive for avoiding relegation, and an incentive for finishing top, scaled down through as many as the first ten positions.

This led to the League studying the many bonus-schemes appearing in players' contracts—all of which were legal—and to calling in the players' trade union to see if it would co-operate in working for a rationalization. The League secretary, Alan Hardaker, revealed the concern of his management committee at the rise in bonus payments and their further resolve to

investigate a possible connection between bonuses and trouble on the field.

No question of a return to the maximum wage was envisaged, just a suggestion as to how bonuses could be generally agreed upon so that each club could offer the same kinds of incentive to players. One reason for the probe was that clubs such as Chelsea, Fulham and Sunderland paid players so much—£30 in one case—for each League point they gained. But under League rules the bonus payable on the result of a match was limited to £4 or £2.

There were strong criticisms of the moves to restrict payments; indeed an argument was made that the League's own £4-a-win ruling was the one that should be scrapped since it was outdated. Some clubs suggested that there should be no restriction for winning matches. Taking the view that it was purely a club responsibility. They contended, too, that an employer and employee had the right to negotiate their own contracts, as in other businesses, without outside interference.

In what an older generation of soccer followers likes to call the 'good old days', the restriction on wages and bonuses led to under-the-counter dealings and lurid tales of players being 'on £50-a-man' to win a certain game. In the 1970s the tales are of the thousands of pounds offered—legitimately—to teams to prosper in European and other competitions involving national prestige and pride.

Whatever the merits of the various arguments it must be unrealistic to ask a player to accept £4 for winning a match when the gate-receipts net his club several thousands of pounds.

Violence . . . cash bonuses—these are just two current examples of the problems which the organizers of world soccer tackle every year.

This page: Puskas, above, leads the FIFA team from the pitch and, below, Denis Law flies through the air for the Rest of the World to challenge England's Maurice Norman. Opposite page, above: the East German team run round Mexico's University City Stadium after a friendly match in 1966. Below: Chile score from the penalty-spot against North Korea, the surprise side of 1966.

8
Running a Top Club

Every Saturday afternoon during Britain's long winter some three-quarters of a million people watch the English Football League programme, while a lesser, but equally enthusiastic number support the Scottish and Irish League fixtures.

The majority of these fans are devotees of one particular club. Often they will put up with primitive accommodation and uncomfortable travelling facilities just to watch *their* team in action. So far as most of them are concerned it is only the players who matter. The manager is frequently forgotten in victory. Occasionally the club chairman becomes identified but, more often, he remains in the background. The secretary is an anonymous figure.

Yet, without these officials and hundreds of others, organized football could not continue. The fans turn up knowing that the teams will appear from the tunnel at the appointed time. But few stop to consider what has gone on behind the scenes.

Soccer, however, is far from an eleven-man production. In this highly competitive and commercial game, when success or failure can mean the difference between thousands of pounds to both player and club, England's leading sides need at least fourteen men working in the background for every one commanding the limelight on the field of play. Clubs like Tottenham, Manchester United, Liverpool and Sunderland need a staff of at least 150 for every home League match.

The turnstile operators, crowd controllers, stewards, gate men, policemen, ambulancemen, dressing-room attendants, announcers, caterers and bandsmen are the part-timers without whom no match could possibly take place.

At White Hart Lane, home of Tottenham Hotspur, London's most successful club during the last decade, such part-time and casual staff take up more than four pages in the wages book, which shows forty names to a page!

'Nobody hears about them, nobody considers them. But without them we would never get through,' explained the Tottenham secretary, Geoffrey Jones. 'The players on the field provide the action. These others give them the support that makes that action possible.'

From the manager through his assistant, club secretary, scouts, trainers, office staff, groundsmen, to the smallest boy on the groundstaff, each one plays his part in making soccer the best-supported game in the country.

It is more than a weekend job. For many of these people football is a religion, occupying every spare minute of their waking life. Everyday home comforts are put aside. Even on Sundays, football is rarely forgotten. There are team injuries to check and telephone calls to handle from reporters seeking comments on the match.

Some managers find the game even invades their sleeping hours. One manager admits to going to sleep with a pencil and notebook by his side. When he wakes up he makes a note of any subconscious thoughts he can recall about his club. None of his players knows it, but some owe their first-team place to those bedside jottings.

On Sundays many managers play in friendly matches for charitable causes. Such matches can mean a round-trip of up to 200 miles. In the summer months there are tours and next season's team to occupy his attention.

Opposite page: Jimmy Greaves bends the Burnley net with a quickly taken goal during a League match at Turf Moor.

And nothing, perhaps, can compare with a manager's life during the long, hard winter, when he becomes a stranger to his own family. The shoals of letters received each week by football clubs show that for every one of the ninety-two managers in the Football League there are dozens of people outside who believe they can do the job better.

Yet there is more to a manager's job than checking on the fitness of players and naming the most suitable side on a Friday morning. He knows that his present side is only as good as its last result. Past glories are soon forgotten. Football fans are fickle. They want

more than promises, they want to see their team winning the League titles and Cup competitions which are the stepping-stones into Europe.

No manager is more conscious of this need than Bill Nicholson, the man who made the Tottenham side which reached a triumphant peak in the early 1960s. In that period they became the first side this century to complete the Football League and FA Cup double; they won the FA Cup a second time and then became the first English side to win a major European tournament by taking the European Cup Winners' Cup. That was in 1963, and in 1967 they were at

Of those players who appeared at Wembley only two others apart from Greaves were with Tottenham in 1963, Dave Mackay and Frank Saul. Mackay missed the European Cup Winners' Cup Final through injury, while Saul was still learning the finer arts of his trade.

The others who had contributed to Tottenham's greatest years were gone. Injuries had robbed Nicholson of some. Age had crept up on others. Tragedy, too, struck when Scottish-international inside-forward John White was killed by lightning in July 1964 while he was out on a London golf course.

A manager can make allowances for players slowing up because of advancing years. Nobody can cater for injuries or sudden death. But for the spirit and determination of Dave Mackay, qualities which have always been his hallmark, Nicholson might also have lost the player who was to captain his 1967 team at Wembley.

Mackay spent two seasons out of football, fighting to recover his fitness and mobility after twice breaking his left leg inside ten months. They were injuries which would have forced a less courageous footballer to retire.

Wembley again, beating Chelsea 2—1 in the Final.

Only four years separated those notable events in the history of the North London club—but they were four years which epitomized the trials and struggles facing a manager in this modern age, when success is all that counts.

Only Jimmy Greaves, of the side that beat Atletico Madrid 5—1 in Rotterdam in May 1963, remained to play in the Wembley FA Cup Final in 1967. Of that 1963 side only three others were still on Spurs' books four years later, Maurice Norman, Ron Henry and Cliff Jones.

Opposite page, above: Tottenham manager Bill Nicholson adds the European Cup Winners' Cup to the club's other trophies after their victory in 1963. Below: members of the 1967 FA Cup-winning side. This page, above: rival managers Nicholson and Busby separately watch Spurs play Manchester United high up in the crowded stand at White Hart Lane. Below: captain Dave Mackay is crowned with the FA Cup.

Mackay had no doubts that he would play again. Neither did Nicholson, as he set about rebuilding the side he had lost, filling every vacancy but that at left-half to allow for the return of the club captain, a man who has won more honours in British football than any other player.

In doing so Nicholson illustrated one quality needed by a first-class manager—the quality to sum up character as well as technical skill. He showed it also in his signing of left-back Cyril Knowles from Middlesbrough, when the same club also had two *full* international full-backs available for transfer. Knowles had then made only thirty-nine first-team appearances, but was soon pressing for a place in England's national squad.

This ability to assess individuals showed again when Nicholson bought the Northern Ireland international goalkeeper, Pat Jennings, from Watford. Jennings was then keeping regularly for his country but many doubted Nicholson's choice when Jennings started badly in Tottenham's first team. He was soon replaced by the goalkeeper he had been bought to succeed. Nicholson knew that Jennings would need time to adjust to the higher standards of the First Division. His judgment has been amply justified.

It is this search for strength of character as well as ability that takes Nicholson to an average of five matches a week during the season. These games range from first-team matches in England and Scotland to schoolboy fixtures on a Saturday morning in the parks of London.

Supporting Nicholson in his ceaseless search for fresh talent are his assistant manager Eddie Baily, himself a former Spurs' player, scouts Charlie Faulkner and Dick Walker and eight part-time scouts strategically placed to cover every part of Britain.

Their presence is essential to Tottenham's drive to be one step ahead of their rivals. This highly organized group of assessors not only studies players. Each of them checks, too, on techniques and tactics used by other teams.

Such a network of football 'espionage' enables Tottenham to keep a trace on each player of promise, to card-index him so that when the time is ripe to buy, manager Nicholson has a ready-made list of possible replacements. He has been known to watch a player for two years before making up his mind.

Some managers ease the pace by employing coaches to take care of the everyday work back at the club. Nicholson prefers to be out on the training field in a tracksuit—keeping a close personal check on the ability of his first-team squad.

For Tottenham that means being at White Hart Lane four mornings a week—sometimes on Monday as well, before a mid-week match. Most of the early-season work is done on their training ground a few miles away in the Hertfordshire countryside at Cheshunt, which is large enough to include a tennis court as well as three soccer pitches. In mid-winter, training often takes place at White Hart Lane, where the gymnasium can house a five-a-side football match while the ground is being spiked and rolled. The car-park space can also be used in an emergency.

Close contact with players can prove a valuable guide for managers. Often it is only by playing with them that they can tell whether the footballer's mind

This page: Nicholson holds the FA Cup with Chelsea manager Tommy Docherty, left, and with Dave Mackay, right, on the balcony of Tottenham Town Hall. Opposite page, below: the Cup comes to Tottenham on the top of a bus—and the fans go wild. Above: Spurs supporters at Wembley in 1961, to see their team clinch the Cup and League double.

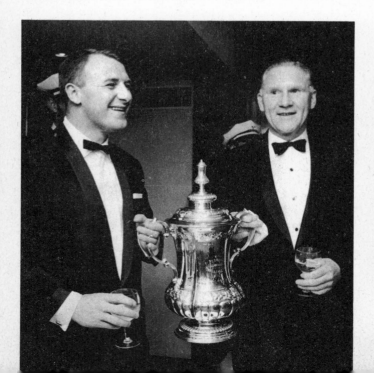

This page, above: Danny Blanchflower, captain of the 1960–1 double-winning side. Below: Bill Nicholson in his playing days as right-half for Spurs, left, and at the manager's desk with assistant manager Eddie Baily, also a former Spurs player. Top picture: John White, left, beats Leicester goalkeeper Banks in the 1961 Cup Final but just misses the net. Opposite page: the team train together at Cheshunt.

is on the job or whether he may be worrying about something unconnected with the game.

One manager, before a match on a snow-covered ground, noticed that his goalkeeper was slow to get changed. Then he remembered that at a previous club this goalkeeper had objected to training in the cold

without a track suit. The player was promptly told he was being replaced. 'I knew he was worrying about the cold and frozen ground,' explained the manager afterwards. 'It was pointless playing him because he was unhappy and his mind would not be entirely on the game.' This kind of an eye for detail can mean the difference between success and failure at the end of a season.

Between scouting missions, training sessions and tactical discussions, Nicholson provides time for his players to consult him on various personal problems. There are reports from scouts and fitness reports to scrutinize, inquiries from the Press, radio and television to be answered, transfer requests to be considered.

In addition to these duties there is the normal day-to-day running of the club, making sure transport arrangements have been made, hotels booked, the opposition studied, postponed matches re-arranged, setting aside time to interview parents of possible young players. 'If there were thirty-six hours in a day,' said Nicholson, 'a manager would still not have enough time to do all the things he wants to do.'

One of a manager's most important tasks is the pre-match briefing, usually on Fridays—a time when the manager's tactical judgment is put to the test. The procedure is the same at almost every British club.

Alex Stepney, Manchester United and England Under-23 goalkeeper, once said that before the players left a briefing session with Matt Busby at Old Trafford they knew everything there was to know about the opposition. 'We are told about the tactics they use, free-kick gimmicks they employ. In fact the strengths and shortcomings of every player. It's a tremendous help for me in goal to know whether the opposing forward shoots left- or right-footed or is strong in both feet. It makes it easier for positioning if I have an idea from which boot the shot is coming. Matt is seldom wrong.'

While Nicholson is kept busy with present-day problems and with planning for the immediate future, Tottenham's long-term prospects are mainly in the hands of full-time scouts Charlie Faulkner and Dick Walker, whose job is to be permanently on the look-out for young talent.

This page, above: goalkeeper Pat Jennings faces a barrage at the Cheshunt training-ground. Below: weight-training in the gymnasium. Opposite page, above: Jimmy Greaves warms up on the indoor pitch. Below: Alan Mullery, centre, shortly after his transfer from Fulham, takes a tea-break with his new colleagues, left to right, Peter Baker, Laurie Brown, Terry Dyson and Terry Medwin.

Because of highly specialized coaching and the pace at which soccer is played today, youngsters are maturing earlier. It means that clubs have to secure them earlier. Professional clubs are allowed to sign schoolboys from the age of thirteen, but that often means trailing them from the time they start senior school at the age of eleven.

The life of a scout is as full as that of the manager. 'Sometimes I've managed to watch five matches in a day, as many as ten or twelve in a week,' explained Faulkner, who was responsible for building up the youth teams at West Ham United and Queen's Park Rangers before he joined with Nicholson.

Parkland, school pitches, army grounds and amateur matches are his territory. Youngsters from twelve or thirteen upwards are his speciality. 'When I say watching five matches in a day I don't spend ninety minutes at all the matches. Often I look in just to take a look at one particular player. In most cases five minutes is enough to say whether he is worth checking again.'

Faulkner is never short of players to watch. Many write to the club asking for a trial. Schoolmasters, friends, old players, boys' club leaders all send in names of players they believe should be watched.

'Checking each one takes up a lot of the time but

we can't afford to overlook one recommendation. Who knows, we might be missing another Jimmy Greaves, Mike England or Dave Mackay. If we don't check, another club will.

'Finding the players we want is half the battle. The other half is persuading parents that Tottenham can offer their lad the right future, that football is a worthwhile career. We're not allowed to sign any schoolboy player unless we have the permission of his headmaster and his parents.'

Once the contact has been established, and permission granted for Tottenham to make the approach, then begins the long process of training and sifting. Clubs are not allowed to have more than fifteen apprentice professionals on their staff at any one time. Tottenham keep their number down to around ten. Room must be left for any young player who suddenly hits the kind of form which makes him a 'must'.

It is not only in soccer skill that the large clubs can educate youngsters. Many of them encourage boys who have just left school to continue their academic studies. The Football Association also offers grants for players to study a second career to serve them when their playing days are over.

Several clubs such as Tottenham, Chelsea, West Ham, Manchester United and Liverpool also take young players away with them for first-team matches. This gives the youngster an introduction to the atmosphere of big-time soccer.

On the training side, the healing hands at Tottenham belong to Cecil Poynton, a former player at White Hart Lane who became trainer at the finish of his playing days. His long experience of all types of injury makes him one of the most valuable members of the staff.

Prompt and efficient action by the trainer on the field can make all the difference between a star player missing one match or several matches. 'It is a ticklish problem making an on-the-spot decision in the middle of a match,' he explained. 'Persuading a player to stay on and therefore risk aggravating an injury which might keep him out for weeks. On the other hand taking him off could result in the loss of the match. The introduction of substitutes has made this decision-taking easier.'

Poynton works in an expensively equipped medical room that would do credit to the casualty section of

This page, above: Mike England works to recover fitness after being troubled by injury. Below: Alan Mullery, behind, plays squash with Peter Baker. Opposite page, above: Pat Jennings punches the ball off Jackie Charlton's head during a League match against Leeds. Below: Dave Mackay in the treatment room with trainer Cecil Poynton, watched by Cliff Jones.

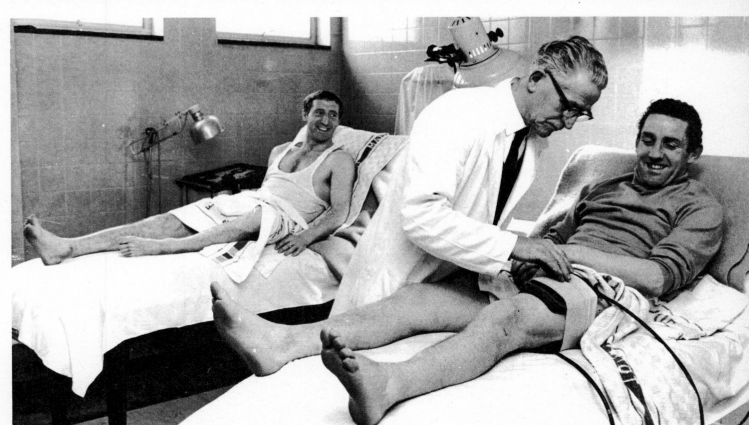

285

285

most leading hospitals. Most clubs in the First Division are equipped with such impressive-sounding equipment as ultra-short-wave diathermy, ultra-sonics, generalized ultra-violet, infra-red, galvanism, faradism and sterilizing units for instruments. Some even house portable X-ray machines.

Clubs have found this necessary because hospitals lack the time, space and facilities to give the intensive treatment needed to restore a footballer to full health in a short space of time. Specialists are often consulted on the recommendation of the club medical adviser; at Tottenham he is Dr Brian Curtin. And under the guidance of the specialists Poynton can supervise the players' treatment and progress in his own miniature hospital.

The trainers are helped by players being briefed on the nature of injuries they can expect. This helps them to give sensible answers to probing questions by the trainers whenever they are injured. Few English trainers rush on without their plastic bag, sponge and a bottle of ointment. But they are never loaded down with the large boxes of medicines which are favoured by most Continental countries. 'Cold water or methylated spirits is generally all that is needed on the field,' said Poynton. 'It just helps to relieve the pain. The serious work is done inside the medical room.'

Poynton seldom has a Sunday free to himself. It is a rare weekend when a first-team player does not report for treatment from the previous day's game.

Some clubs employ physiotherapists in addition to trainers and doctors, but Spurs are fortunate in having a trainer of Poynton's experience available. 'He doubles in for the role of physiotherapist and we have no need to employ one specially,' said the club secretary, Geoff Jones.

Tottenham fans, the people who follow the team round the country during the season, queue all night for Cup tickets, rush to their favourite positions when the gates open on match days, and go mad when Spurs win. On the opposite page, bottom, are the Tottenham Angels—a particularly devoted bunch—rousing the crowd on one of Tottenham's European nights, v. Benfica in the European Cup.

These are the men who are immediately concerned with the finished article watched by the spectators on the Saturday afternoon—the team. Yet, even with these exacting roles compelling a deep sense of loyalty and dedication, the job of producing a game is only half complete.

To cope with the staging of between fifty and sixty matches a year at White Hart Lane and the general day-to-day administrative problems, Tottenham employ an office staff of ten. In charge is secretary Mr Jones, who provides the link between the playing and administrative staffs. His other link is doubly important—that between the permanent staff and the board of five directors who provide the cash, the backing and the business acumen needed to run a flourishing concern. With the huge transfer-deals involved, and the healthy support which Tottenham's success has made them able to command, their type of soccer is undoubtedly big business.

On Mr Jones's shoulders rests the responsibility for the smooth running of the club, the wages, arranging board meetings, dealing with correspondence from the Football League and Association, looking after the legal matters and dealing with the accounts.

His assistant is generally in charge of the more domestic items such as arranging travelling, hotels, looking after the referee and match officials, assisting with the programme, which is organized by a professional journalist, and helping to administer the property which Spurs own around the ground.

In some respects the lifting of the maximum-wage restriction on a player's earnings has helped the club. Before this happened, most top clubs provided houses for players at a nominal rent. Now the established players prefer to buy their own as added security for the time when their playing days are over.

In addition many footballers are taking extra safeguards for their future by ploughing their soccer earnings into businesses outside the game. This involves them employing their own accountants and business advisers, so that clubs seldom get those problems to handle which they did ten years ago.

The competition from television, the attraction of a fireside on a cold winter's afternoon, has forced many of the clubs to alter their attitude towards

This page: Spurs players at the airport, above, and posing for the Press, below, at Cheshunt. Opposite page, top: the crowd at the Spurs v. Benfica match in 1962, just after Blanchflower scored from the penalty-spot. Centre: a typically poached goal by Jimmy Greaves. Fortunately for Sheffield Wednesday it was offside. Bottom: captains past and present—Dave Mackay (now Derby County) and Alan Mullery.

spectators. Too often in the past they were ignored during the week, then beckoned on Saturday with few amenities to comfort them.

As a result of various attractions offered to the public, clubs have spent more on ground rebuilding in recent seasons than they have ever done. For Tottenham it means employing Len Warren as clerk of the works to handle all their football property.

To assist him there is a staff of ten groundsmen including one who doubles as a gateman. Their job is to keep the pitch, stand and terracing in first-class condition. Watering, rolling, replacing the divots torn up in matches, levelling the piles of mud during the rainy seasons, protecting the ground from frost during the cold nights of January and February—these form just part of the routine battle against changing weather conditions. Too many matches postponed can mean a great backlog of fixtures

remaining to be played at the finish of the season.

To help with the administrative duties Tottenham employ one full-time typist and one part-time, two general office staff plus a part-time telephonist.

The advance bookings and ticket office is an entirely separate department occupying two people. Tottenham have their own pools organization requiring a staff of two. On top of these come the 150 casuals needed for each first-team home match.

This page above: Cup Final action. Jimmy Greaves and Chelsea's Ron Harris race for the ball. Below: Pat Jennings dives to save from Tommy Baldwin. Opposite page, above: League action. Martin Chivers, Tottenham's expensive signing from Southampton, heads a superb goal against Leeds for his new club while, below, Frank Saul (transferred to Southampton as part of the same deal) challenges former clubmate Alan Mullery for the ball.

Few people realize the personal sacrifices made by the directors, who get nothing out of the game except the pleasure of seeing their team become champions. There is no financial benefit to be gained from being a football-club director. The theoretical $7\frac{1}{2}$ per cent dividend permitted to shareholders is, in fact, seldom paid by any club.

Even those clubs earning sufficient to justify the payment of a dividend prefer to keep the money in the game. Again, in theory, directors can be reimbursed for out-of-pocket expenses but few directors trouble to collect them. And no payment is permitted for 'services rendered'.

These then, are the men whose dedication sustains the modern Football League club. The three-quarters of a million fans who pour through the turnstiles are living testimony to the thoroughness of their planning.

Glossary & Laws of the Game

This section is designed to give a brief guide to common footballing terms and to supplement information contained in the Laws of the Game, which follow on p. 295 (supplied by courtesy of the FA).

CAUTION. This is an official warning given by the referee to a player who persistently breaks the Laws of the Game, is guilty of ungentlemanly conduct, or shows dissent from any decision by the referee. In the Football League three cautions in a season can lead to suspension.

CORNER-KICK. A corner-kick is taken when the ball passes over the goal-line—outside the goal-posts and the cross-bar—and was last touched by a player of the defending side. The attacking team are permitted to centre the ball from the corner of the pitch, which is marked by a flag and a quarter-circle. The player who takes the corner-kick cannot touch the ball until it has been played by another player, but a player can score direct from a corner-kick.

DROPPED BALL. If the referee halts play when the ball is on the field for reasons other than a foul (i.e. injury), he must restart the game by dropping the ball at the spot where it was last touched when he stopped play. He must drop the ball between one player of each side and it is not in play until it has touched the ground. Should a player touch the ball before it has touched the ground, the referee must drop it again.

DURATION OF MATCH. A senior game is divided into two halves of forty-five minutes with a rest period of at least five minutes. At the end of each half the referee shall add time which has been lost through injury, or other cause, for example, a loose dog which runs on the pitch and holds up play. Some matches require extra-time. This is normally thirty minutes and is also divided into two equal halves with the sides changing ends at half-time. Extra-time is restarted as for the beginning of the game, the captains tossing a coin for choice of ends or kick-off.

EQUIPMENT. It is generally accepted that players take four items of outer equipment with them on to the field of play: shirt, shorts, socks and boots. Some players, though, wear shin-guards for protection against injury. The ten outfield players on each team must wear the same colours, but different colours from the opposing side. Goalkeepers, however, must wear a jersey of distinctive colour from outfield players. The Football League have approved the following colours: scarlet, royal blue, royal green and white. Great emphasis is placed on safety nowadays and nails must not protrude from the studs on players' boots and players must not wear anything which might endanger an opponent, i.e. rings, watches. Although spectacles can be worn by players at their own risk, contact-lenses which fit securely to the eye-ball are becoming more popular among players needing such aids to vision.

FLAG-POSTS. Although these must be used at the four corners of the pitch, they are optional at the half-way line. They must be not less than five feet high with a non-pointed top. Players are not allowed to remove corner-flags in order to give themselves more space when taking corner-kicks.

FREE-KICKS. There are two types of free-kick, direct and indirect. A goal can be scored straight from the former but, in the case of an indirect free-kick, the ball must be played by a player other than the kicker before a goal can be scored. The raising of one hand above his head by the referee indicates to players and supporters that he has awarded an indirect free-kick. If a player is

fouled but still manages to retain the ball, the sensible referee will wave play on. This is known as playing the advantage rule.

GOAL. This is the method of scoring in Association Football. A goal is awarded each time the *whole* of the ball legally passes over the goal-line between the goal-posts and beneath the cross-bar. The goal itself is situated at each end of the pitch and comprises two eight-feet-high upright posts eight yards apart and joined at the top by a cross-bar.

GOAL-KICK. This is a kick used to re-start play when the ball, having last been played by one of the opposing team, goes over the goal-line outside the goal-posts and cross-bar. The kick is usually taken by the goalkeeper, and from such a kick the ball cannot be touched by another player until it passes outside the penalty-area.

GOAL-NETS. These are fitted behind the goal and should be properly pegged down and examined by the referee or linesmen before the match to see that there are no tears in them. Nets were introduced in 1890.

HANDLING. To be guilty of a handling offence a player must *intentionally* strike the ball anywhere from the top of the arm to the tip of his fingers. A player should not be penalized if he touches the ball accidentally. Handling the ball is punished by a direct free-kick and, therefore, a penalty-kick if the offence is committed by a defender in his own penalty-area. Goalkeepers, of course, can handle the ball but only in their own penalty-area.

INJURIES. A referee should stop play if he considers that an injury is serious, and call on the team's trainer. Minor injuries should not be treated on the field. The injured player should be directed to the touchline for attention and there is no need to halt play while this is given. A player who leaves the field for treatment is allowed to re-enter while the ball is in play, provided he is authorized to do so by the referee. If a substitute is used to replace an injured player, the injured player cannot return to the field.

KICK-OFF. This is the term used for the start of play. The ball is kicked from the centre-spot at the start of each half of the game (by alternate sides) and after the scoring of each goal (by the team which conceded that goal). At the beginning of the match the side to kick-off is decided by the tossing of a coin which gives the captain winning the toss the choice of kicking-off or the direction in which he wishes his team to play. The kick-off and the penalty-kick are the only two situations in which the ball *must* be kicked forward.

LINESMAN. Each match must be officiated by a referee and two linesmen, and while the referee concentrates on the play on the field, the linesman's job principally is to signal when the ball goes out of play, to indicate to the referee any player who is in an offside position and to point out any other infringement which the referee may not see. Each linesman has a flag with which he can signal to the referee. Linesmen, however, are not authorized to give decisions.

OBSTRUCTION. This is one of the most controversial subjects in football. In many Latin countries it is a common occurrence for a player to step into the path of an opponent and prevent him playing the ball. This is known as the body-check and, according to International Board ruling, is punishable by an indirect free-kick. A player can legitimately shield the ball, from an opponent, though, provided it is considered to be within playing distance. But he must not try to prevent the opponent reaching the ball. Shirt-tugging is one form of obstruction which often creates bad feeling.

OFFSIDE. This is one of the most difficult Laws to understand and, indeed, to enforce. Players and supporters often have difficulty appreciating the deciding factor: where the player was at the moment the ball was played by a member of his own side—*not* where he is when he himself plays the ball. The enforcement of this Law is very much a matter of interpretation by the individual referee. A player can be offside in theory, but if he is not interfering with play or gaining an advantage for his team by being offside the referee is not bound to penalize him. He cannot be offside if he makes sure that when the ball is played by a member of his own team he is not in front of the ball or that there are at least two opponents between him and the opposing goal-line; he cannot be offside direct from a goal-kick, a corner-kick, a throw-in, or when the ball is dropped by the referee. Moreover, if he is in his own half of the field or if the ball was last touched by an opponent, the referee cannot penalize him for offside.

PENALTY-KICK. The penalty-kick is awarded to the attacking team if one of their players is fouled in the opposing penalty-area. Theoretically, every penalty-kick should produce a goal as the taker, shooting unhampered from twelve yards, has only the goalkeeper to beat. Yet statistical research has shown that, in the heat of the moment, approximately one in every four penalties is missed. The goalkeeper must stand on his goal-line and must not move until the penalty has been kicked. If he does so, the kick has to be retaken. If the ball rebounds into play off a post or cross-bar the player who took the kick must not play it again until it has been touched by another player. The referee must extend play at half-time and full-time to allow a penalty to be taken even if time has expired.

REFEREE. His task is to enforce the Laws of the Game throughout the duration of play. He has to keep a record of the scoring and any incidents which might need disciplinary action. Apart from his clothing, the referee should take with him on the field ten items of personal equipment: two whistles, two pencils, two watches (one of which must have a 'stop' action), scorecard, notebook, pen-knife and a coin. He is also responsible for the match-ball.

SENDING-OFF. The referee should send off the field any player who persists in misconduct after being cautioned. He can also dismiss a player for violent conduct, abusive language, or serious foul play.

SHOULDER CHARGE. The shoulder charge is being used less and less in the international game because physical contact is frowned upon in many countries. Nevertheless, the Law permitting fair shoulder-charging has never been altered and several European countries, sometimes referred to as the Nordic group, which includes Britain, still consider it an essential part of soccer.

SUBSTITUTES. The substitute is becoming a familiar part of the modern game. In season 1965–6 the Football League decided that each club could use one substitute per match for reasons of injury. The innovation proved so successful that most British competitions adopted the use of substitutes on the same basis the following season. Then, in season 1967–8, the Football League amended its substitute regulation to permit one player to be replaced for reasons other than injury. Substitutes are not yet allowed in the World Cup or many of the top club and international tournaments, particularly in Europe. This is for fear of abuses such as substituting an off-form rather than an injured player. Nevertheless, it seems likely that these competitions will follow Britain's lead in allowing one substitute per match for any reason.

THROW-IN. The throw-in is employed as a method of re-starting the game when the ball has crossed the touchline and is therefore out of play. The thrower, who is a member of the team which did not put the ball into touch, must face the field of play where the ball went over the touchline. With part of each foot either on or behind the line, he must throw the ball two-handed over his head. Once the ball has been thrown back into play it cannot be touched again by the thrower until it has been played by another player. Some specialist throwers can propel the ball as far as some players are capable of kicking it.

Law 1/The Field of Play

The Field of Play and appurtenances shall be as shown in the following plan:

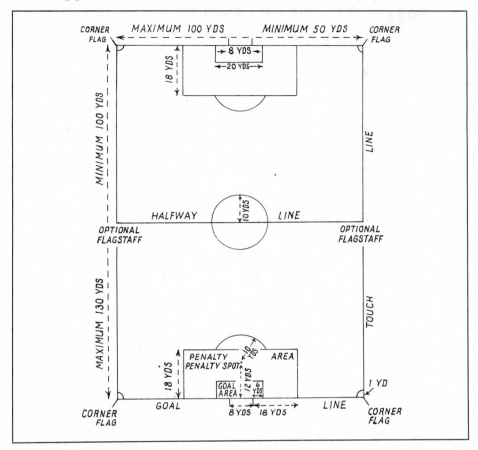

(1) **Dimensions.** The field of play shall be rectangular, its length being not more than 130 yards nor less than 100 yards and its breadth not more than 100 yards nor less than 50 yards. (In International Matches the length shall be not more than 120 yards nor less than 110 yards and the breadth not more than 80 yards nor less than 70 yards.) The length shall in all cases exceed the breadth.

(2) **Marking.** The field of play shall be marked with distinctive lines, not more than 5 inches in width, not by a V-shaped rut, in accordance with the plan, the longer boundary lines being called the touch-lines and the shorter the goal-lines. A flag on a post not less than 5 feet high and having a non-pointed top, shall be placed at each

corner; a similar flag-post may be placed opposite the halfway-line on each side of the field of play, not less than 1 yard outside the touch-line. A halfway-line shall be marked out across the field of play. The centre of the field of play shall be indicated by a suitable mark and a circle with a 10-yards radius shall be marked round it.

(3) **The Goal-Area.** At each end of the field of play two lines shall be drawn at right-angles to the goal-line, 6 yards from each goal-post. These shall extend into the field of play for a distance of 6 yards and shall be joined by a line drawn parallel with the goal-line. Each of the spaces enclosed by these lines and the goal-line shall be called a goal-area.

(4) **The Penalty-Area.** At each end of the field of play two lines shall be drawn at right-angles to the goal-line, 18 yards from each goal-post. These shall extend into

the field of play for a distance of 18 yards and shall be joined by a line drawn parallel with the goal-line. Each of the spaces enclosed by these lines and the goal-line shall be called a penalty-area. A suitable mark shall be made within each penalty-area, 12 yards from the mid-point of the goal-line, measured along an undrawn line at right-angles thereto. These shall be the penalty-kick marks. From each penalty-kick mark an arc of a circle, having a radius of 10 yards, shall be drawn outside the penalty-area.

(5) **The Corner-Area.** From each corner-flag post a quarter-circle, having a radius of 1 yard, shall be drawn inside the field of play.

(6) **The Goals.** The goals shall be placed on the centre of each goal-line and shall consist of two upright posts, equidistant from the corner-flags and 8 yards apart (inside measurement), joined by a horizontal cross-bar the lower edge of which shall be 8 feet from the ground. The width and depth of the goal-posts and the width and depth of the cross-bars shall not exceed 5 inches (12 cm). The goal-posts and the cross-bars shall have the same width.

Nets may be attached to the posts, cross-bars and ground behind the goals. They should be appropriately supported and be so placed as to allow the goalkeeper ample room.

International Board Decisions
1. In International matches the dimensions of the field of play shall be: maximum 110 metres × 75 metres; minimum 100 metres × 64 metres.
2. National Associations must adhere strictly to these dimensions. Each National Association organizing an International Match must advise the visiting Association, before the match, of the place and the dimensions of the field of play.
3. The Board has approved this

table of measurements for the Laws of the Game.

			Metres
130 yards	..	..	120
120 yards	..	..	110
110 yards	..	..	100
100 yards	..	..	90
80 yards	..	..	75
70 yards	..	..	64
50 yards	..	..	45
18 yards	..	..	16·50
12 yards	..	..	11
10 yards	..	..	9·15
8 yards	..	..	7·32
6 yards	..	..	5·50
1 yard	..	..	1
8 feet..	..	..	2·44
5 feet..	..	..	1·50
28 inches	..	..	0·71
27 inches	..	..	0·68
5 inches	..	..	0·12

4. The goal-line shall be marked the same width as the depth of the goal-posts and the cross-bar so that the goal-line and the goal-posts will conform to the same interior and exterior edges.

5. The 6 yards (for the outline of the goal-area) and the 18 yards (for the outline of the penalty-area) which have to be measured along the goal-line, must start from the inner sides of the goal-posts.

6. The space within the inside areas of the field of play includes the width of the lines marking these areas.

7. All Associations shall provide standard equipment, particularly in International Matches, when the Laws of the Game must be complied with in every respect and especially with regard to the size of the ball and other equipment which must conform to the regulations. All cases of failure to provide standard equipment must be reported to FIFA.

8. In a match played under the rules of a competition if the cross-bar becomes displaced or broken play shall be stopped and the match abandoned unless the cross-bar has been repaired and replaced in position or a new one provided without such being a danger to the players. A rope is not considered to be a satisfactory substitute for a cross-bar.

In a Friendly Match, by mutual consent, play may be resumed without the cross-bar provided it has been removed and no longer constitutes a danger to the players. In these circumstances, a rope may be used as a substitute for a cross-bar. If a rope is not used and the ball crosses the goal-line at a point which in the opinion of the Referee is below where the cross-bar should have been he shall award a goal.

The game shall be restarted by the Referee dropping the ball at the place where it was when play was stopped.

9. National Associations may specify such maximum and minimum dimensions for the cross-bars and goal-posts, within the limits laid down in Law 1, as they consider appropriate.

10. Goal-posts and cross-bars must be made of wood, metal, or other approved material as decided from time to time by the International FA Board. They may be square, rectangular, round, half-round, or elliptical in shape. Goal-posts and cross-bars made of other materials and in other shapes are not permitted.

11. 'Curtain-raisers' to International Matches should only be played following agreement on the day of the match, and taking into account the condition of the field of play, between representatives of the two Associations and the Referee (of the International Match).

12. National Associations, particularly in International Matches, should restrict the number of photographers and have a line marked at least 2 metres and not more than 10 metres from the goal-lines and a similar distance from the angle formed by the goal-line with the touchlines; they should prohibit photographers from passing over these lines and finally forbid the use of artificial lighting in the form of 'flash-lights'.

Law 2/The Ball

The ball shall be spherical; the outer casing shall be of leather or other approved materials. No material shall be used in its construction which might prove dangerous to the players.

The circumference of the ball shall not be more than 28 inches and not less than 27 inches. The weight of the ball at the start of the game shall not be more than 16 ounces nor less than 14 ounces. The pressure shall be equal to atmospheric pressure (15 lb per sq in, i.e. 1 kg per sq cm) at sea-level. The ball shall not be changed during the game unless authorized by the Referee.

International Board Decisions

1. The ball used in any match shall be considered the property of the Association or Club on whose ground the match is played, and at the close of play it must be returned to the Referee.

2. The International Board, from time to time, shall decide what constitutes approved materials. Any approved material shall be certified as such by the International Board.

3. The Board has approved these equivalents of the weights specified in the Law:

14 to 16 ounces = 396 to 453 grammes.

4. If the ball bursts or becomes deflated during the course of a match, the game shall be stopped and restarted by dropping the new ball at the place where the first ball became defective.

5. If this happens during a stoppage of the game (place-kick, goal-kick, corner-kick, free-kick, penalty-kick or throw-in) the game shall be restarted accordingly.

Law 3/Number of Players

(1) A match shall be played by two teams, each consisting of not more than eleven players, one of whom shall be the goalkeeper.

(2) Substitutes, up to a maximum of two per team, are permitted in a Friendly Match and also, provided that the authority of the International Association(s) or National Association(s) concerned has been obtained in a match played under the rules of a competition. The Referee shall be informed of the names of substitutes (if any) before the start of the match.

(3) One of the other players, or a named substitute (if allowed) may change places with the goalkeeper, provided that notice is given to the Referee before the change is made.

Punishment. If, without the Referee being notified, a player or a named substitute, changes places with the goalkeeper during the game, at the half-time interval, or at any other interval in a game in which extra-time is played, and then handles the ball within the penalty area, a penalty-kick shall be awarded.

International Board Decisions

1. A minimum number of players in a team is left to the discretion of National Associations.

2. The Board is of the opinion that a match should not be considered valid if there are fewer than seven players in either of the teams.

3. Before the start of a match the Referee shall be informed of the names of any possible substitutes up to a maximum of five from whom the two substitutes may be chosen. The number of substitutes who may be named shall be determined by the International Association(s) or National Association(s) concerned.

4. A player who has been ordered off before play begins may only be replaced by one of the named substitutes. The kick-off must not be delayed to allow the substitute to join his team.

A player who has been ordered off after play has started may not be replaced. A named substitute who has been ordered off, either before, or after play has started, may not be replaced. (This decision only relates to players who are ordered off under Law 12. It does not apply to players who have infringed Law 4.)

5. A player who has been replaced shall not take any further part in the game.

6. The Referee must be informed if a player is to be substituted. A substitute may only be permitted to enter the field of play during a stoppage in the game and after he has received a signal from the Referee authorizing him to do so.

7. A substitute shall be deemed to be a player and shall be subject to the authority and jurisdiction of the Referee whether called upon to play or not.

Law 4/Players' Equipment

A player shall not wear anything which is dangerous to another player. Boots must conform to the following standard:

(a) Bars shall be made of leather or rubber and shall be transverse and flat, not less than half an inch in width and shall extend the total width of the boot and be rounded at the corners.

(b) Studs shall be made of leather, rubber, aluminium, plastic or similar material and shall be solid. With the exception of that part of the stud forming the base, which shall not protrude from the sole more than one quarter of an inch, studs shall be round in plan and not less than half an inch in diameter. Where studs are tapered, the minimum diameter of any section of the stud must not be less than half an inch. Where metal seating for the screw type is used, this seating must be embedded in the sole of the boot and any attachment screw shall be part of the stud. Other than the metal seating for the screw type of stud, no metal plates even though covered with leather or rubber shall be worn, neither studs which are threaded to allow them to be screwed on to a base screw that is fixed by nails or otherwise to the soles of boots, nor studs which, apart from the base, have any form of protruding edge rim, or relief marking, or ornament, should be allowed.

(c) Combined bars and studs may be worn, provided the whole conforms to the general requirements of this law. Neither bars nor studs on the soles or heels shall project more than three-quarters of an inch. If nails are used they shall be driven in flush with the surface.

(NB—The usual equipment of a player consists of a jersey or shirt, shorts, stockings and boots. A goalkeeper shall wear colours which distinguish him from the other players.)

Punishment. For any infringement of this Law, the player at fault shall be sent off the field of play to adjust his equipment and he shall not return without first reporting to the Referee, who shall satisfy himself that the player's equipment is in order; the player shall only re-enter the game at a moment when the ball has ceased to be in play.

International Board Decisions

1. In International Matches the jerseys of the goalkeepers shall be distinct from the colours of the other players taking part in the game.

2. The Law does not insist that football boots must be worn, but the Board is of opinion that, in competition matches, Referees should not allow one or a few

players to play without wearing football boots, when all the other players do wear them.

3. In International Matches, International Competitions and friendly matches between clubs of different National Associations, the Referee, prior to the start of the game, shall inspect the players' boots and prevent any player whose boots do not conform to the requirements of Law 4 from playing until they comply with the Law.

Leagues and Competitions may include a similar provision in their rules.

4. If the Referee finds that a player is wearing articles not permitted by the Laws and which may constitute a danger to other players, he shall order him to take them off. If he fails to carry out the Referee's instruction, the player shall not take part in the match.

5. A player who has been prevented from taking part in the game or a player who has been sent off the field for infringing Law 4 must report to the Referee during a stoppage of the game and may not enter or re-enter the field of play unless and until the Referee has satisfied himself that the player is no longer infringing Law 4.

6. If a player has been prevented from taking part in a game or has been sent off because of an infringement of Law 4, and enters or re-enters the field of play to join or rejoin his team in breach of the conditions of Decision No. 5 the Referee shall stop the game, unless by doing so the offending team would gain an advantage. The player shall be cautioned, and if the game has been stopped to administer the caution it will be restarted by the Referee dropping the ball at the place where the infringement occurred.

Law 5/Referees
A Referee shall be appointed to officiate in each game. He shall:
(a) Enforce the Laws and decide any disputed point. His decision on points of fact connected with the play shall be final so far as the result of the game is concerned. His jurisdiction begins from the time he signals for the kick-off, and his power of penalizing shall extend to offences committed when play has been temporarily suspended or when the ball is out of play. He shall, however, refrain from penalizing in cases where he is satisfied that by doing so he would be giving an advantage to the offending team.
(b) Keep a record of the game; act as timekeeper and allow the full or agreed time, adding thereto all time lost through accident or other cause.
(c) Have discretionary power to stop the game for any infringement of the Laws and to suspend or terminate the game whenever, by reasons of the elements, interference by spectators, or other cause, he deems such stoppage necessary. In such a case he shall submit a detailed report to the competent authority, within the stipulated time, and in accordance with the provisions set up by the National Association under whose jurisdiction the match was played. Reports will be deemed to be made when received in the ordinary course of post.
(d) Have discretionary power, from the time he enters the field of play, to caution any player guilty of misconduct or ungentlemanly behaviour and, if he persists, to suspend him from further participation in the game. In such cases the Referee shall send the name of the offender to the competent authority, within the stipulated time, and in accordance with the provisions set up by the National Association under whose jurisdiction the match was played. Reports will be deemed to be made when received in the ordinary course of post.
(e) Allow no person other than the players and Linesmen to enter the field of play without his permission.
(f) Stop the game if, in his opinion, a player has been seriously injured; have the player removed as soon as possible from the field of play, and immediately resume the game. If a player is slightly injured, the game shall not be stopped until the ball has ceased to be in play. A player who is able to go to the touch- or goal-line for attention of any kind, shall not be treated on the field of play.
(g) Have discretionary power to suspend from further participation in the game, without previous caution, a player guilty of violent conduct.
(h) Signal for recommencement of the game after all stoppages.
(i) Decide that the ball provided for a match meets with the requirements of Law 2.

International Board Decisions

1. Referees in International Matches shall wear a blazer or blouse the colour of which is distinctive from the colours worn by the contesting teams.

2. Referees for International Matches will be selected from a neutral country unless the countries concerned agree to appoint their own officials.

3. The Referee must be chosen from the official list of International Referees. This need not apply to Amateur and Youth International matches.

4. The authority of the Referee, and the exercise of the powers granted to him by the Laws of the Game, commence as soon as he enters the field of play, and consequently any players, or named

substitutes, at fault may be sent off the field before the game has actually commenced. The Referee shall report to the appropriate authority misconduct or any misdemeanour on the part of spectators, officials, players, named substitutes or other persons which take place either on the field of play or in its vicinity at any time prior to, during, or after the match in question so that appropriate action can be taken by the Authority concerned.

5. Linesmen are assistants of the Referee. In no case shall the Referee consider the intervention of a Linesman if he himself has seen the incident and from his position on the field, is better able to judge. With this reserve, and the Linesman neutral, the Referee can consider the intervention and if the information of the Linesman applies to that phase of the game immediately before the scoring of a goal, the Referee may act thereon and cancel the goal.

6. The Referee, however, can only reverse his first decision so long as the game has not been restarted.

7. If the Referee has decided to apply the advantage clause and to let the game proceed, he cannot revoke his decision if the presumed advantage has not been realized, even though he has not, by any gesture, indicated his decision. This does not exempt the offending player from being dealt with by the Referee.

8. The Laws of the Game are intended to provide that games should be played with as little interference as possible, and in this view it is the duty of Referees to penalize only deliberate breaches of the Law. Constant whistling for trifling and doubtful breaches produces bad feeling and loss of temper on the part of the players and spoils the pleasure of spectators.

9. By paragraph (c) of Law 5 the Referee is empowered to terminate

a match in the event of grave disorder, but he has no power or right to decide in such event, that either team is disqualified and thereby the loser of the match. He must send a detailed report to the proper authority who alone has power to deal further with this matter.

10. If a player commits two infringements of a different nature at the same time, the Referee shall punish the more serious offence.

11. It is the duty of the Referee to act upon the information of neutral Linesmen with regard to incidents that do not come under the personal notice of the Referee.

12. The Referee must not allow trainers or any other persons to enter the field of play while the game is in progress unless they receive a signal from him to do so; he must also prevent coaching by trainers and club officials from the boundary lines.

Law 6/Linesmen

Two linesmen shall be appointed, whose duty (subject to the decision of the Referee) shall be to indicate when the ball is out of play and which side is entitled to the corner-kick, goal-kick, or throw-in. They shall also assist the Referee to control the game in accordance with the Laws. In the event of undue interference or improper conduct by a Linesman, the Referee shall dispense with his services and arrange for a substitute to be appointed. (The matter shall be reported by the Referee to the competent authority.) The Linesmen should be equipped with flags by the Club on whose ground the match is played.

International Board Decisions

1. Linesmen where neutral shall draw the Referee's attention to any breach of the Laws of the Game of which they become aware if they consider that the Referee may not have seen it, but the Referee shall always be the judge of the decision to be taken.

2. National Associations are advised to appoint official Referees of neutral nationality to act as Linesmen in International Matches.

3. In International Matches, Linesmens' flags shall be of a vivid colour—bright reds and yellows. Such flags are recommended for use in all other matches.

4. A linesman may be subject to disciplinary action only upon a report of the Referee for unjustified interference or insufficient assistance.

Law 7/Duration of the Game

The duration of the game shall be two equal periods of 45 minutes, unless otherwise mutually agreed upon, subject to the following:

(a) Allowance shall be made in either period for all time lost through accident or other cause, the amount of which shall be a matter for the discretion of the Referee.

(b) Time shall be extended to permit of a penalty-kick being taken at or after the expiration of the normal period in either half.

At half-time the interval shall not exceed five minutes except by consent of the Referee.

International Board Decisions

1. If a match has been stopped by the Referee, before the completion of the time specified in the rules, for any reason stated in Law 5 it must be replayed in full unless the rules of the competition concerned provide for the result of the match at the time of such stoppage to stand.

2. Players have a right to an interval at half-time.

Law 8/The Start of Play

(a) At the beginning of the game, choice of ends and the kick-off shall be decided by the toss of a coin. The team winning the toss shall have the option of choice of ends or the kick-off.

The Referee, having given a

signal, the game shall be started by a player taking a place-kick (i.e. a kick at the ball while it is stationary on the ground in the centre of the field of play) into his opponents' half of the field of play. Every player shall be in his own half of the field and every player of the team opposing that of the kicker shall remain not less than 10 yards from the ball until it is kicked-off; it shall not be deemed in play until it has travelled the distance of its own circumference. The kicker shall not play the ball a second time until it has been touched or played by another player.

(b) After a goal has been scored, the game shall be restarted in like manner by a player of the team losing the goal.

(c) After half-time; when restarting after half-time, ends shall be changed and the kick-off shall be taken by a player of the opposite team to that of the player who started the game.

Punishment. For any infringement of this Law, the kick-off shall be retaken, except in the case of the kicker playing the ball again before it has been touched or played by another player; for this offence, an indirect free-kick shall be taken by a player of the opposing team from the place where the infringement occurred. A goal shall not be scored direct from a kick-off.

(d) After any other temporary suspension; when restarting the game after a temporary suspension of play from any cause not mentioned elsewhere in these Laws, provided that immediately prior to the suspension the ball has not passed over the touch- or goal-lines, the Referee shall drop the ball at the place where it was when play was suspended and it shall be deemed in play when it has touched the ground; if, however, it goes over the touch- or goal-lines after it has been dropped by the Referee, but before it is touched

by a player, the Referee shall again drop it. A player shall not play the ball until it has touched the ground. If this section of the Law is not complied with the Referee shall again drop the ball.

International Board Decisions
1. If, when the Referee drops the ball, a player infringes any of the Laws before the ball has touched the ground, the player concerned shall be cautioned or sent off the field according to the seriousness of the offence, but a free-kick cannot be awarded to the opposing team because the ball was not in play at the time of the offence. The ball shall therefore be again dropped by the Referee.

2. Kicking-off by persons other than the players competing in a match is prohibited.

Law 9/Ball In and Out of Play
The ball is out of play:
(a) When it has wholly crossed the goal-line or touch-line, whether on the ground or in the air.
(b) When the game has been stopped by the Referee.

The ball is in play at all other times from the start of the match to the finish including:
(a) If it rebounds from a goal-post, cross-bar or corner-flag post into the field of play.
(b) If it rebounds off either the Referee or Linesmen when they are in the field of play.
(c) In the event of a supposed infringement of the Laws, until a decision is given.

International Board Decisions
1. The lines belong to the areas of which they are the boundaries. In consequence, the touch-lines and the goal-lines belong to the field of play.

Law 10/Method of Scoring
Except as otherwise provided by these Laws, a goal is scored when the whole of the ball has passed over the goal-line, between the goal-posts and under the cross-bar, provided it has not been thrown, carried or propelled by hand or

arm, by a player of the attacking side, except in the case of a goal-keeper, who is within his own penalty-area.

The team scoring the greater number of goals during a game shall be the winner; if no goals, or an equal number of goals are scored, the game shall be termed a 'draw'.

International Board Decisions
1. Law 10 defines the only method according to which a match is won or drawn; no variation whatsoever can be authorized.

2. A goal cannot in any case be allowed if the ball has been prevented by some outside agency from passing over the goal-line. If this happens in the normal course of play, other than at the taking of a penalty-kick, the game must be stopped and restarted by the Referee dropping the ball at the place where the ball came into contact with the interference.

3. If the ball is going into goal, but before it passes wholly over the goal-line, a spectator enters the field and tries to prevent the goal but fails to make contact with the ball which then goes into goal, the Referee shall allow the goal.

Law 11/Off-side
A player is off-side if he is nearer his opponents' goal-line than the ball at the moment the ball is played unless:
(a) He is in his own half of the field of play.
(b) There are two of his opponents nearer to their own goal-line than he is.
(c) The ball last touched an opponent or was last played by him.
(d) He receives the ball direct from a goal-kick, a corner-kick, a throw-in, or when it was dropped by the Referee.

Punishment. For an infringement of this Law, an indirect free-kick shall be taken by a player of the opposing team from the place where the infringement occurred.

A player in an off-side position shall not be penalized unless, in the opinion of the Referee, he is interfering with the play or with an opponent, or is seeking to gain an advantage by being in an off-side position.

International Board Decisions
1. Off-side shall not be judged at the moment the player in question receives the ball, but at the moment when the ball is passed to him by one of his own side. A player who is not in an off-side position when one of his colleagues passes the ball to him or takes a free-kick, does not therefore become off-side if he goes forward during the flight of the ball.

Law 12/Fouls and Misconduct
A player who intentionally commits any of the following nine offences:

(a) kicks or attempts to kick an opponent;
(b) trips an opponent, i.e. throwing or attempting to throw him by the use of the legs or by stooping in front of or behind him;
(c) jumps at an opponent;
(d) charges an opponent in a violent or dangerous manner;
(e) charges an opponent from behind unless the latter be obstructing;
(f) strikes or attempts to strike an opponent;
(g) holds an opponent with his hand or any part of his arm;
(h) pushes an opponent with his hand or any part of his arm;
(i) handles the ball, i.e. carries, strikes or propels the ball with his hand or arm (this does not apply to the goalkeeper within his own penalty-area);

shall be penalized by the award of a direct free-kick to be taken by the opposing side from the place where the offence occurred.

Should a player of the defending side intentionally commit one of the above nine offences within the penalty-area he shall be penalized by a penalty-kick.

A penalty-kick can be awarded irrespective of the position of the ball, if in play, at the time an offence within the penalty-area is committed.

A player committing any of the five following offences:

1. Playing in a manner considered by the Referee to be dangerous, e.g. attempting to kick the ball while held by the goalkeeper;

2. Charging fairly, i.e. with the shoulder, when the ball is not within playing distance of the players concerned and they are definitely not trying to play it;

3. When not playing the ball, intentionally obstructing an opponent, i.e. running between the opponent and the ball, or interposing the body so as to form an obstacle to an opponent;

4. Charging the goalkeeper except when he:
   (a) is holding the ball;
   (b) is obstructing an opponent;
   (c) has passed outside the goal-area;

5. When playing as goalkeeper:
   (a) takes more than 4 steps whilst holding, bouncing or throwing the ball in the air and catching it again without releasing it so that it is played by another player, or
   (b) indulges in tactics which, in the opinion of the Referee, are designed merely to hold up the game and thus waste time and so give an unfair advantage to his own team;

shall be penalized by the award of an indirect free-kick to be taken by the opposing side from the place where the infringement occurred.

A player shall be cautioned if:

(j) he enters the field of play to join or rejoin his team after the game has commenced without first having received a signal from the Referee showing him that he is in order to do so. If the game has been stopped (to administer the caution) it shall be restarted by the Referee dropping the ball at the place where the infringement occurred, but if the player has committed a more important offence he shall be penalized according to that section of the Law infringed;

(k) he persistently infringes the Laws of the Game;

(l) he shows by word or action, dissent from any decision given by the Referee;

(m) he is guilty of ungentlemanly conduct.

For any of these last three offences, in addition to the caution, an indirect free-kick shall also be awarded to the opposing side from the place where the offence occurred.

A player shall be sent off the field of play if:

(n) in the opinion of the Referee, he is guilty of violent conduct or serious foul play;

(o) he uses foul or abusive language;

(p) he persists in misconduct after having received a caution.

If play be stopped by reason of a player being ordered from the field for an offence without a separate breach of the Law having been committed, the game shall be resumed by an indirect free-kick awarded to the opposing side from the place where the infringement occurred.

International Board Decisions

1. If the goalkeeper either intentionally strikes an opponent by throwing the ball vigorously at him, or pushes him with the ball while holding it, the Referee shall award a penalty-kick, if the offence took place within the penalty-area.

2. If a player deliberately turns his back to an opponent when he is about to be tackled, he may be charged but not in a dangerous manner.

3. In case of body-contact in the goal-area between an attacking player and the opposing goalkeeper not in possession of the ball, the Referee, as sole judge of intention, shall stop the game if, in his opinion, the action of the attacking player was intentional, and award an indirect free-kick.

4. If a player leans on the shoulders of another player of his own team in front of him in order to head the ball, which he succeeds in doing, the Referee shall stop the game, caution the player for ungentlemanly conduct and award an indirect free-kick to the opposing side.

5. A player's obligation when joining or rejoining his team after the start of the match to 'report to the Referee' must be interpreted as meaning to 'draw the attention of the Referee from the touchline'. The signal from the Referee shall be made by a definite gesture which makes the player understand that he may come into the field of play; it is not necessary for the Referee to wait until the game is stopped (this does not apply in respect of an infringement of Law 4), but the Referee is the sole judge of the moment in which he gives his signal of acknowledgment.

6. If play is stopped in order to caution a player who infringes Law 12(i) the game must be restarted by the Referee dropping the ball at the place where the infringement occurred and not at the place where the ball was at the moment of the stoppage. In this respect, the letter and spirit of Law 12 do not oblige the Referee to stop the game to administer the caution, but that he can always apply the advantage clause.

7. If a player covers up the ball without touching it in an endeavour not to have it played by an opponent, he obstructs but does not infringe Law 12, para. 3, because he is already in possession of the ball and covers it for tactical reasons whilst the ball remains within playing distance. In fact, he is actually playing the ball and does not commit an infringement; in this case, the player may be charged because he is in fact playing the ball.

8. If a player intentionally stretches his arms to obstruct an opponent and steps from one side to the other, moving his arms up and down to delay his opponent, forcing him to change course, but does not make 'bodily contact' the Referee shall caution the player for ungentlemanly conduct and award an indirect free-kick.

9. If after a Referee has awarded a free-kick a player protests violently by using abusive or foul language and is sent off the field, the free-kick should not be taken until the player has left the field.

10. If, during the half-time interval, a player strikes an opponent or behaves in an ungentlemanly manner towards the Referee, he shall be debarred from taking any further part in the match, and shall not be replaced.

11. If two players of opposing sides should be outside the boundary of the field of play and one intentionally trips or strikes the other, the ball being still in play, the Referee shall stop the game and caution or send off the guilty player according to Law 12. The game shall be restarted by the Referee dropping the ball, in conformity with Law 8, at the place where it was in play at the moment the game was stopped.

12. If in the opinion of the Referee a goalkeeper intentionally lies on the ball longer than is necessary, he shall be penalized for ungentlemanly conduct and:

(a) be cautioned, and an indirect free-kick awarded to the opposing team;

(b) in case of repetition of the offence, be sent off the field.

13. Any player leaving the field during the progress of the game (except through accident) without the consent of the Referee, shall be deemed guilty of ungentlemanly conduct and shall be dealt with accordingly.

Law 13/Free-kick

Free-kicks shall be classified under two heads: 'Direct' (from which a goal can be scored direct against the offending side), and 'Indirect' (from which a goal cannot be scored unless the ball has been played or touched by a player other than the kicker before passing through the goal).

When a player is taking a direct or an indirect free-kick inside his own penalty-area, all of the opposing players shall remain outside the area, and shall be at least ten yards from the ball whilst the kick is being taken. The ball shall be in play immediately it has travelled the distance of its own circumference and is beyond the penalty-area. The goalkeeper shall not receive the ball into his hands, in order that he may thereafter kick it into play. If the ball is not kicked direct into play, beyond the penalty-area, the kick shall be retaken.

When a player is taking a direct or an indirect free-kick outside his own penalty-area, all of the opposing players shall be at least ten yards from the ball, until it is in play, unless they are standing on their own goal-line between the goal-posts. The ball shall be in play when it has travelled the distance of its own circumference.

If a player of the opposing side encroaches into the penalty-area, or within ten yards of the ball, as the case may be, before a free-kick is taken, the Referee shall delay the taking of the kick, until the Law is complied with.

The ball must be stationary when a free-kick is taken, and the kicker shall not play the ball a second time, until it has been touched or played by another player.

Punishment. If the kicker after taking the free-kick, plays the ball a second time before it has been touched or played by another player an indirect free-kick shall be taken by a player of the opposing team from the spot where the infringement occurred.

International Board Decisions
1. When the Referee awards an indirect free-kick he shall signal it by raising his arm and this signal must precede the blowing of the whistle for the free-kick to

be taken; no signal is required in the case of a direct free-kick.
2. Players who do not retire to the proper distance when a free-kick is taken must be cautioned and on any repetition be ordered off. It is particularly requested of Referees that attempts to delay the taking of a free-kick by encroaching should be treated as serious misconduct.
3. If, when a free-kick is being taken, any of the players dance about or gesticulate in a way calculated to distract their opponents, it shall be deemed ungentlemanly conduct for which the offender(s) shall be cautioned.

Law 14/Penalty-kick
A penalty-kick shall be taken from the penalty-mark and, when it is being taken, all players with the exception of the player taking the kick, and the opposing goalkeeper, shall be within the field of play but outside the penalty-area, and at least 10 yards from the penalty-mark. The opposing goalkeeper

must stand (without moving his feet) on his own goal-line, between the goal-posts, until the ball is kicked. The player taking the kick must kick the ball forward; he shall not play the ball a second time until it has been touched or played by another player. The ball shall be deemed in play directly it is kicked, i.e. travelled the distance of its circumference, and a goal may be scored direct from such a penalty-kick. If the ball touches the goalkeeper before passing between the posts, when a penalty-kick is being taken at or after the expiration of half-time or full-time, it does not nullify a goal. If necessary, time of play shall be extended at half-time or full-time to allow a penalty-kick to be taken.

Punishment. For any infringement of this Law:

(a) by the defending team, the kick shall be retaken if a goal has not resulted;

(b) by the attacking team, other than by the player taking the kick, if a goal is scored it shall be disallowed and the kick retaken;

(c) by the player taking the penalty-kick, committed after the ball is in play, a player of the opposing team shall take an indirect free-kick from the spot where the infringement occurred.

International Board Decisions

1. When a penalty-kick is being taken the Referee must not give the signal for the restart until the players have taken up the position ordered by the Law.

2. If, after having given the signal, the Referee sees that the goalkeeper is not in his right place on the goal-line, he must not blow his whistle for the offence by the goalkeeper, but await the result of the penalty-kick. The proper position of the goalkeeper is on the goal-line between the goal-

posts. If the goalkeeper moves his feet after the blowing of the whistle but before the penalty-kick is taken and no goal is scored, the penalty-kick must be retaken.

3. If a player of the defending side encroaches into the penalty-area or within ten yards of the penalty-mark before the ball has been kicked the Referee will not intervene. If a goal has been scored it shall be awarded.

4. If, when a penalty-kick is being taken, the player taking the penalty-kick is guilty of ungentlemanly conduct he shall be cautioned. If the kick has been taken and a goal has resulted it shall be retaken.

5. If, in the circumstances (described in 4), the ball had passed the goal-line outside the goal, the Referee would restart the game with a goal-kick.

6. If a colleague of the player taking the penalty-kick, encroaches into the penalty-area or within 10

yards of the penalty-mark before the ball is in play, and the ball rebounds into play from the goal-posts, cross-bar or goalkeeper, the Referee shall stop the game and caution the player at fault. The game shall be restarted by an indirect free-kick.

7. If a player or players of each side encroach into the penalty-area or within 10 yards of the penalty-mark before the ball is in play, the penalty-kick must be retaken.

8. When a match is extended to allow a penalty-kick to be taken or retaken, the extension shall last until the moment that the penalty-kick has been completed, that is when:

(a) the ball goes direct into the goal. A goal is scored and the match ends the moment the ball passes wholly over the goal-line;

(b) the ball rebounds from either goal-post or cross-bar into goal.

A goal is scored and the match ends the moment the ball passes wholly over the goal-line;

(c) the ball passes out of play outside the goal-posts or over the cross-bar. The match ends the moment that the ball passes beyond the boundary of the field of play;

(d) the ball strikes a goal-post or the cross-bar and rebounds into play. The match is terminated at the moment the ball rebounds into play;

(e) the ball having been touched by the goalkeeper, enters the goal. A goal is scored and the match ends the moment the ball passes over the goal-line;

(f) the ball is clearly saved by the goalkeeper. The Referee should blow for 'Time' at once. Should the goalkeeper by mischance, then drop the ball over his goal-line it is not a goal, for the game has ended;

(g) the ball is stopped in its course

by an outside agent. The game should be further extended to allow the penalty-kick to be taken properly;

(h) and in addition if any defending player infringes the Law and encroaches, play shall be extended for the penalty-kick to be retaken under the provisions of this Law.

9. If, when a penalty-kick has been taken, the ball is stopped in its course, by an outside agent, the kick shall be retaken.

Law 15/Throw-in

When the whole of the ball passes over a touch-line, either on the ground or in the air, it shall be thrown in from the point where it crossed the line, in any direction, by a player of the team opposite to that of the player who last touched it. The thrower at the moment of delivering the ball must face the field of play and part of each foot shall be either on the touch-line or on the ground outside the

touch-line. The thrower shall use both hands and shall deliver the ball from behind and over his head. The ball shall be in play immediately it enters the field of play, but the thrower shall not again play the ball until it has been touched or played by another player. A goal shall not be scored direct from a throw-in.

Punishment:

(a) If the ball is improperly thrown in the throw-in shall be taken by a player of the opposing team.

(b) If the thrower plays the ball a second time before it has been touched or played by another player, an indirect free-kick shall be taken by a player of the opposing team from the place where the infringement occurred.

International Board Decisions

1. If a player taking a throw-in plays the ball a second time by handling it within the field of play before it has been touched or played by another player, the Referee shall award a direct free-kick.

2. A player taking a throw-in must face the field of play with some part of his body.

3. If, when a throw-in is being taken, any of the opposing players dance about or gesticulate in a way calculated to distract or im-

pede the thrower, it shall be deemed ungentlemanly conduct, for which the offender(s) shall be cautioned.

Law 16/Goal-kick

When the whole of the ball passes over the goal-line, excluding that portion between the goal-posts, either in the air or on the ground, having last been played by one of the attacking team, it shall be kicked direct into play beyond the penalty-area from a point within that half of the goal-area nearest to where it crossed the line, by a player of the defending team. A goalkeeper shall not receive the ball into his hands from a goal-kick in order that he may

thereafter kick it into play. If the ball is not kicked beyond the penalty-area, i.e. direct into play, the kick shall be retaken. The kicker shall not play the ball a second time until it has touched or been played by another player. A goal shall not be scored direct from such a kick. Players of the team opposing that of the player taking the goal-kick shall remain outside the penalty-area whilst the kick is being taken.

Punishment. If a player taking a goal-kick plays the ball a second time after it has passed beyond the penalty-area, but before it has touched or been played by another player, an indirect free-kick shall be awarded to the opposing team, to be taken from the place where the infringement occurred.

International Board Decisions

When a goal-kick has been taken and the player who has kicked the ball touches it again before it has left the penalty-area, the kick has not been taken in accordance with the Law and must be retaken.

Law 17/Corner-kick

When the whole of the ball passes over the goal-line, excluding that portion between the goal-posts, either in the air or on the ground, having last been played by one of the defending team, a member of the attacking team shall kick the ball from within the quarter-circle at the nearest corner flag-post, which must not be moved, i.e. a corner-kick. A goal may be scored direct from such a kick. Players of the team opposing that of the player taking the corner-kick shall not approach within 10 yards of the ball until it is in play, i.e. it has travelled the distance of its own circumference, nor shall the kicker play the ball a second time until it has been touched or played by another player.

Punishment. For an infringement of this Law, an indirect free-kick shall be awarded to the opposing team, to be taken from the place where the infringement occurred.

Index

Page numbers in italics refer to illustrations

Monti 190
Moore, Bobby 65, 127, *137*, 263
Moreno 210
Mortensen, Stan 57, 119, *124*, 146, 228
Morton, Alan 37, *110*
Moscow Dynamo *120*, 144
Motherwell 48, 110
Mullen, Jimmy 116, 228, 231
Muller, Benny *182*, *184*
Mullery, Alan *282*, *284*, *289*, *290*
Munich 65, 80
Munich air crash, 1958 122, *129*, 189
Munoz 210
Mutch, George *54*
Mynti 143

Nacional (Uruguay) 217
Naples 104
Needham, E. *109*
Nep Stadion (Budapest) 189
Netto, Igor 144, 146
Netherlands 44, *163*, *184*
Netherlands FA 36
New York Brookhattan Club 227
New York Generals 234, *240*
New Zealand FA 37
Newcastle United 23, 34, 42, *42*, 49, 74, 110, 111, 113, 115, 116, 117, 118, 123
Newton, Graham *242*
Nicholson, Bill *30*, 122, 123, 276, *276*, 277, 278, *278*, 280, 281, 282
Nigeria 96
No Names, Kilburn 17
Norman, Maurice 123, 277
North American League 235
North Koreans 89, 90, 91, *94*, 95, 104, *272*
Northampton Town 77
Northern Ireland 54, 55, *118*, 137, 142, *144*
Norway 151, 163, 174, 180
Norwich City 47, 51
Nottingham 36
Nottingham Forest 17, 29, *84*, 123, *161*
Notts County 17, *26*, 35, 37, 46, 121
Novak 142
Nou Camp (Barcelona) 185
NPSL 235, 236, 237, 244, 245, 247, 248, 249

Ocwirk 142
OFK Belgrade *172*
Old Carthusians 30, 46
Old Etonians 20, 30, 34, 46, 54, 106
Old Harrovians 15, 106
Old Trafford (Manchester) 47, 48, 53
Old Westminsters 46
Oldham 47, 48, 54
Olympic Bowl (Berlin) 185
Olympic Stadium (Rome) 185
Onega Ermindo *206*, 208
Orlando 202
Oval, Kennington 20, 23, *23*, *26*, 30, 32, 34, 46, 106, 109
Overath *181*, *182*
Oxford University 17, 29

Padilla 222
Pallo 13
Paraguay 190, *220*, 222
Parker, Tom 113
Parkhead Stadium (Glasgow) 47, *187*
Partick 23, 32
Partizan (Belgrade) 83, 167
Payne, Joe ('Ten-Goal Payne') 54
Pedernera 210
Peiro 60
Pele 56, 87, 102, 104, *140*, *141*, 142, 146, *190*, *196*, 198, 200, *201*, 202, 206, 267
Pember 17
Penarol (Uruguay) 74, 100, 213, *215*, 217, 257
Perry, Bill 119
Peru 190, *218*, 221, 222
Peters, Martin 58, 60, 127
Philadelphia Nationals 227

Philadelphia Spartans 234, 241
Pianetti *206*
Pickering, Fred 115
Pinga *192*
Pittsburgh Phantoms 234
Planicka 143
Plumstead 44
Pluskal *163*
Poland 45, 96, 151, 163, 185
Ponomarev *182*
Pools, The 66
Port Elizabeth City 101
Port Vale 49
Portsmouth 49, 115, *143*
Portugal 17, *73*, *90*, 91, *94*, 154, 158, 164, 174, 189
Poynton, Cecil 284, 286
Prague 32, 44
Prater Stadium (Vienna) 185
Preston North End 17, *26*, 31, 34, 35, 37, 44, 49, 50, *51*, 54, *109*, 109, 113, *120*, 168
Prieto 220
Prince Rainier 171
Professionalism, legalization of 34
PSV Eindhoven 167, 170
Puskas, Ferenc *64*, 100, *107*, 125, 143, *150*, 151, *247*, 272
Pythian, Ernie *168*

Queen's Park (Glasgow) 15, 17, 20, 23, 37, *40*, 55, *110*
Queen's Park Rangers 77, 96, *179*, 283

Racing Club of Buenos Aires 69, 74, 80, 171, 190, *204*, *208*, 213
Racing Club de Paris 69, *83*, 171
Ramsey, Sir Alf 69, 80, 122, 125, 127, *134*, *135*, 228, *256*
Rattin, Antonio 69, 76, 80, 190, 208, *259*
Real Madrid 60, *62*, *64*, 70, 74, 96, 100, 116, 143, *150*, *151*, *153*, *159*, 164, 170, 185, 245
Real Zaragoza 74
Red Banner (Bulgaria) 101, 167
Red Star (Belgrade) *129*
Red Star (Paris) 174
Referees' Association 36
Reigate Priory 20
Revie, Don 118
Richardson, W. G. *112*
Riera, Fernando 220
Rimet, Jules 57, *139*, *201*, 226, *250*, 264, 265
Rio Stadium 58
River Plate 213
Rivera, Gianni *157*, *271*
Rhodes, Peter 244
Roberts, Herbie *49*, 113
Robledo, George 116, 117
Rocha, Pedro 212, 217
Rogers, Alan 240
Roker Park 74, *168*
Roma AS 60, 62, 74, 82, *159*, 167
Ross, James 109
Ross, Nick 109
Rotherham 51
Rowe, Arthur 122
Rowley, Arthur 110
Rous, Sir Stanley *35*, 89, 231, 245, *250*, 253, *253*, *256*, 257, *260*, 264, *266*, *266*, 268
Royal Belgian FA 48
Royal Engineers 18, *18*, 20
Rugby League 30
Rugilio 146
Rumania 34, *138*, 163, 167
Russia 34, *61*, *72*, *87*, 90, *90*, *142*, ·143, 144, 150, 151, 163, 167, 185, *188*, 196, *198*

St Albans 48
St Johnstone 72
St Louis Stars 234, 237, 240, *240*
San Siro (Milan) 185
Sanchez, Leon 218, 220
Santamaria 100
Santisteban 237

Santos (Brazil) 56, 74, 142, *196*
Santos, Djalmar, *201*, 202, 267
Saul, Frank 277, *290*
Schiaffino 100, 217
Schön, Helmut 181
Scotland 30, 31, 42, 51, 53, 57, 58, *127*, 139, *184*
Scotland v. England 23, *23*, 29, *29*, 44, 53, 54, 121
Scottish Cup 18, 32, 46, 54, *148*
Scottish FA 49
Seeler, Uwe *146*, *182*, 212
Servilio *141*
Sheffield Association 23, 27
Sheffield Norwich 17
Sheffield United *13*, 15, *30*, 42, *42*, 44, 49, *109*, 168
Sheffield Wednesday 17, 40, 47, *84*, 104, *109*
Shepherds Bush (London) 46
Shipman, Len 64
Silva, Hector *73*, *210*, 212, 214, 217
Simpson, Ron 55
Sims, Nigel 237
Sipos, Ferenc 81
Sivori 96, 190, 212
SK Slavia 32, 167
Slovan Bratislava 70
Smith, G. O. 32, 40, *109*
Smithfield 12
Sormani, Angelo 60, *62*
South Africa 32, 96, 101
South Korea 91
South Shields 51
Southampton *30*, 44, 49, 53
Spain 34, 44, *45*, 53, 58, 96, 100, 143, 146, 154, *158*, *163*, 164, 174, 180, 181, 185
Sparta, AC (Prague) 32
Spartak 116, 146, 167
Spiksley, F. *109*
Sporting Lisbon 70
Stade de Paris 172
Stade de Reims *83*, 170
Stadio Communale (Turin) 185
Staffordshire County Challenge Cup *24*
Stamford Bridge (Chelsea) 23, *41*, 111, *116*
Standard Liège 80
Steel, Billy 121, 149
Steele, Danny *54*
Stefano, Alfredo di *62*, *64*, 96, *150*, *151*, 190, 212
Stein, Jock *148*
Stiles, Nobby *88*, 127
Stockholm 46
Stockport 48, 54
Stockton 30
Stoke City 24, 35, 53, *122*, *124*, 127
Strutt, Joseph 15
Suarez, Luis 60, *62*, *163*
Sudell, Major 34, 109
Sunderland *33*, 37, 45, *50*, *51*, 74, 112, 123, 272, 274
'Super League' 257, 258, 260, 261, 263
Surbiton 17
Sutar, Fergus 32
Suter, R. 51
Svensson *140*, 143
Swan, Peter 104
Sweden 44, 57, *61*, 96, 123, *139*, *140*, 144, 151, 163, 174, 180, 196
Swift, Frank *119*, 146
Swifts 30, 37, 46, *109*
Swiss FA 163
Switzerland 44, 57, *57*, 58, 81, 96, 151, 154, 163, 167, 174, 180
Szymaniak, Horst 237

Taylor, Ernie 117, 119
Taylor, Tommy 122
Torino AC *157*, *159*, 189
Toronto Falcons 234, 241
Torres *90*, *94*
Tottenham Hotspur 23, *30*, 34, 40, 44, 70, 74,

122, 123, 127, *131*, *137*, 149, *172*, *186*, 274–291
Townley, W. J. 37
Toye, Clive 95
Tranmere 54
Trapattoni *153*, *240*
Troche, Horacio 214, 217
TSV Munich 65, 80
Turkey 150, 185

UEFA 253
United Soccer Association 245, 247, *253*
United States 224, 227, 228, 231
Universidad de Santiago 220
Upton Park 20, 34
Uruguay 32, 42, 51, 53, 56, 57, *73*, 87, 88, 100, 146, 190, 192, *210*, *212*, 213, 214, 217

Vale of Leven 17
Van Heel 143
Vasas 245
Vava *195*, 203
Venezuela 190
Viera, Ondion 214, 217
Villa Park (Birmingham) 44, 114
Viollet, Denis 236, 247

Wales 23, 36, 42, 55, 57, *86*, *136*, 137, 139

Wales v. England 42
Walker, Billy 'Knocky' 120
Walker, Dick 278, 282
Walsall 40, 114
Walter, Fritz 143
Walters, Sonny 122
Wanderers 15, 18, 20, 23, 106
War Office 17
Wembley Stadium 18, 23, 38, *39*, *44*, 46, 48, 49, 51, 53, 55, *58*, 76, *84*, 111, 119, 123, *133*, 139, 146, *176*, 185
Werder Bremen 82
West Bromwich Albion 24, *26*, 35, 37, *44*, 53, 55, 109, *109*, *112*, *116*
West Germany 56, 57, *57*, *58*, 59, *62*, *73*, *83*, 86, 88, 123, *135*, *142*, *146*, 158, 167, 174, 180
West, Gordon *72*
West Ham United 23, 38, 39, 48, 49, 57, *65*, 70, 232, 245, 283, 284
Western Association 30
Westminster School 15
White, John 123, 277, *280*
White City Stadium (London) 35
White Hart Lane (Tottenham) *34*, *130*, 274, 278, 287
'White Horse Final' 48
Widdowson, Samuel W. 29
Willis, Arthur 122

Wilson, Ray 127, 137
Winterbottom, Walter 264
Wolverhampton Wanderers 35, 47, 55, 115, 116, 125, *126*, 253
Woodley, Vic 146
Woodward, Vivian 40
Woolwich Arsenal 44
Woosnam, Phil 95, *232*, 237, 240
Workington 68
World Cup 56, 57, *57*, *58*, *58*, 60, *61*, *73*, 76, *78*, 81, 87, 89–90, *134*, *135*, *138*, *140*, 142, 143, 264, 265, 266, 271
Wrexham *168*
Wright, Billy 116, 125, *126*, 127, *134*, 228

Yankee Stadium (New York) 247
Yashin, Lev *72*, *142*, 143, 144, *182*, *184*
Yeats, Ron *172*
Young, George *127*, 239
Yugoslavia 104, 154, 158, *164*, 167, *169*, 189

Zagallo *195*, 203
Zakarias 125
Zamora, Ricardo *45*, 146
Zebec 143
Zemaria 237
Zito *141*, 202
Zozimo 203

Acknowledgments

ABC Television
Albanaise de Football
Associated Newspapers
Associated Press
Atkins Photos
Atlanta Chiefs
Baltimore Bays
Bethlehem Steel
BIPPA (Barratt's)
Brazilian Embassy
British Broadcasting Corporation
Camera Press
Central Press Photos
Columbia Pictures Corporation
B. O. Corbett
Fox Photos
Mrs Grace Graham-Doggart
R. J. Hayter's Service
Imperial War Museum
Keystone Press Agency
Koningklijke Nederlandsche Voetbalbond
Sergio Larrain—Magnum Photos
Littlewoods Pools

London Express News and Feature Service
Mansell Collection
Milt Miller
'Olympia'
Geo. Outram & Co.
Portsmouth *Evening News*
Press Association Photos
Publifoto
Radio Times Hulton Picture Library
Schirner
Chris Smith, courtesy *The Observer*
Mrs D. L. Stewart
Syndication International
Topix
United Press International
United Soccer Association, N.Y.
Vernons Pools
Franco Villani
A. Wilkes & Son
Arthur J. Winder
Carlo J. Ziliani
100 Years of Soccer in Pictures
(William Heinemann Ltd)